HISTORY
OF THE
MOGUL DYNASTY IN INDIA

HISTORY

OF THE

MOGUL DYNASTY IN INDIA

FROM ITS FOUNDATION BY TAMERLANE, IN THE YEAR 1399,

TO THE

ACCESSION OF AURENGZEBE, IN THE YEAR 1657

TRANSLATED BY

FATHER FRANCOIS CATROU

GYAN

Published by

Gyan Publishing House
5, Ansari Road
Daryaganj, New Delhi-110002
Phone: 011-47034999, 9811692060
E-mail: books@gyanbooks.com

Distribution Network
gyanbooks.com
India, USA, Canada, UK, Australia, France

ISBN: 978-81-212-8874-3 (PB)
First Published, 1826

2nd Impression 2023

Printed at: Gyan Press, Delhi.

HISTORY OF THE MOGUL DYNASTY IN INDIA
TRANSLATOR: FATHER FRANCOIS CATROU

HISTORY

OF THE

MOGUL DYNASTY

IN

INDIA.

HISTORY

OF THE

MOGUL DYNASTY

IN

India,

FROM ITS FOUNDATION BY TAMERLANE, IN THE YEAR 1399,

TO THE

ACCESSION OF AURENGZEBE, IN THE YEAR 1657.

TRANSLATED FROM THE FRENCH OF

FATHER FRANCOIS CATROU,

Of the Society of Jesus;

Founded on the Memoirs of Signor Manouchi, a Venetian,

Forty-Eight Years Physician in the Service of the Imperial Family, at the Court of Delhi and Agra.

ACCOMPANIED WITH

A DETAILED DESCRIPTION OF THE COURT AND HARAM, MILITARY STRENGTH, RESOURCES, POLITY AND CHARACTER OF THE MOGUL GOVERNMENT, AT THE EPOCH, WHEN THE GLORY OF THIS DYNASTY WAS IN ITS ZENITH.

London:

PUBLISHED BY J. M. RICHARDSON, 23, CORNHILL;

AND SOLD BY ALL BOOKSELLERS.

1826.

ADDRESS

OF THE

TRANSLATOR.

THE volume, published at the Hague in the year 1708, containing the history here offered to the public, had many years been in the possession of the translator, and undergone frequent perusal, before he began to entertain the design of transfusing the contents into his native language. Commenced, at first, as an amusement for the employment of his hours of leisure; as the translation progressed, and the interest of the narrative developed itself, he became impressed with the idea, that an historical work, founded on such, apparently, authentic and valuable materials, merited to be introduced to the notice of the public. Independent of the great variety and interest of the incidents; a chief feature, and it may be said, excellence of the narrative consists, in an animated and faithful delineation of the human character, as dis-

played in the conduct and deportment of the prominent actors, which are introduced throughout its pages.

The translator has endeavoured to render his author strict justice, by a faithful adherence to the genuine sense of his text; and by declining the exercise of a discretion, which might have led him, either to engraft any foreign matter upon, or to abridge the narrative. He has left it to his readers to make the comments their good sense will suggest, upon such passages, as may be calculated to stagger their confidence in the truth of the facts related. A charge of credulity will, perhaps, in some places, be thought to attach to the author; or, at least, to those persons, from whom he has taken his incidents: but a liberality may, nevertheless, be due, wherever these relations appear supported by Protestant testimony, though they should have proceeded from members of a communion to which Protestants are opposed. The fact, which possesses the most extraordinary character, relates to an occurrence, reputed to have taken place in the vicinity of Lahor, nearly at the close of the reign of the Emperor Akebar. The translator felt an inclination to omit altogether this passage, from its, apparently, very extravagant nature; but a little reflexion induced him to abide by his first determination, namely, to give a faithful and ungarbled translation of his author's history. The transactions, in which the missionaries of the Romish church sustain a conspicuous part, he could not but regard as worthy of being preserved, on account of the interest they excite, and the very singular nature of the occurrences to which they led; as well as their tendency to shew the intercourse which subsisted, at that era, between the great men of Indostan and Europeans, and the private sentiments and biasses of the Mogul princes.

The rise and fall of states and dynasties, so fertile in events of the most influential character, as operating on the interests and passions of mankind, will ever afford themes of the most impressive nature, and such as are calculated to awaken public curiosity; it is presumed, that the history, which the translator now submits to the public, will be found the very reverse of tedious or dull; but, teeming with instructive, curious, and entertaining matter. A relation so complete, of the military, political, and domestic history of a dynasty of sovereigns, ruling an empire of such vast extent, for the space of three hundred years, is scarcely, perhaps, to be found extant, apart from the sphere of European history. A work so curious, and, it is presumed, generally interesting, may, perhaps, be thought worthy the notice of that class of the public, particularly, which may be disposed (from the interest it takes in Indian affairs, or a partiality for research and information upon the political history of India,) to encourage the exertions of the humble translator, to contribute to the historical notices, which have been attempted to be furnished to the public, upon the topics of Indian government and policy.

The translator, without pledging himself to a continuation of the History of the Mogul Dynasty in India, to its later period; a dynasty, which is generally understood to have attained its zenith in the reign of Aurengzebe (with whose accession to the empire this volume closes), and to have gradually declined in power and celebrity from that epoch (contingent as such an undertaking must necessarily be, on finding the requisite materials), presumes, nevertheless, to say, that should the present volume meet with a favourable reception, he shall feel encouraged to ascertain how far the attempt may be practicable.

THE

AUTHOR'S PREFACE.

IF my good fortune had not enabled me to overcome all the difficulties of the undertaking, the idea of giving to the Public a General History of the Mogul Empire, never would have once entered my imagination. The necessity of making researches for materials in so distant a climate, for the purpose of obtaining an acquaintance with the history of the race of sovereigns which governs at the present day in Indostan, would have deterred me from the design. It was impossible, besides, to have avoided reflecting, how little the people of Europe feel interested in the lives of princes, whose rule is unconnected with our politics. Moreover, the lives of many eminent persons, illuminating our own sphere, remain enveloped in obscurity, from the neglect of records, or the want of curiosity in the Public. By a strange perversion of the imagination, or from a false pride, we affect to class, as barbarous, those nations, whose education differs from our own; how, then, could I think it meet to travel to the Indies in search of heroes, and men of note? So many prejudices, and so many discouragements, would have made me abjure a work, which I have just happily completed; or, rather, the idea of attempting it would never have suggested itself to me.

Chance, then, has embarked me in an undertaking, which I should never have embraced through choice or inclination. A person, of well known integrity, who has exercised in the Indies the first employments in our Colonies, placed in my hands a Portuguese Manuscript, the work of M. Manouchi, a Venetian. I read it over, at first, with that common curiosity with which we are accustomed to peruse the adventures of the traveller; but I found that it contained something more than a narrative of mere journeyings. It seemed to me, that something better than a simple description of a strange country might be extracted from the Manuscript. I found that the Chronicles of the Mogul Empire had been communicated to M. Manouchi; that he had caused them to be translated into the Portuguese Tongue; and that they were inserted in the work which I held in my hands.

On contemplating so valuable a document, my reflexions ultimately determined me to found a work on the memoir I had before me. I considered, that a General History of a Great Empire, from its foundation, was a work which would be valued by Men of Letters; that the History of the Mogul Dynasty was wanting to universal history; that some traits of it had appeared in all the languages of Europe, and had been greeted with the public approbation;

that after all, the diversity which is perceivable between the manners of the Orientals and our own might awaken the curiosity of the Public; that the heroes of Asia would have their attractions, if pourtrayed in their natural colours; and that the taste of the Public might be gratified by a change in the costume of heroes, who had hitherto been offered to them after the European fashion only, and prejudices; that the history of a distant country is as susceptible of ornament as that of our own; that it has beauties which are peculiarly and properly its own; that the human passions, which are the soul of great events, are the same in Asia as in Europe; that the people of France might acquire instruction from the example of Indian virtues, as did formerly the people of Greece from the models of genuine integrity and true generosity furnished them by the Scythians; lastly, that the example of Padmani would not be a less impressive lesson of conjugal fidelity, than was to the Athenians, the constancy of the heroes of Toxaris, of the most exalted friendship.

I had no reason, besides, to doubt the existence, in the archives of the Mogul Empire, of an exact Chronicle, in which the principal events were narrated at length. It is from memoirs drawn from the Chronicle, that Jean Laet has composed his notice of the Mogul States. He speaks of it in the following terms:—*Nos fragmentum e Belgico, quod genuino illius Regni Chronico, expressum credimus, libere vertimus.*

I had, moreover, the most convincing evidence attainable in such matters, of the veracity of the Mogul Chronicle, of which I possessed a translation in the Portuguese Tongue. M. Manouchi assures us that he has caused it to be translated, with great care, from the originals, lodged in the palace, written in the Persian language. The Venetian does not appear to have been sparing of expense, that he might be enabled to transmit to Europe exact documents of the empire in which he resides. He has procured portraits to be painted, at a great charge, by the artists of the haram, of the Emperors and the eminent men of the Mogul Empire. The fear of rendering a first edition too costly has prevented my furnishing the Public with impressions.

The Author of the Manuscript is not one of those traders of Europe, obliged, by his commercial interests, to undertake a rapid progress through particular districts, or to take up his residence in the sea ports of Indostan, at a distance from the capital. M. Manouchi is a physician, whose profession has for a long time attached him to the service of the Emperors. Having resided at the court forty years, and from the nature of his employment been admitted, with a familiarity denied to others, into the recesses of the haram, it can by no means be considered as extraordinary, that he should have procured valuable memoirs, and been introduced to an acquaintance with the genuine Chronicle of the Empire. In comparing this document with the European writers, who have treated of the Mogul Empire, I have been the more convinced of its authenticity, from having found that the best informed speak conformably to his Chronicle.

A better account than M. Manouchi's, of the two last reigns, it is evident cannot be expected. He came to the Indies in the reign of Cha-Jaham, and attached himself to the person and fortunes of Dara, the eldest son of the Emperor. He was present at all the battles fought by this young sultan, which terminated in the destruction of his hopes of empire, and finally in the death of that unfortunate prince. If he is found at variance, at times, with that judicious writer, Monsieur Bernier, who has given us a history of the revolution which placed Aurengzebe on the throne, it is because the Venetian has written his account subsequent to that of the Frenchman, and has had an opportunity of verifying on the spot certain events, which M. Bernier has advanced on the faith of popular belief.

I have experienced another advantage, in taking M. Manouchi for my guide. Notwithstanding his having written in that dialect of the Portuguese Tongue, which is spoken in the Indies, and which is not the most pure; although he often blends with it Italian phraseology, and French turns of expression; in the stile of his narrative there is an indescribable fire and elevation of the imagination, which sustains and aids an historian who has to labour on the materials of his furnishing. It is true, that I have not always rigidly followed him. I have not unfrequently assumed a privilege, which is not unjustifiable, when our discretion is to be exercised upon the memoirs of others. I have even collected from other quarters materials in aid of the brevity of the Chronicle. Sometimes it is a French or an English writer, sometimes an Italian, but more frequently they are Portuguese or Dutch writers, whom I have consulted. I have not entirely neglected the writings of travellers, but I have made a cautious use of their assistance. However, after glancing at the productions of others, I have always returned to the Chronicle, as the basis and support of this history. I would even make no difficulty of attributing the entire work to M. Manouchi, and of inscribing it with his name only, if I could be persuaded of his entire approbation of that accessary matter, which I have taken from other writers, and have engrafted upon his manuscript.

The Oriental Library of Mons. D'Herbelot has been of great assistance to me, in explaining and amplifying whatever the brevity of the Chronicle had left obscure. Maffei, Tossi, Texeira, Pietro Della Valle, Thomas Rhoe, Jean de Laet, Messieurs. Bernier and Tavernier, are the principal sources whence I have drawn the matter, in which the Chronicle appeared to me to be defective. I have consulted in Paris with persons of ability, who have long resided in the Mogul States. Another, Mons. Landes, (not the person of that name from whom I received the Portuguese Manuscript) who has had a considerable share in the work of Mons. Tavernier, has had the kindness to communicate to me the results of his experience and acquaintance with the Empire, the history of which I have written, and in which he long resided.

The treasure, which M. Manouchi has transmitted us from the Indies, is not entirely exhausted. His Manuscript contains, besides, independently of the relation of his own adventures, almost a complete history of the reigning Emperor. In the volume which I give to the Public, I have been content with placing Aurengzebe upon the throne. Nevertheless, I have entitled the work, "A General History of the Mogul Empire." May it not be allowed, that the history of a nation is complete, when it has been carried to the epoch of the accession of the reigning sovereign. Should this Work find favor with the Public, I shall continue the life of Aurengzebe, of which I have the memoirs in a prepared state. The Public will, probably, be gratified, in having presented to their view the oldest sovereign in the world, with the most refined policy, reforming and extending an empire, to the throne of which he attained by the instrumentality of intrigue and dissimulation.

If I should be accused of having furnished a simple Abridgment of the Life and Conquests of the First Founder of the Mogul Empire, my reason for taking this course, is, that I might avoid giving to the Public a repetition of what has been already written. Tamerlane is almost as well known in France, as our heroes of Europe. I have, therefore, in tracing his history, entered into a detail only of the events of the life of this conqueror which are found in no other place than in the Mogul Chronicle. I have confined myself to a description of the exploits of Tamerlane in the Indies, and the species of rule, which he established in that country, after his conquests. This is a point of history which had never been hitherto communicated, and which has the strongest bearing on the subject of which I had to treat. It will afford me pleasure, should the curiosity, which is commonly inspired by the history of foreign empires, occasion the one that I now introduce to the Public, to be sought after as the agreeable occupation of a leisure hour; and have the effect of causing those pernicious books, the reading of which has a tendency to corrupt the heart, to be thrown aside.

CONTENTS.

TAMERLANE,

FIRST EMPEROR.

MIRACHA,

SECOND EMPEROR.

ABOUCHAID,

THIRD EMPEROR.

SEC-OMOR,

FOURTH EMPEROR.

BABAR,

FIFTH EMPEROR.

AMAYUM,

SIXTH EMPEROR.

AKEBAR,

SEVENTH EMPEROR.

JEHAN GUIR,

EIGHTH EMPEROR.

CHA-JAHAM,

NINTH EMPEROR.

ERRATA.

Page 53, last line, *for* he established court, *read* established his court.
—— 134, line 25, *for* supported, *read* surmounted.
—— 229, line 11, *for* where, *read* were.
—— 251, line 30, *for* made a profession, *read* made profession.

HISTORY OF THE

MOGUL DYNASTY

IN INDIA.

TAMERLANE,

FIRST EMPEROR.

His Birth. Is chosen King of the Shepherds. Makes War upon his Neighbours. Seizes upon the Throne of Samarcand. Tamerlane compared with Alexander. His first Expedition to India. His Conquests in Persia. His Conquest of Indostan. Establishment of the Mogul Empire. Defeat of Bajazet. Death of Tamerlane.

A COMPLETE relation of the life and exploits of this prince, born in a country which was the ultima Thule of the conquests of Alexander; of a prince who made the ebbing tide of victory to return nearly to the very land whence Alexander had entered upon his career, would require a volume of unusual dimensions. Tamerlank, or Timurlenk, is a name compounded of two Tartar words. Timur signifies iron. This hero was thus called from living constantly amidst the din of arms. Lenk means halting, and this prince was born with a defect in one of his legs. The place of his nativity was Casch, a town in a province of Tartary, known to Europeans as Transoxiana, on account of its situation on the other side of the river Oxus, but called at the present day, Abiamu, by the Orientals. The Chronicle has signalised the birth of this conqueror, by a fable to be found no where but in its own records, and which is worthy of a place among those tales only, with which the Asiatics never fail to embellish the origin of their princes.

The mother of Tamerlane, before her marriage, appeared suddenly pregnant. The father of the young princess took an alarm ; he broke out into invectives against his daughter, and was on the point of avenging the dishonor done to his family, by shedding the blood of his guilty child, when the young princess, throwing herself at the feet of her father, discovered to him the origin of an event, which had caused even her own astonishment. A sunbeam pierced through a cleft, which had been left in one of the windows of her apartment, and winding itself around her, seemed to clothe her as it were with a garment of light, and affectionately to caress her. "Such," said the princess to her father, "is the origin alone of that event, which has so justly exasperated you." The father was convinced, upon inspection, of the truth of so extraordinary a circumstance, and conjectured that a son who was indebted to the earth's great luminary for his birth, would surpass all his ancestors in glory.

It is probable, that a story so little worthy of belief, and which seems to have been transplanted from the mother of Gengiskan to the mother of Timur, had its origin in the name borne by the father of Tamerlane. He was called Targay, which signifies "the source of light," and was a nobleman of distinguished reputation at the court of Houssain, at that time sovereign of all Turquestan, and of the province of Transoxiana, which was dependant upon it. Tamerlane was related to the king, and was descended from a Mogul stock. This word "Mogul," in its original signification, is not the name of a country, or of an empire, but of a family, which was almost always upon the throne in the more southern regions of Tartary. From this family Tamerlane derived his origin. In the person of Gengiskan, his ancestors had already given to Asia one of its most celebrated captains. This illustrious Mogul subjected all those extensive countries, which at the present day are comprehended under the name of the Two Tartaries, and having carried his arms victoriously into the heart of China, established in that country an empire, which was inherited by his posterity.

Houssain, one of the descendants of Gengiskan, reigned over the Southern Tartars at the time of the birth of Tamerlane, which happened in the year 736 of the Hegira, answering to the year 1335 of the Christian epoch. Though a scion of the royal race of the Moguls, he was educated at a distance from courts and cities, and agreeably to the customs of his country, was employed in his youth in taking care of his father's flocks. From his earliest years he gave indications of an intrepid spirit; and the ascendancy he obtained over the young shepherds of the neighbourhood, evinced that he was born for command. The children of the vicinity deferred to him the superiority, and elected him for their judge. In the contests which took place respecting the right of pasturage, they addressed themselves to Tamerlane, and his decisions were certain of execution without appeal. A camel, which had strayed from its companions, was found in the pastures, which the young subjects of the captain elect assumed as belonging to them by the award of Tamerlane. Not being able to decide whether they should keep it or send it back, they enquired of their oracle, young Tamerlane, who thus adjudged the case. "If the camel entered your pastures from a level country, it is incumbent upon you to let him return to the herd from which he strayed; but if he came from a hilly country, and it is probable he may not be able to rejoin his companions without being exposed to be devoured by wild beasts, it will be proper to retain him." Thus the most extensive monarchy ever known originated in the play of children. The young shepherds grew up, and the influence acquired over them by Tamerlane increased with the years of his subjects.

Some instances of sovereignty which he exercised rendered him formidable to his followers. He was informed that a wolf had carried off a sheep. Tamerlane gave directions that the shepherd should be punished for his negligence. A little while afterwards, one of his subjects was detected in stealing cattle: the young king had him impaled. This act of justice revealed to the leader of the shepherds the secret of his strength, and inspired him with the desire of attempting conquests. The parents of the deceased thought that Tamerlane had carried to an unjustifiable extent the power delegated to him by the young shepherds, and took arms against the judge and the ministers of his cruelty. The inhabitants of two villages, or rather two families, encamped in the neighbouring pasturages, united to avenge a death, not indeed unmerited, but directed by an authority they did not recognize. Tamerlane led to the battle his young warriors, and by the discomfiture of the two families, his followers served their first apprenticeship to victory. The report of the valour and ability of Tamerlane soon rallied around him the boldest youths of the country. They arrived in crowds to range themselves in the number of his subjects, and they prided themselves on maintaining towards him the same fidelity which would be due to the most legitimate prince.

As the lands of his family were not sufficient for the pasture of so many flocks, or for the extension of the liberties of so many shepherds, it became necessary to acquire new. Sultan Mahmoud was the nearest neighbour. They decided to make him the first object of their attack, and determined to carry the war into the heart of his country, and to surprise his capital, which served as a place of retreat for all the young shepherds of his province.

Young shepherds, without experience in war, led by a chief of years equally immature, presented themselves before the city, and were soon obliged to raise the siege. The army of Tamerlane was dissipated, and he was obliged to return begging his way, on foot, and without attendants. In passing a village he endeavoured to procure a supply of food. An old woman, who knew him, received him into her cottage, and served to the prince of the shepherds some hot rice, in rather a narrow dish. Tamerlane, pressed with hunger, took the rice from the centre of the dish, and eating with too great precipitation, burnt his mouth. The old woman, laughing, addressed him thus: "Be advised, my lord, from this accident to begin with the sides rather than in the centre; and that we expose ourselves to danger and misfortune, by carrying war with too great eagerness into the heart of a country, without having first possessed ourselves of the extremities."

This was a lesson never forgotten by Tamerlane, and which he constantly practised in all his subsequent expeditions. He never left any thing behind which might incommode him in his march, distress his retreat, or embarrass him in his conquests. This check, almost the only one he ever experienced, did not discourage him. His dispersed adherents, who had escaped by different routes, again rallied around him. They continued the same devotedness to their chief, and he affected in his misfortune a greater degree of haughtiness, and more severity, than prior to his disgrace. The usurpation of Tamerlane extended itself by degrees over the neighbouring lands; and the king of the shepherds, by constantly gaining ground, at last found himself sufficiently near the scene of his former failure, to justify a second attempt. Tamerlane made himself master of the city, and by its capture beheld himself in a condition to spread the terror of his arms to a distance.

The audacity of the shepherds, and of their chief, created alarm at the court of Houssain, who claimed the supremacy of the Canton of the Tartars, in which Tamerlane had usurped a species of sovereignty. Houssain deemed it requisite to put a stop, by force of arms, to the progress of the young conqueror. The defeat of Mahmoud had justly rendered Tamerlane an object of jealousy. Houssain was persuaded, that with a small number of disciplined and experienced troops, he might easily defeat a handful of raw young shepherds, without experience in war. Never did two armies engage upon more unequal terms, as regarded the quality of their arms. The troops of the king, clothed in resplendent steel, were armed with the bow and the cimetar. Although the Tartars were at this time familiar with the use of fire-arms, the musquet appears not to have been yet applied to the purposes of war, but to have been used only for field sports. On the side of Tamerlane were displayed only long pikes, and a kind of javelin, used by the Tartarian shepherds in defending their flocks. But, on the other hand, his subjects were all in the flower of their age, in that season of youth, which possesses a vigour capable of maintaining a lengthened action without any sense of fatigue, and a fervour of courage, which rushes into danger unapprehensive of consequences. Their attachment besides to a chief chosen for their leader from his very infancy, and the confidence inspired by his late victory, increased their boldness. The native sagacity of Tamerlane, who seemed a warrior by inspiration, supplied the want of experience. The battle was fought; the squadrons of young shepherds, bristling with long pointed pikes, were impenetrable. Tamerlane, who fought at the head of his followers, performed prodigies of valour. Finally, Houssain lost both his life and his crown.

From this time Tamerlane became sensible that with the cavalry he had formed, it would be easy to subdue all Asia. The shepherds, his subjects, had selected from their studs the most active of their horses, trained them to war, and used them, while yet young, to exercise in squadrons. Their skill as horsemen, and the habit of attending to the cure of their horses when diseased, was in the sequel of great service to these new conquerors, in the strange regions whither they carried their arms.

Tamerlane, in consequence of his victory, entered Samarcand without resistance. The capital of the kingdom of Houssain opened its gates, and a prince of the Mogul stock was beheld, without regret, on a throne, which had been filled by his ancestors. Tamerlane established in this city the seat of the vast empire, which he acquired by his victories, and preserved by his wisdom. Samarcand became the depôt of all the wealth of Asia; of the spoils of Indostan, Persia, Syria, and Egypt; countries which the conqueror either ravaged, or brought into subjection.

The capture of Samarcand may be regarded as the commencement of the reign of Tamerlane. It happened, according to the Chronicle, in the year 771 of the Hegira, and of the Christian era 1370, when Tamerlane was thirty-five years of age. Certain it is, that the Tartarian conqueror commenced his career of victory at an age when Alexander had brought his to a close; but, the Macedonian monarch possessed advantages from birth to which the other was a stranger. Alexander was born heir to a kingdom; Tamerlane acquired one by his ability. The first inherited, the other gave himself subjects. The Macedonian found disciplined phalanxes prepared for service, the Tartar formed himself to discipline his squadrons. The homage and attachment of his subjects were the consequence of legitimate succession in the one; in the other, of a superior mind, and that ascendancy over other men, which is the gift of nature alone. Without the advantage of having had an Aristotle for his preceptor, Tamerlane had all the virtues without the vices of Alexander. He was temperate, chaste, moderate, attached to the duties of his religion; and, notwithstanding the assertions of one of his enemies, who has written his history, not too cruel for a conqueror.

The new king, continuing to pursue the plan of conquest which he had traced out, began by subjecting the people in the vicinity of Samarcand. The enterprising chiefs, who have at different times quitted the frozen regions of the north with their followers, have commonly effected an establishment in the more wealthy and inviting climates of the South. It was therefore on the side of the Indies that the torrent first poured its overwhelming tide. Tamerlane found, on the banks of the Indies, a people of a very different faith from his own. The Tartars, of his time, were in general disciples of Mahomet. He followed himself the religion of Gengiskan, which had been preserved in the family of the Moguls. He adored the eternal God, invisible, infinite, and almighty, without distinction of nature or persons, one only in unity. He observed the law of nature, contained in eight precepts, which are nearly the same with those of the Decalogue. He contemned the reveries of the Alcoran, and was equally the enemy of idolaters and of Mussulmen. To the law of Jesus Christ he had no aversion. The wife of Gengiskan is said to have professed the Christian faith, and that she had inspired her children with a respect for that religion. Thus, ambition, and a zeal for the extermination of idolatry, engaged Tamerlane to make war upon the Indian nations.

Cabul, one of the most northern of the cities of India, situated between Persia, Tartary, and the river Indus, gives its name to a kingdom called Cabulestan. The king of this region, the most exposed to the incursions of Tamerlane, experienced the entire shock of the first war, which this conquerer undertook against a foreign state. Cabulestan was delivered up to pillage, was ravaged, and made tributary to the Tartar. The circumstances which suddenly diverted the storm, and caused it to fall upon Persia are not known; but it is certain that Tamerlane without having passed the river Indus, transferred the march of his victories, which had commenced their career on the side of the east, to the west.

Different writers have described the progress of the Tartar Prince in his conquests of Persia and Syria. The capture and destruction of Herat rendered him master of Korasan. The kingdom of Georgia submitted to his dominion, on the reduction of the city of Nichabour. The conquest of Persia was a task of greater difficulty; Tamerlane was two years occupied in accomplishing this enterprise. At last, having made himself master of Shiraz, the Persians offered no further resistance, and were brought into complete subjection, as much through the influence of the conciliatory policy of their conqueror, as by the strength of his arms. Thence he directed his victorious progress towards those distant northern regions, where the sun is seen for forty successive days never to dip beneath the horizon. The Imans, who followed the army, dispensed the soldiers on this occasion from the duty of the evening prayer; as between the rising and the setting of the sun, they remarked, there was no longer any visible distinction.

In this expedition Tamerlane made himself master of the two Tartaries; but the attraction of the climate, and a sedition which broke out in Persia, occasioned him quickly to return to that country. Bagdat yet preserved some semblance to the ancient Babylon. It was the capital of a country, of which Sultan Ben-Avis, himself a Mogul and of the race of Gengiskan, had taken possession. Tamerlane attacked him in his new acquisition, drove him from Bagdat, and compelled him to repass the Tigris, and to fly for refuge to the Sultan of Egypt.

The Indies, the first country assailed by his arms, in the meantime had been allowed to recover itself, and to take measures to guard against the future attacks of its ravager. The enslaved condition of the kingdom of Cabul, gave all the nations which inhabited the country on the other side the Indus just reason to apprehend a similar fate.

The Rajas who ruled these provinces, and had partitioned among themselves the different states of this rich country, had made great preparations to withstand the conqueror if he should again direct his enterprises on the side of India. Their fears were not without just grounds, nor were their preparations void of utility. The revolt of Cabul recalled from Syria the Tartar army, and diverted the whole strength of the conqueror to the side of Indostan, who availed himself of the opportunity now afforded him, to complete the subjection of a country, in which his posterity still reign, and where by the establishment of the Mogul Empire, the name of his family will be perpetuated.

The return of Tamerlane to India is noted in the Chronicle for the year 800 of the Hegira, or 1399 of the Christian era. Tamerlane was then sixty-four years of age. It is this epoch to which the origin of the Empire, whose history is about to be recorded, ought to be ascribed.

The destruction of Cabul only served as a means of enabling Tamerlane to penetrate to the centre of those beautiful regions, still known as Indostan, but which are gradually losing that distinctive appellation, and will probably be known in a short time no longer under any other than that of Mogulstan, or the States of the Mogul. These regions, situated between the Indus and the Ganges, are watered by an infinite number of rivers and canals, which nature or art have formed for the transport of the immense riches collected on their bosom.

The Indus on their western side, flows from north to south, and discharges itself into the Indian Ocean. The Ganges having its source from the north in nearly as high a latitude as the Indus, enters the Gulph of Bengal on the south. All the country included between these two rivers was subdued by Tamerlane. This hero found in India a braver and more obstinate resistance than in all the rest of Asia. A new Porus obliged the new Alexander to encounter in the same regions dangers worthy of his great mind. Rana was an idolatrous Prince, whose country was situated nearly in the centre of Indostan. Tamerlane addressed to him one of those menacing letters, an expedient, by which he had often succeeded in effecting the submission of kingdoms and provinces, without being obliged to have recourse to the shedding of blood. He threatened him with his vengeance unless he acknowledged himself his tributary and his vassal. The young prince treated the threats of the Tartar with contempt, and replied only by marching to attack him at the head of a formidable army. This army was more numerous than that of Tamerlane, the troops of Rana being entirely composed of those Rajepoot soldiers who are esteemed in India as almost invincible.

All Indostan seemed to have taken arms to combat with Tamerlane. The cavalry in the army of Rana was computed to number more than one hundred thousand horsemen. Tamerlane at the utmost had only twelve thousand horse, but the Tartars whom he led to the fight were experienced troops, and the confidence they reposed in their chief, joined to their familiarity with victory, elevated their hopes. When the two armies came in sight, the principal Tartar chiefs, alarmed at the multitude of their enemies, began to think of retiring. Have we not already, they said to one another, served long enough this rash cripple, to whom the late combat has added to his lameness the privation of a hand. Is Tamerlane not satisfied that our bodies should be scarred and mutilated like his own; does he also desire that we should sacrifice our lives in a climate so opposite to that of our native regions; a climate in which the intolerable heat will destroy all who may escape the poisoned arrows of the Indians. Language so seditious repeated through all the ranks of the army, had made the Tartars resolve to abandon India, and leave Rana in unmolested possession of his power and independence, Tamerlane, during these tumultuary proceedings, was reposing in his tent, undisturbed by any fears, confiding in the valour and experience of his soldiers, and not at all alarmed at the multitude of his enemies; when he was apprised of the design entertained by his troops of renouncing the enterprise of the Indies. As he had not been used to appease seditions, and perhaps doubted himself of his ability to succeed in a conflict against an innumerable host, supported only by a small number of intimidated soldiers, he thought only of retreating. The tents were already furled, and the baggage had began to move, when a muleteer of the army presented himself to the king, and prostrating himself before him, thus addressed him—"We have beheld you, my lord, hitherto victorious over all the kings who entered the lists against you, and give laws to Persia and to Syria. After having subjected the country which gave you birth, you have chosen, among the vanquished, the means of extending your power over the rest of the universe.—The Tartars have hitherto been fearless of their enemies, having you for their leader, and now the chief himself sanctions the timidity of his soldiers.—Go on, continue to fly before a tumultuary army of badly armed and undisciplined Indians. You may peradventure escape with your life, but the profit and the glory of the conquests which awaited you will be lost for ever." These words, pronounced with an air of enthusiasm, by a man employed in the meanest duties of the army, seemed to have the character of inspiration. Each regarded the other, and sought in the countenance of his comrade a disavowal of their common fears. Tamerlane, who perhaps had himself instructed the muleteer to play his part in this scene, availed himself of the conjuncture to restore confidence to his troops.—The order of battle was formed, they presented themselves before the enemy, and the following stratagem was made use of by Tamerlane, that he might engage, with less danger, an army, whose numbers threatened to invelope him on every side. He placed in his rear a defile, where it was impossible to form an extended front, and stationed some of his best troops at the entrance. Feigning terror, as soon as the enemy commenced the assault, his Tartars took to flight. The cavalry, with a swiftness of which the Tartarian horse alone are capable, sheltered itself in the rear of a mountain, where it lay concealed from the enemy. The Indians pursued the fugitives at full speed, and passed the defile, where their first squadrons experienced little resistance. As soon as one half of their army had gained the plain, the enemy who had fled turned about, and attacking the Indian cavalry, whose horses were exhausted in the pursuit, with their cimetars, made a most dreadful havoc of the foe. This victory made Tamerlane master of Indostan. Rana was obliged to accept peace upon the best terms he could obtain from the conqueror. The Indian was compelled to pay every year a heavy tribute. Tartar governors were placed in the principal fortresses of Indostan, and especially at Delhi, the metropolis of India, which then acknowledged for its sovereign a Patan prince, in religion a Mahometan. From this time, the Rajas adopted a policy, which they have ever since maintained with unwearied consistency; never attacking their adversaries, but contented with acting on the defensive, they defend their possessions with obstinate perseverance against the encroachments of the Mahometans. Tamerlane returned victorious to Samarcand, laden with the spoils of India, having laid the foundation of an empire, which of all his conquests, has alone remained subject to his posterity.

The remainder of the exploits of Tamerlane have no further connexion with this history, than as they may serve to exhibit a true picture of the founder of the Mogul dynasty. Ambition would not allow the conqueror to enjoy in repose the fruit of his enterprise. At an age when the decay of bodily vigour ordinarily entails a relaxation of the energies of the mind, Tamerlane went forth from Samarcand in all the strength and vivacity of youth. Sultan Ben-avis was the first victim of his resentment. This Mogul, whom Tamerlane had formerly vanquished and driven from Bagdat, had been able to re-establish himself in his dominions, by the assistance he had received from Egypt. He even extended his incursions into Persian Irae, the government of which Tamerlane had conferred on his son Miracha. This was provocation sufficient to make the conqueror resolve on exacting reparation from a prince whom he had formerly vanquished. Sultan Ben-Avis was driven from Persia, and obliged to take refuge in Natolia, at the court of Bajazet. Tamerlane, after making himself master of Damascus, took and pillaged Bagdat. On every side he spread terror, wherever he appeared nations submitted to him. The Sultan of Egypt himself, who had been the first to protect

Ben-Avis, respected the power of Tamerlane, and commanded prayers to be put up for this conqueror in all the mosques of Egypt.

Bajazet alone had not as yet experienced the valour of the Tartar, and seemed to defy him. He had even dared to commit spoil on some princes of Caramania who were allies of Tamerlane. The reputation of Bajazet increased every day with his conquests.—The defeat of Sigismond, king of Hungary, and of the duke of Nevers accompanied by the flower of the nobility of France, near Nicopolis, in Bulgaria, had emboldened the Ottoman to attempt the siege of Constantinople. He had already compelled the Emperor Emanuel to cede to the Mahometans a suburb of the city; to allow mosques to be erected there, as well as the residence of a Mussulman judge; and finally, he succeeded in obtaining a recognition, by the Sultan of Egypt, of the title he had assumed of Sultan of Roum, or of the Greek and Roman empire. These magnificent titles, especially that of Ilderim or the Thunderbolt, assumed by Bajazet; the recent victories and audacity of this prince, as well as compassion for the Emperor Emanuel, drew upon the Ottoman all the vengeance of Tamerlane. The Tartar could not endure a rival conqueror in Asia. He therefore turned his arms against Bajazet, and marched to combat a Mussulman, whose sect he hated, in aid of a Christian prince, whose religion he respected.

The whole Tartar army marched with the greatest alacrity against Bajazet, and already viewed the spoil of this Sultan as the richest booty, which they ever conveyed within the walls of Samarcand. Tamerlane alone during the march appeared silent and thoughtful. Some attributed his apparent melancholy to the temperament induced by advanced years, which is disposed to irratibility and over anxiety; others imputed it to his apprehensions for the result of an enterprise, undertaken against a prince covered with laurels; and against troops accustomed to victory. One of his captains took the liberty to ask Tamerlane, in a circle of his principal officers, the cause of this apparent disquietude.—"If I appear thonghtful," he replied, "it is through a state of indecision in which I am placed, from which it will be difficult for you to emancipate me—I am reflecting whether I shall be able to find among you, a man of sufficient capacity to support the weight of the diadem to the conquest of which we are marching, and of sustaining with dignity the vacant throne of Bajazet." A reply so full of confidence gave renewed courage to the Tartars. Some cities were secured by way of protecting their retreat in the event of a check; and the two armies met in that fine plain which extends between Ancyra and Mount Stella, the very spot where Pompey formerly defeated Mithridates.

Tamerlane had forseen that the Mussulmen would have the advantage in a close combat, the sabre being as formidable a weapon in the hands of the Ottomans, as was the bow in those of the Tartars; and that by engaging at a certain distance without allowing the enemy to approach too near, a greater carnage would be made of their antagonists, while his own troops would be less exposed to suffer. He had, therefore, directed his followers to approach within bowshot only of the Mussulman squadrons, and to take to flight immediately after discharging their arrows, that they might return to the charge when they had refitted their bows. In effect, the first attack of the Tartars was lively and terrible. The air was darkened with arrows, and the earth in an instant strewed with dead bodies. The Ottomans pursued the Tartars with the sabre, and whenever they were able to come in contact with a squadron, they were sure to throw it into disorder; with the force of their blows penetrating and dispersing it: but a shower of arrows would again fall upon the Ottomans, and enable the Tartars to recover the ground they had lost. The chiefs in the meanwhile, gave their orders with all the ability which was peculiar to the two greatest captains in Asia. Bajazet fought in the manner of the Romans, Tamerlane after the fashion of the Parthians.

Victory remained for a long time suspended between the two armies; it declared at last in favor of Tamerlane. A body of Tartar auxiliaries, which Bajazet had taken into his service, and had joined his army by the way of Russia, began to murmur at being obliged to fight against their countrymen, and at the prospect of the victory being snatched from the greatest man their nation could ever boast—they deserted Bajazet and went over to Tamerlane. Victory then no longer hesitated; complete disorder took possession of the Ottoman army. The Tartar cavalry attacked the flying enemy with the sabre, a weapon of which they had made no use in the heat of the action. A long pursuit took place. Bajazet was unable to escape the fleetness of the Tartar horse, and fell into the hands of the conqueror. The Ottoman experienced in his misfortunes the kindness and humanity of the Tartar. Tamerlane never exulted over his fallen foe. Every day a tent was ordered to be set up for his accommodation immediately adjacent to that of Tamerlane, who entertained him at his own table, treating him with the greatest distinction, and procuring him every diversion calculated to sooth his mind, and make him forget his disgrace. Such a deportment towards him by no means agrees with the story of the iron cage, in which Bajazet is reported to have been exposed by the order of Tamerlane. It is an ornament, of which I would not willingly deprive history, if I believed there were just grounds for giving credence to it; but as some of the best historians make no mention of it, and the Mogul Chronicle is altogether silent concerning it, I am induced to believe the story of the cage an agreeable fiction invented by the Greeks, who were the enemies of Bajazet. It would seem, that they had a pleasure in representing the captivity of this unfortunate prince as attended with circumstances the most gratifying to their vindictive feelings.

The death of Bajazet, who, according to the Chronicle, took poison, either through disgust of life, or from the apprehension of being exposed in triumph by his conqueror, was quickly succeeded by that of Tamerlane. The Mogul Chronicle varies in the account it gives of the circumstances from that given by the different historians of Europe. I do not pretend to pronounce whether it is more or less meriting credence than theirs; it is at least a contrariety in history with which the reader ought to be made acquainted. It is no longer then at Otrar, at the moment he was on the point of leading his army against Kathay and China, that Tamerlane expired, neither is it at Samarcand, surrounded by his family. It is in India, and at Cabul, when preparing to penetrate into Indostan, and push his conquests in that vast empire to the shores of the ocean.

"Tamerlane," says the Chronicle, "had forbidden on pain of death, those sanguinary combats of squadron against squadron, an exercise to which his bravest soldiers had been accustomed. It was a point of discipline, which he had so much the more at heart, as his army suffered greater loss by this species of mock engagements, than they did through disease, or in conflicts with the enemy. In spite of this prohibition, Miracha, third son of Tamerlane, disobeyed the injunctions of his father and his commander. He put himself at the head of a troop of Tartars, and engaged another troop with so much fury, that a small number only on both sides survived the combat. This act of disobedience irritated Tamerlane to such a degree, that he became incapable of consolation.

Twice he gave orders that his son should be put to death, and as often repented, and retracted the order. Distracted between his zeal for discipline, and his paternal affection for Miracha ; these two passions so preyed upon his mind, that he fell sick. His great age, mortification, anxiety of mind, a fever, and the heat of the climate, all contributed to make his case desperate. It was then that he excluded every one from his presence with the exception of an Iman, who was well acquainted with his sentiments upon matters of faith. He was exhorted according to the principles of Deism, a fatal poison, which corrupts the hearts of all the princes of Asia. He was affected by the exhortations of the Mahometan doctor. Full of confidence in the mercy of God, and of fear of his justice, he expired at the age of sixty-six years, in confessing the unity of one God. A prince unhappy in having believed that he could attain to God without the mediation of Jesus Christ, who is the only way and the life. It becomes us to adore the decrees of Heaven in regard to a hero, who knew the Christian religion, who loved it, who always protected it, but who never professed it. The Mogul Chronicle assigns to him only six years, nine months, and twenty-two days of reign ; doubtless, computing the term of its duration from the date of his last conquests in Indostan. Tamerlane died in the year of the Hegira 806, and of the Christian era, 1405. He was, it is said, buried at Cabul.

MIRACHA,

SECOND EMPEROR.

Succeeds his Father in a part of his dominions. Establishes the seat of his Empire at Herat. Maintains the Sovereignty of his Father in Inodstan. Is Slain by the King of Cascar.

MIRACHA, who was the cause of the death of Tamerlane, his father, succeeded him in the empire of India. In the distribution of the kingdoms made by the conqueror to his children, Persian Irac, Cabulestan, and India fell to the lot of Miracha. It often happens that the sons of a powerful monarch are indolent in their dispositions, and devoted to sensual pleasures, and that the heirs of a conqueror become in their turn the prey to some more enterprising adventurer. This was not strictly true as it respected Miracha. If he did not improve the conquests made by his father, or indeed preserve entire the inheritance he derived from him, it was less the consequence of a degeneracy in valour than through an abandonment of fortune, which seemed weary of having so long and so constantly favoured his father. In the lifetime of Tamerlane, Miracha, who had the government of Persia, was almost always at war, and for the most part unfortunately. Sultan Ben-Avis was very near forcing him to take refuge in Tartary; had not the father arrived to the assistance of the son, this fine portion of the conquests of Tamerlane would have been irrecoverably lost.

After the death of Tamerlane, Miracha made choice for his residence of eastern Persia, in preference to India; this country being situated in a more temperate climate than Indostan. In fixing his ordinary residence at Herat, he placed himself in the centre of his states. The power, besides, of the Moguls was not yet sufficiently strong in the Indies, to justify hazarding the establishment of his court in that country. Tamerlane had indeed possessed himself of the strongest fortresses of Indostan, had placed in them trusty governors, and exacted heavy tribute from all the Rajas; but his authority was maintained in India by the terror of his name alone. Miracha, who was less feared than his father, had great difficulty in levying at Cabul, and throughout Indostan, the tributes which Tamerlane had imposed on those countries. He shewed himself every year at the head of a formidable army, with the view of overawing the Indians, and enforcing payment of the tributes; maintaining by these means an appearance of sovereignty and dominion.

All the Rajas were not equally submissive to the son of their vanquisher. The king of Cascar took arms against Miracha, and the evil genius which constantly persecuted the son of Tamerlane, delivered him into the hands of the Indian king. He was made prisoner in a combat; but the conqueror made a generous use of his victory. He restored his captive to liberty on the sole condition of the kingdom of Cascar being for the future exempted from tribute. Miracha, who had as often as seven times experienced fortune adverse to his arms in his wars with this prince, was at last so fortunate as to defeat and take him prisoner in his turn. The Tartar proved that he had less humanity and generosity than the Indian. So far from giving liberty to his prisoner, with the greatness of soul and disinterestedness which had been displayed towards himself; on the contrary, he kept him prisoner, and put out his eyes.

Ingratitude of so deep a dye was punished by the very individual who had been the subject of it. The Raja, notwithstanding the deprivation of his sight, was able to destroy Miracha by transfixing his breast with a poisoned arrow.—He made use of the following artifice.

The Tartars have always had the reputation of being superior in archery and in darting the javelin, to all other nations. The Tartar soldiery were daily accustomed to the exercise of shooting at a mark. Miracha himself excelled in this kind of diversion, and as he fancied himself unrivalled, he was astonished to learn that the Raja of Cascar, blind as he was, could hit a mark with the greatest precision, provided he heard a sound to proceed from the spot, at which it was necessary to take aim. The story, of this surprising skill of the Raja, appeared to the king quite fabulous. He therefore commanded that his prisoner should be brought into his presence, being surrounded at the time by all the officers of his court. A bow and arrows were placed in his hands, and he was ordered to suspend drawing the bow till the word commanding him to do so should be given. The Raja assuming in his misfortunes an air of haughtiness which became him; "I shall not obey," he said, "in this place, any one but my conqueror; no other person has a right to command me. As soon as I hear the king's voice commanding me to let fly the arrow, I shall obey his mandate." Having thus spoken, he placed himself in an attitude to obey the prince, as soon as he should give the word. Miracha then raising his voice, ordered him to let fly the arrow at the spot whence his voice proceeded. At these words, the Raja obeyed; the bow was drawn, and the arrow entered the body of Miracha. He was carried off expiring, and the Raja was hewn in pieces by Miracha's guards. The king of Cascar, in relinquishing a painful existence, had at least the barbarous consolation of having punished an ingrate. Miracha died in the year of the Hegira 852, and of the Christian era 1451. He reigned forty-six years, and left the kingdom to his son Abouchaid.

ABOUCHAID,

THIRD EMPEROR.

The beginning of his reign. Is driven from his Throne. The Throne occupied by his Brother. Recovers his Crown. Makes amends by his Valour for his former Indolence. Enters India with an Army to exact the Tributes imposed by Tamerlane. Takes possession of Samarcand. Defeats the young Ibrahim. Distributes his Dominions among his Children. Is defeated and beheaded by Usum Cassan.

TAMERLANE had acquired the esteem of his subjects by his superior merit, and Miracha gained their affection by the mildness of a government which cultivated the arts of peace. Abouchaid, in the first years of his reign, was alike wanting in merit and humanity. He passed at Herat a life of slothful ease in the pleasures of the haram, and appeared to be of a disposition equally remote from the clemency of his father, and the valour of his grandfather. He held no further correspondence with his people than such as served to answer the purposes of extortion, and the indulgence of his cruelty. This conduct made him detested, and his apparent want of talent inspired his subjects with a contempt for him. They resolved to be delivered from the tyrant and to put him to death. Abouchaid was not ignorant of the designs which were plotting against him. Sensible of his inability to escape from the fury of the people, or the treason of the nobles, he embraced a design worthy of his inclinations. He put on the habit of a Faquir, a class of religious penitents, who live on alms, and go from town to town, imposing on the credulity of the people by an appearance of austerity. Abouchaid thus disguised went from province to province, attended by two confidants only, who were the companions of his wanderings.

The people in the mean while placed on the throne, in the room of Abouchaid, one of his brothers, flattering themselves with the hopes of better treatment from a king who owed his crown to their choice. They found however to their cost, that the second son of Miracha was of a disposition yet more barbarous than the elder. The new king, in the severities he exercised upon his subjects, did not judge it requisite to excuse his conduct with a colour of administering justice. The blood of his subjects flowed, from the dictates of an arbitrary will and a naturally sanguinary disposition. All ranks were equally persecuted; the rich and the poor, nobles and slaves, were put to death amidst excruciating torments.

So many cruelties made the people regret the loss of Abouchaid, the younger brother having become a greater object of their detestation than ever the elder had been, notwithstanding their former experience of his natural ferocity. A search was made for the fugitive monarch, and a conspiracy was entered into, to reinstate him on the throne from which he had been driven. So much diligence was used, that he was at last discovered among the prodigious multitude of Faquirs, who wander from place to place in India. Abouchaid resumed the crown, and after his new elevation, applied himself seriously to render himself worthy of it. He had been taught by adversity the use of moderation in his good fortune.

The beginning of the new reign was as agreeable to the people as the government which it supplanted had been intolerable. Abouchaid treated with indulgence those who had forced him into exile. My people, he said, are sufficiently punished for their revolt by the persecution they suffered from the tyrant they had chosen to rule them. The only cruelty he exercised was upon his brother, who had usurped his power, whom he ordered to be beheaded.

By this act he revenged his own injuries, as well as those of his subjects, who had suffered by the cruelties and usurpation of the tyrant. It is from the example of Abouchaid that the Mogul Emperors derived the practice of massacreing their brothers ; we shall find in the sequel of this history but too many instances of such melancholy catastrophes.

Abouchaid repaired his passed indolence, and the recent crime of the murder of his brother, by a conduct full of valour. Ulubeg, his cousin-german, also a grandson of Tamerlane, was but an indifferent father. Through jealousy of the preference given by Ulubeg to his younger brother, his eldest son, Abdalatif, had quitted Samarcand. This Ulubeg reigned in Southern Tartary, having succeeded his father Schahrokh. In the division of the empire of Tamerlane, the provinces on the other side of the Oxus had fallen to the lot of this eldest son of the conqueror, to whom Ulubeg was indebted for his birth. Abdalatif, after having taken arms against his father, had retired to Herat, and placed himself under the protection of Abouchaid. The opportunity which this circumstance afforded Abouchaid of quitting that state of inaction in which he had so long languished, and of recovering the esteem of his people by acts of valour, was not neglected by him. He furnished aid to Abdalatif, and placed himself at the head of an army, with which he marched in person to Samarcand, carrying war into the country from which he derived his origin, against the head of his family. Ulubeg was at this time occupied at a distance from Samarcand, in a war with some of the neighbouring states. Abdalaziz, the brother of Abdalatif, and the object of his jealousy, commanded in the city in the absence of his father. The young Tartar made a defence worthy of a descendant of Tamerlane. Princes of the Mogul blood were then beheld armed against each other, contending for glory and their private interests. Abdalatif, the eldest son of Ulubeg, was indignant at the preference his father gave to his younger brother. Abouchaid, eager to efface by the glory of his arms the shame of his past inactivity, maintained the rights of an elder brother, whose just claims it was sought to frustrate. Abdalaziz combated at the same time for his country, the rights of his father, and a kingdom which he hoped to inherit, to the exclusion of his elder brother. The siege was long and bloody; but in the end, Abouchaid made himself master of Samarcand; placed the presumptive heir upon a throne, which would have been lawfully his after the death of his father, and returned to Herat covered with laurels. Abdalatif pushed too far the advantages which the taking of Samarcand had given him over his father. He marched against Ulubeg, engaged him in battle near Balk, gave him a total defeat, and deprived of life him to whom he was indebted for it. This unfortunate prince enjoyed but a short time the fruit of his crime; he perished after a reign of a few months; Abdalaziz having been put to death by him, the kingdom of Samarcand was inherited by his third brother, Abdalla.

Abouchaid, in the mean time, enjoyed quietly at Herat the reputation he had acquired by the capture of Samarcand. Full of the confidence which victory inspires, he imagined, that by shewing himself in the Indies like his predecessors at the head of a gallant army, he should be able to levy the tributes which Tamerlane had imposed on the Rajas. He found the authority of the Moguls greatly enfeebled in Indostan. The contempt which he had drawn upon himself at Herat, during the first years of his reign, had spread to India. The Tartar governors, whom his predecessors had appointed over the principal fortresses of Indostan, had almost all thrown off their allegiance, and erected themselves into so many petty sovereigns. Abouchaid repressed their insolence on his arrival, exacted from the idolatrous Rajas the tributes which were his due, and succeeded in re-establishing in India a dominion equal to that of his predecessors.

A great change had apparently taken place in the character of Abouchaid, and the virtues he now displayed seemed to have supplanted the vices which disgraced his early years. His natural disposition, nevertheless, remained the same, as was at times but too apparent. His two associates, who had attached themselves to his fortunes, and had followed him in the habit of Faquirs, trusted to experience a return of gratitude proportioned to their services, and their fidelity. They presented themselves to their sovereign, at a moment when he was distributing in the Indies the governments of which he had deprived many of his Tartar officers, whose fidelity he suspected; and solicited employment as a reward for the proofs they had given of attachment to their master. Nothing could be more equitable than to confer on affectionate servants those benefits which had been forfeited by rebels. But the ungrateful Abouchaid spurned the persons who had made him their debtor by their services. He commanded them to leave his presence, and release him from a sight which was offensive to him. They did not however take their departure without a remonstrance. "By what means have we offended you, my lord?" resumed the two ancient servants of the monarch: "we attached ourselves to your fortunes at a season when they were the most adverse to you; we were the companions of your wanderings, we assisted you with our counsel, and we have partaken with you the severities of an austere and laborious ministry." It is for that very cause, replied Abouchaid, with a manifestation of rage which terrified the two applicants; it is because your claims upon my gratitude are greater than I can ever repay. It is a reflection I can never bear, that I have subjects to whom I am so deeply indebted; and your presence only serves to accuse me, without ceasing, of the crime of ingratitude. Begone for ever from my presence; never shall your names be enrolled among those of the officers of my crown.

This record of ingratitude on the part of Abouchaid has become proverbial among the Moguls; M. Manouchi had seen it in the Mogul Chronicle, but he received one day a confirmation of it from one of the officers of the sultaness, the mother of Aurengzebe, when M. Manouchi was expressing his surprise at the little generosity of the princes whom he served in his capacity of their physician. Such, the officer replied, is the character of the Moguls; they bestow upon you a thousand caresses when they have occasion for your services, and give as many proofs of ingratitude, when they are no longer wanted. They are indeed the true heirs of Abouchaid.

The king did not resign himself to his pleasures, or to the enjoyment of repose, upon his return from his expedition into India. He had already experienced too severely the dangerous results of a life of indolence, to be disposed to resign himself to the enervating delights of his haram. The possession of Samarcand was the immediate object of his ambition, to which he had paved the way by his first successes, and to which point he now purposed to conduct a new army. Abdalla still reigned in that capital, and filled a throne for which his two elder brothers had long contended. The Chronicle does not explain the motives which influenced Abouchaid to make war upon a prince of his blood. The grandsons of Tamerlane, doubtless, resembled their progenitor, and had few scruples in regard to the equity of their enterprises, provided they were successful.

Uzbec-Khan, who afterwards gave his name to a Tartar dynasty, known at the present day as that of the Uzbecs, was grandson of the famous Houssain, whom Tamerlane in his early years had deprived both of life and empire. This prince governed at this time a very small kingdom in Western Tartary, on the banks of the Caspian Sea. Abouchaid formed an alliance with the successor of Houssain, that he might be able to wrest, with his assistance, the sceptre from a Mogul prince, his near relation. Samarcand was then besieged a second time, but Uzbec-Khan and Abouchaid were repulsed with loss. The first retired into Bokhara, where he passed the winter, and the other took up his quarters in the neighbourhood of Samarcand, till the return of spring. On the opening of the campaign, Abouchaid on one side, and Uzbec-Khan on the other, advanced again to Samarcand. Abdalla did not judge it proper to wait for the enemy in his capital, as the preceding year. He took the field, and marched with his troops to encounter the two confederate monarchs. The combat was sanguinary on both sides: Tartars were seen fighting against Tartars, and the descendants of Tamerlane armed for their mutual destruction. Abouchaid, who commanded the wing of his army opposed to that in which Abdalla fought, was at first routed, but that illustrious chief Uzbec-Khan, whose name has been perpetuated by his victories, and by the great empire of which he was the founder, fell with so much impetuosity upon Abdalla, that he lost both the victory and his life. Samarcand received the two conquerors, and the inhabitants of that great city beheld within their walls the grandsons of two kings, who had both reigned over them. Uzbec-Khan represented the rights of Houssain, who had been driven from the throne by Tamerlane; and Abouchaid had on his side the rights of Tamerlane, whose descendants had reigned over them from the days of Houssain. Abouchaid, apprehensive lest the people of Samarcand might hesitate in their choice of a ruler between him and Uzbec-Khan, made use of a stratagem to get himself acknowledged as sole master. Causing his army to march in by the eastern gate, he hastened in a disguised habit to the western gate, by which the troops of Uzbec-Khan were to be introduced, and ordered it to be shut against his allies; making a merit afterwards of suffering their chief, who had imprudently entered the city before his army, to retire and rejoin his troops. Thus Abouchaid remained in sole possession of the famous capital, to which Tamerlane brought every year the spoils of the nations he had subdued.

Whilst Abouchaid was occupied in the conquest of Samarcand, and in establishing his authority in that city, he was dispossessed of his own capital, the city of Herat. Ibrahim Mirza, a young prince of great beauty, had inspired a princess of the Mogul race, whom Abouchaid had compelled to reside in his haram in a state of celibacy, with a passion for him. Some authors pretend she was the sister, others the cousin of Abouchaid. The princess, who, in the absence of the king, found herself under less restraint than usual, procured Ibrahim easy access to the haram, gained him the affection of the eunuchs, and caused him to be proclaimed king in Herat. The new sultan was the son of Alaeddoulet, who possessed the sovereignty of some provinces in the vicinity of Persian Irac. Having obtained assistance from his father, and persuaded the people of Korasan, of which Herat was the capital, to revolt, he made preparations to maintain possession, by force of arms, of a crown which he had received from the hands of his princess. He trusted that he should be able to oppose, with success, the army of Abouchaid on its return from Samarcand; and waited for the king in a camp, well supplied with provisions, resolved to give him battle before he could reach Herat. Abouchaid was never exposed to greater peril. His soldiers, after the fatigues of a long march, stood in need of repose, while those of Ibrahim were fresh, occupied advantageous posts, and were drawn up in order of battle. A considerable part of the army of Abouchaid was yet at a distance, when he appeared in the presence of Ibrahim, accompanied by some of his squadrons. He beheld the enemy in a large plain, situated between the cities of Sarkas and Merou. Abouchaid was too near to have it in his power to avoid an engagement, and already Ibrahim, superior in number, had began to surround the army of the king; when the remainder of his troops arrived. Ibrahim, who made war from motives which have the greatest sway over the human heart, attacked with fury, and fought valiantly; but he was too young to be able to contend with the experience of Abouchaid. At the first shock the tumultuary army of Ibrahim was put to the rout, and the young prince fled towards Damegan, more distressed at the prospect of the fate which awaited the young princess, than for his own misfortune. In effect, the news of the flight of Ibrahim was no sooner made known at Herat, and conveyed to the haram, than every one gave himself up for lost. They were sensible of the severity of Abouchaid from the melancholy experience of former days. The women, and the eunuchs of the palace, thought proper to anticipate the justice of the conqueror. Some destroyed themselves by poison, others with the sword: but the young sultaness, with superior resolution, had the courage to put to death her little son, whom she yet suckled, the sole fruit of her intercourse with Ibrahim, by forcing into its throat a piece of gold, and producing strangulation. After which, taking poison, which she had preserved sometime in a ring, she instantly expired. It was thus that the rebels exercised upon themselves the vengeance due to their crime, sparing their conqueror the odium of putting them to death.

Abouchaid having returned in triumph to his capital, the city of Herat, made a merit of pardoning several of the guilty who had been wanting in the courage to execute justice upon themselves. By this act of clemency, the prince gained the affection of his people, and entirely effaced the stain of his former cruelty. He made some further conquests upon his neighbours, who were nearly all of Mogul race, and descended from the sons of Tamerlane. He took Asterabad, the capital city of Mazanderan, from Sultan Houssain, and vanquished in battle Sultan Khalil, Prince of Segestan, obliging him to return into his own country with a ruined army. Finally, having restored tranquillity in Herat, and in all Korasan, he returned to Samarcand, which seems to have been his favorite conquest.

The son of Abdalatif, Sultan Gioughi, appeared to Abouchaid ungrateful for the assistance which he had formerly granted to his father. This young prince preserved a secret intelligence in Samarcand, and laid claim to a kingdom, of which he insisted his family had been deprived, under the pretext of rendering them assistance. Availing himself of the absence of Abouchaid, he advanced often to the gates of Samarcand, made inroads into the provinces of Transoxiana, and ravaged the open country. The audacity of Gioughi obliged Abouchaid to hasten, by some months, his march towards Tartary; but he had scarcely passed the river Gihon, when, seized with alarm, Gioughi retired to Skarokhia, which he fortified, and there waited the attack of his enemy. The young prince defended the fortress with courage, but was at last obliged to surrender at discretion; and as an act of grace on the part of his conqueror, was condemned to a perpetual captivity. The life of Abouchaid seemed to be a continual progress from Herat to Samarcand, and from Samarcand to Herat. About this time a religious ceremony recalled him to the capital of Korasan. The Imans had long pressed the king to give orders for the circumcision of his children. Abouchaid had, by different wives, eleven sons, and they were nearly now all of an age capable of being placed in posts of honor and authority. Reverence for his religion had hitherto prevented his placing them at the head of his troops, till such time as they had received the mark of true Mussulmen. It was in Herat that the ceremony of the circumcision of the princes was kept, accompanied by feasts, dances, the combat of elephants, and other rejoicings, which are practised on such extraordinary occasions. What enhanced the value of the ceremony to the sons of Abouchaid, was, their being proclaimed sultans; and the father distributing to his children the government of the kingdoms which belonged to his empire, either by inheritance or conquest. The Chronicle does not explain the particular territory apportioned to each prince. It is however certain that Samarcand and Southern Tartary fell to the lot of Sec-Omor, fifth son of Abouchaid, from whom the Mogul Emperors, who now reign in Indostan, are descended.

Doubtless, Abouchaid ought to have been satisfied with terminating in repose the remainder of a life which had been so much occupied in warlike enterprise. The fault of this prince was always to deal in extremes. He gave himself up, during the early years of his reign, which ought to have been a season of action, to repose; and in his old age he abandoned himself to wars, which he should have shunned. That which he undertook against Usum Cassan was both rash, and unfortunate. I trust that the recital will be the more agreeable to the reader, as he will thereby learn the origin of the Dynasty which rules, at the present day, the empire of Persia.

Miracha, the son of Tamerlane, to whom, in the distribution of the states of his father, the province of Persian Irac had fallen, did not long enjoy entire his extensive dominions. Different princes despoiled the son of the best part of the conquests of his father, and forced him to be content with the kingdoms of Sindy, Segestan, Cabul, and Korasan, of which Herat was the capital. He preserved also the species of sovereignty which the posterity of Tamerlane have always enjoyed in the Indies. To these remains of the vast empire which had been acquired by Tamerlane, Abouchaid joined the conquest of Transoxiana and Samarcand. The extensive kingdom he had thus acquired ought to have satisfied his ambition, but the natural restlessness of the Tartars, when they have entered upon a successful career, prompted Abouchaid to renounce a repose in which he might safely have indulged. He sighed incessantly for the possession of Western Persia, that beautiful portion of the conquests of his grandfather. Two Turkish princes, at this time, divided the territory between them; Hassan Beg, known in Europe by the name of Usum Cassan, of the family of the white sheep; and Gehan-Schah, of the family of the black sheep. These two sultans had formerly been the principal chiefs of the army of Ben-Avis, whom Tamerlane had expelled from Bagdat. Ben-Avis had divided his troops into two bodies, of which one, commanded by Cara-Muhammed, carried in their ensigns a white sheep; and the other, commanded by Cara-Joseph, carried in his a black sheep. After the death of Tamerlane, and of Ben Avis, the princes, who descended from the chiefs of these two families, took possession of the best provinces of Southern Persia; and, as it often happens to ambitious conquerors, they quarrelled, made war upon each other, and seized upon the fruits of each others spoil. Usum Cassan, not contented with Mesopotamia, of which he had dispossessed one of the successors of Tamerlane, turned his arms against Gehan-Schah. Georgia and Gurgestan were subject to this sultan. Usum Cassan coveted these fine provinces, and was besides instigated by that jealousy, which from the earliest times had existed between the families of the white and of the black sheep. The two Turcomans gave battle to each other, and Usum Cassan, who remained victor, slew, in the heat of the action, Gehan-Schah, and the eldest of his sons. There only remained of the family of the black sheep, Hassan Ali, who with the wreck of his father's army had recourse to the protection of Abouchaid. The Mogul was stimulated by various considerations to make war on the Turcoman. Compassion for a young prince despoiled of his inheritance, hatred to the vanquisher of the successors of Tamerlane, but especially by his desire for the conquest of Persia, and for rendering his empire equal to that of his grandfather. Such were the motives which determined him to march towards the west with those gallant troops, which had been so often victorious in the north. Abouchaid accordingly entered the provinces of Aderbigiam and Fars, without encountering any resistance

All Persia was in a state of alarm at beholding the grandson of Tamerlane marching in the steps of his grandfather, and inundating extensive countries with still more numerous armies. Usum Cassan especially, terrified at the approach of so formidable an enemy, was desirous of deprecating the storm, by making the most humble submissions. He dispatched ambassadors to the Tartar prince, offering to restore to the family of the black sheep the conquered territory, and to relinquish to Abouchaid all the country between Korasan. and the Caspian Sea. It was in vain; the haughty Mogul insisted upon harder conditions. He required that the Turcoman should deliver himself into his hands, and become guarantee in his own person for the fulfilment of his engagements. The gallant Turcoman was indignant at these propositions, and determined to reject them; but not being in a condition to make head against the swarms of Indians and Tartars which accompanied Abouchaid, he supplied by art his want of force. Avoiding the risque of coming to blows, he intrenched himself between lakes, and inaccessible mountains; whence harrassing continually the enemy with small detachments, he cut off his provisions, and left the incredible multitude of his foes to waste itself in inaction, and perish for want. Abouchaid then became too late sensible, that it is often dangerous to refuse peace to an enemy who solicits it at the price of great sacrifices. The haughty Mogul, constrained to attempt a retreat, which had the character of a flight, was taken by the son of Usum Cassan. Being brought into the tent of the Turcoman, he affected, in the presence of the victor, a haughty demeanor; reproaching Usum Cassan that he had not dared to encounter him in fair and open combat in the field. This behaviour exasperated the sultan, who had received him at first with humanity, and was inclined to treat him with generosity. This unseasonable pride was fatal to Abouchaid; he was beheaded in the year 1469. The victor carried his resentment still further; he ordered the eyes of the three eldest sons of Abouchaid, who had been taken with their father, to be seared with a hot iron. It was thus that Usum Cassan found himself master of all Persia, to the frontiers of India. Happy, had he known how to enjoy the fruit of his victories!

The fate of Abouchaid might have taught Usum Cassan, that to cultivate the arts of peace would be the best policy of conquerors in their old age. At a very advanced age he engaged in a distant war in Natolia, and was defeated by Mahomet the Second. His children even did not reign after him in Persia, and the family of the white sheep did not long survive that of the rival colour. Ismail Sophi, profiting by the defeat of Usum Cassan, possessed himself of the spoil too much neglected by Mahomet the Second. Thus the family of Ali, son-in-law to Mahomet, from whom Ismail was descended, mounted the throne of Persia, whose posterity still enjoy it, and retain the title of Sophi.

The children of Abouchaid availed themselves of the misfortunes of Usum Cassan, to recover some part of their father's inheritance.

Abouchaid reigned eighteen years; a prince unhappy in the beginning, and in the close of his reign; but always fortunate when he merited it by his conduct. He suffered equally by indulging in indolence, and in too much action. At a time it became him to be enterprising, he resigned himself to ease; and he engaged in perilous undertakings, when he might have enjoyed an honorable repose. The Chronicle complains, that he left to his successors two bad examples; that of putting to death his brothers, and acting the ingrate to his most faithful servants.

It is not altogether certain, that Abouchaid was the son of Miracha, or that he was his immediate successor, and the grandson of Tamerlane. The great seal of the Mogul emperors, places among the number of sovereigns a Mirza Sultan Mahamed, between Miracha and Abouchaid. Some authors represent this Mahamed as the father of Abouchaid. However, the Mogul Chronicle, and the best historians, are agreed that Abouchaid succeeded immediately to his father Miracha. In order to reconcile these contradictory statements, it may be surmised, that Mahamed, whose name is engraved on the imperial seal, was the brother of Abouchaid, whom the people raised to the throne at the time of the flight of this monarch. The word Mirza, which is a title bestowed on princes of an inferior rank only, is some evidence that Mahamed's pretensions as sovereign were of a doubtful character. However, granting even that he was the father of Abouchaid, and actually reigned before him, he was doubtless a prince of so little merit, that history has deemed the mere record of his name the only notice to which it is entitled.

SEC-OMOR; OR, SCEICK-OMAR.

FOURTH EMPEROR.

His peaceable Character. Reigns at Samarcand. His Death.

THE sons of Abouchaid, during the lifetime of their father, had already commanded as governors in the provinces, of which it was intended they should one day possess the sovereignty. Sec-Omor had for his inheritance the province of Maveranahar, known in Europe as Transoxiana. It may be concluded also, that he retained the dominion which Abouchaid had established in the Indies, either as part of his inheritance, or by possessing himself of it after the death of his three elder brothers, who perished in Persia, in the defeat of their father. Never was a Tartar prince of a more tranquil character than Sec-Omor. Content with the kingdom assigned him by Providence, he never by his ambition gave disturbance to his neighbours, or tormented his subjects with tributes and laborious enterprises.

The Tartars, notwithstanding their natural restlessness, soon acquired a taste for the sweets of a tranquil life, which they seem at this period to have required. Tamerlane and his sons had much thinned the country of inhabitants by their warlike enterprises, and by the colonies which they had established. Their cities had become desart, and their lands were left without culture. Sec-Omor seemed destined by Providence to repair, by a long peace, all the evils which the Tartars had suffered in making war.

Samarcand was the capital of the states of Sec-Omor. It is situated in a pleasant territory, watered by a large river, which, after gently meandering through the neighbouring plains, passes through the centre of the city, and making a circle round it, fills the channel of the fosse which surrounds and protects it. It has been said, that Alexander the Great built Samarcand, and gave his name to it. Tamerlane took a pleasure in enriching and adorning it; and he rendered it one of the largest and most opulent cities in Asia. Its air is pure and temperate, and the vast plain, which encircles it, is varied with meadows and cultivated grounds. It is still called Sogd, a word which may sanction the belief, that this part of Southern Tartary was the ancient Sogdiana, a country which the writers of the life of Alexander have so much extolled.

It was in this charming country, and in this agreeable residence, that Sec-Omor enjoyed tranquilly the fruit of the labours, and of the conquests of his predecessors. His sole occupation consisted in re-establishing in its purity throughout his states the Mahometan law. Tamerlane always entertained an aversion to the Alcoran, and professed a species of Deism, exempt from the superstitions of the east. Sec-Omor applied himself, especially, to the study of the Mahometan law, to which he was scrupulously attached. He caused its precepts to be carefully observed, and suffered the Imans to have rather too much influence over him. The Tartar princes, his neighbours, respected the mildness of his character, and never troubled his repose. He lived till the year 1493, having reigned twenty-four years. The Chronicle gives the following account of the manner of his death:—

"Almost the only diversion in which this good prince indulged was that of rearing pigeons, and teaching them to engage in certain combats. Two dove houses had been constructed in his haram, at the two extremities of a terrace, upon which the king was accustomed to assemble these birds, who gathered about him at the least signal. At times the king made use of a long cane, to which was attached a sort of standard, composed of white satin. All the pigeons of one of the dove houses would collect around the flag, and accompany the monarch, who led them to the attack of the opposite dove house. These animals, notwithstanding their natural mildness, would defend fiercely their possessions against the irruption of the assailants. Sometimes the besieged quitted their retreat, and gave battle in the open air. The king encouraged them by his voice and gestures, fluttering the standard to inspire them with greater rage, and induce them to come to a closer engagement. One day that Sec-Omor was enjoying this harmless diversion, having his attention fixed on a flock of pigeons, which he was animating to the combat, he did not observe a place where the parapet of the terrace had given way. He fell from a considerable height to the ground, and died two days afterwards from the injuries he received. This prince had nothing of the impetuosity which characterized the Tartars. He was reproached with a rather too great indolence of temper, which appeared in him the more particular, as he was surrounded on all sides by princes of a warlike character."

BABAR,

FIFTH EMPEROR.

Is driven from Samarcand by an Usbec Prince. Retires to Cabul Resolves to establish himself in the Indies. Disguises himself to acquire a knowledge of the Manners of the Indians. Makes War upon an Indian King and defeats him. Establishes Laws in Indostan, after having subjected it. Dies.

THE repose, in which Sec-Omor had indulged his subjects, was fatal to Babar, his son and successor. The courage of his Tartars was enervated by a long peace, and their experience of the sweets of a tranquil life had rendered them inadequate to the maintenance of a conflict with their neighbours. In the person of Schaibekkan they had a formidable enemy. He was an ambitious and enterprising prince, who had not yet forgotten the treachery which had been practised by Abouchaid towards his father, Uzbec-Khan. He called to mind the ingratitude with which his father had been driven from the city of Samarcand, after the co-operation of his arms had been obtained for its reduction. The gallant Uzbec, animated by ambition and revenge, entered Transoxiana, ravaged all the provinces of Andecan, and presented himself before Samarcand. Schaibek found no longer in the Tartars he attacked those gallant Moguls whom the preceding kings had always led to victory. Babar, especially, educated in habits of effeminacy and indolence, had imbibed the quiet spirit of his father, Sec-Omor. Terrified at the approach of Schaibek, and abandoned by his timorous subjects, he retired with a few attendants to Gazna, a city of Tartary, the nearest to the Indian frontier. Thus, by a disposition of Providence, the victory of Schaibek, and the flight of Babar, were the means of establishing two of the greatest monarchies of the world. The Uzbecs took possession of Samarcand, which has ever since been the capital of their empire, and Babar, compelled to flight, carried into India the Mogul domination, which subsists to the present day.

The fugitive sultan did not long remain at Gazna. He was obliged to retire from one city to another, and eventually to seek an asylum in Cabul. This capital of a kingdom of the same name, was governed at the time by one of those Tartar officers whom Abouchaid had placed in authority in the Indian provinces, and who remained faithful to the princes of the Mogul race, and especially to the son of Sec-Omor. This faithful subject received his sovereign with honour, assisted him with his counsel, and assembling an army chiefly composed of Tartars scattered throughout Cabulestan, he placed Babar in a situation to sustain with honour the dignity of his predecessors.

Courage is sometimes inspired by adversity. Babar found virtue revive in his breast, after the loss of his kingdom. Like his grandfather, Abouchaid, he redeemed by his valour the time he had wasted in inactivity. He placed himself at the head of his new army. It was natural that his inclination should lead him in the direction of Samarcand, and that he should seek to recover possession of his former kingdom. Ranguildas, which was the name of the governor of Cabul, (immortalised by his fidelity to his sovereign) did not enter into the views of Babar, and spoke to him to the following effect :—" I do not pretend, my lord, to restrain your inclinations, or to resist the just resentment which you entertain against the usurper. Nothing can be more reasonable than to make war upon him who has despoiled you of your dominions; and I am ready to sacrifice my life to aid you in recovering possession of them. But, when I cast my eyes, first towards the north, whence you come, and next towards the south, which offers so noble a career, I confess that I feel inclined to advise you to neglect your ancient domain, for the more profitable and inviting prospect which a new dominion offers. No, my lord, your ability to measure your strength with that of Schaibek is by no means evident. The Tartar, who has seized your crown is grown, old in the career of arms, and his Usbecs are troops which have taken the place, at the present day, of those invincible soldiers whom Tamerlane formerly disciplined in Tartary. Let us listen no longer, my lord, to the seducing language of passion. To be revenged upon an usurper is sweet, but it is dangerous to attack him with unequal forces. India, on the contrary, offers to your valour a more easy prey. The domination of your predecessors was never completely established in that country, and your own is in a tottering state. Hasten to secure to yourself the finest empire in the universe. Establish beyond the river Indus a power only sketched by your ancestors. Go and fix your court in the centre of Indostan, and learn how much the delicious climes of India are to be preferred to the snows of Tartary. All things concur to attract your attention to the south; the Providence which has led you to Cabul, and placed you on the road to Indostan; the interests of the religion you profess; God and Mahomet engage you to war against the idolatry of the Indians. Consider the facility of the enterprise. The governors of your own nation, whom your fathers have placed in the fortresses of the Indians, will unite their forces with your's, and your army will gather strength every step which you take in Indostan. When we shall have made an essay of victory under your command, we will follow the path you may lead, even to the walls of Samarcand, where you wish to conduct us. It will then be time enough to despoil the Tartar, and make war upon the Usbecs."

A discourse so reasonable determined the prince, who had good sense, to prefer an almost certain victory to an uncertain revenge. He, in consequence, turned his attention to the side of the Indus, and formed the resolution to undertake the conquest of Indostan. Before entering upon so glorious an enterprise, Babar, desirous to attain, in his own person, an acquaintance with the manners, resources, and the mode of conducting military enterprises, of those who were likely to become his antagonists, assumed the habit of a Joguy, a kind of penitent, who is occupied chiefly in making pilgrimages in India to those spots which are particularly consecrated by the devotlon of the people. Babar, then, disguised as a pilgrim, and accompanied by Ranguildas, entered India, visited all the fortresses occupied by the Tartars, and made himself acquainted with the conduct, and the character of his governors. At last he arrived at Delhi, the strongest of the places which had submitted to Tamerlane, and the most distant of all those which the Moguls at that time occupied in India. It will, in this place, then, be proper to explain the state in which he found that fine region, which was soon to become the theatre of his glory.

India, in the year 1501, when Babar entered the country, was peopled by four distinct races of inhabitants. First, the descendants of the Hindoos, the original inhabitants; secondly, the Patans; thirdly, the Parsees; and fourthly, and last, the Tartars, or, as they were usually denominated, the Moguls.

If we are to credit the most learned Bramins of the country, the ancient inhabitants of India were a colony of Egyptians, which is corroborated by the fact, that the manners, customs, and religion of ancient Egypt subsist at the present day in India, nearly in the same state in which they are described by Herodotus. It is besides certain that there has always been an intercourse of commerce between the Indians and the Egyptians, and that the Metempsychosis which Pythagoras learnt in Egypt, makes still a part of the religion of the Indians. These ancient Egyptians, who came to take up their habitation between the Indus and the Ganges, brought with them, doubtless, the knowledge of the true God. They maintained his worship for some time, and preserve it to this day, at least in certain families, who adore only the Lord of Heaven and Earth in temples, in which idols have never been erected. However, to speak more generally, the greater part of the nation soon adopted false divinities, and paid them a profane worship. These corruptions became introduced in the following manner. The Indians persuaded themselves that the Lord of Heaven exercised his care over mankind, without its being necessary to implore his protection by prayer. With respect to the demon, they judged that this malignant and jealous spirit should be appeased by offerings. It was thus that they divided their worship between the Sovereign of Heaven and the demon. They represented not the Sovereign of the Universe under figures; but the demon they represented under the most hideous forms. They painted him under the form of tigers, elephants, lions, or serpents, and often indeed they blended all these animals in one, in order to make a representation of him of the greatest possible hideousness.

The religion of the Indians was for a long time confined to the knowledge of God, and the worship of the demon, without any intermixture. In the sequel they blended with it the worship of Brama, a legislator meriting the veneration of the whole nation, by the good order and admirable policy which he established throughout India. Some

Brahmins pretend that he came from Europe, and give him a name much resembling that of Pythagoras. If the historians of India are, indeed, to be credited, the works of that philosopher may be found at the present day in the hands of the learned of the country. It is more probable, however, both that Pythagoras never made a voyage to India, and that the laws of Brama are more ancient than that philosopher.

This legislator separated the people into four casts, or principal tribes. The first is that of the Brachmans, or Bramins. This cast is the most noble, and has alone the privilege of giving to the nation those persons who are to be set apart for the services of religion, and the office of judges, or of teachers. The second tribe is that of the Rajepoots, which is solely military, their destination being to defend the state, or to extend its limits. The third are the Banians, whose occupation is limited to trade, the employment of artisans, and the sale of their wares either retail or in gross. The fourth class is that of the artisans, which is divided into several other casts, according to their different occupations; one cast not being allowed to marry into that of another. A labourer, for example, a goldsmith, or a weaver, never instructs his son in any other business than his own, and will never marry his children to one of a different trade.

Brama, who was the founder of this species of republic, instituted general laws for all the tribes, and other laws which are applicable to each in particular. The Brahmins are under an obligation to live in great austerity. It is a crime for them to eat fish, birds, four-footed animals, or even any sort of vegetables with a red tinge, which resembles a blood colour. They are prohibited from having more than one wife at a time, and their wives are forbidden from entering again into the marriage state after the death of their husbands. They are permitted to burn themselves on the same funeral pile, on which the bodies of their husbands are consumed. Brama instituted this law to put a stop to a crime which had become too common. The wives, often weary of their husbands, destroyed them secretly by poison. The device of Brama was to render it honorable for women to burn themselves on the bodies of their husbands, or to subject themselves to a perpetual widowhood after their death. Hence, the care and the affection of the wives for those to whom heaven has united them; their life or their liberty being irrevocably attached to the life of their husbands. It is a crime for a Brahmin to have intercourse with an Indian of an inferior cast, to eat with him, or even to allow himself to be touched by him. They are all under the obligation of passing their lives in the study of the law, in the contemplation of the heavens, in ministering in the temples, in burning perfumes, and making sacrifices.

The Rajepoots are not obliged to submit to austerities so severe. Being destined for the services of war, the legislator has not required at their hands abstinence so rigorous. It would be criminal in them to slay animals, but they are permitted to eat the flesh of them when they find them killed. Brama did not exact from them a rigid adherence to one wife. The race of warriors, he said, which is so perishable through the perils and fatigues to which it is exposed, cannot be rendered too prolific.

The Banians are the most rigid observers of the laws, and the most scrupulous in abstaining from eating the flesh of animals or fish. As they live in the cities, and are the only class engaged in commerce, it is their duty, above the rest, to give an example to strangers, and to artisans, of whom they are the chiefs. Charity towards man and animals has never been carried so far by any other tribe. Besides the hospitals which they have built for the reception of sick persons and for orphans, others have been founded for cows, for monkeys, and for birds. The Banians would be the most amiable of human beings, if it were not for those unsociable and rather ferocious manners engendered by the fear of being defiled by intercourse with strangers. Their propensity to trickery makes them rather dangerous in commerce.

The artisans are exempt from the observance of the more severe laws. As their employments are laborious, Brama allows them the use of more solid and nourishing aliments. This indulgence, however, is augmented or decreased in proportion to the degree of labour the different trades require. Those to whom the largest exemptions are permitted, are esteemed the most ignoble. These laws extend generally to the ancient people of India, whatsoever chief or raja they may be subject to.

However repugnant to reason the doctrines of Brama may appear, the moral tendency of his institutions is less questionable. He forbids adultery, and fornication. The greatest of all crimes is that of shedding human blood, or taking away the life of animals, whom they believe inhabited by a human soul. Lying and theft were proscribed society. Cows were to be nourished with care, never used for food, but protected and revered as the mothers of men. This is more a political, than a religious institution. Oxen are of all animals the most useful in India. They are used in carriages for travelling, and for the conveyance of the productions of the soil; supplying for those purposes the place of horses.

The kings are always taken from the cast of the Rajepoots. Never has a Banian or an Artisan been known to mount the throne; these are casts which are despised by the Brahmins. The kings treat their subjects with haughtiness, and oppress them with tributes. As the love of indolence keeps them almost always shut up within the walls of their Haram, it is seldom they are inspired with the ambition of making conquests. A disposition, besides, naturally soft and effeminate, is little calculated to produce gallant soldiers. Such was the state of the native Indians, when visited by Babar.

The Patans are a Mahometan people, who were established in India more than four hundred years before the conquest by Tamerlane. It is probable, that this colony came from Arabia, and after traversing the Indian ocean, was at first seated on the southern coast of Indostan; that the city was founded by them still called Musulipatam, and that penetrating from thence into the interior, they finally became possessed of the city of Delhi, where they ruled at the time of Tamerlane's invasion of India, to whom the place submitted. The Moguls are therefore not the first nation, which introduced Mahometanism into India.

The Parsées are another people scattered more particularly throughout the maritime parts of Indostan. They are most probably the remains of those ancient idolaters of Persia, who were constrained to leave their country, when the Mahometans, by the increase of their power and influence, would have compelled them to forsake their idolatry, and embrace the law of Mahomet. This unfortunate people preferred abandoning their native soil, to the obligation of submitting to a new faith. The Parsées acknowledge one God, and worship the sun, and fire. They suppose a certain something divine in this element; they make offerings, and immolate victims to it. They give the greatest attention to preserve a perpetuity of the ignition on their altars. If by accident it is suffered to expire, it is considered a crime, from which they can only be absolved by the ministers of their religion. They, in consequence, visit them, acknowledge their offence, and after a severe admonition from the priest, they take away with them a brand from his fire, which they bring home in triumph, to the sound of trumpets and hautboys. There are no people in the world more tractable than the Parsées. As they are all poor, and scattered throughout the country, they are regarded with contempt by the state.

As for the Moguls, their origin is traced no higher than the epoch of the arrival of Tamerlane in India. This conqueror established them in the principal fortresses which he had subjected to his power. The whole duty of these governors was originally confined to the exacting, from the Rajas of the country, the tributes which they had submitted to pay to the successors of Tamerlane.

Babar, in his disguise, visited these different nations, made himself acquainted with their manners, and formed his plan of conquest on the result of his personal observation. The kingdom of Delhi, especially, appeared to him the portion of India most worthy of his labours, and the easiest to bring into subjection. Sultan Amwixa, who at this time was in possession of Delhi, was the most powerful prince in Indostan. He was the thirty-first king of the race of those brave Patans, who had established themselves in India by force of arms. It was then resolved to enter upon the conquest of the new empire, by first attacking this monarch.

Babar, having returned to Cabul with his faithful Ranguildas, adopted the most prudent measures to ensure the success of the great enterprise he meditated. He instructed, in the first place, the Mogul officers who commanded in Delhi, to observe the motions and the preparations of Amwixa, and to give him advice of all his proceedings. Some time after, he summoned the Patan monarch to relinquish the title and character of sovereign over a country, the whole of which was a dependancy of the Mogul empire.

He added, that Tamerlane, one of his ancestors, had conquered it for his posterity. Amwixa replied with spirit—that a tributary monarch did not forfeit his rank among sovereigns—that the love of peace had alone influenced him to submit to a symbol of dependance which it became him long since to have renounced to a feeble usurper—that since his rank as a monarch was disputed, he, in his turn, refused to pay to a foreign invader, who had been driven from his own dominions, a tribute to which he was no longer entitled.

So haughty a reply brought down upon the Patan the whole vengeance of the Mogul. He ordered his troops to take their departure from Cabul, and proceed in the direction of Delhi. Amwixa did not think it necessary to stand upon the defensive, and to oppose walls to the impetuosity of Babar; his courage prompted him to take the field, and to encounter the attack of an enemy, of whose means of annoyance he had little dread. The army of Amwixa was indeed formidable in respect to numbers. It was composed of Mahometan Patans, and idolatrous Indians. The natives of the country were accustomed to the quiet domination of the Patan princes, and feared the power of the Moguls, whose severity, and avarice they had experienced. Amwixa commenced the war by taking possession of the citadel of Delhi, occupied by the Tartars, and immediately went to meet Babar, who was advancing by forced marches to engage him in battle. The principal strength of Amwixa consisted iu his elephants, which abound in the vicinity of Delhi. The two rivals met in a plain, where the Patan appeared to have the advantage over his enemy. His elephants had sufficient room to extend themselves, and his innumerable army seemed capable of surrounding with ease the weaker force of Babar. The Mogul prince had learnt from the example of Tamerlane, to regard with little apprehension the most numerous armies, when accompanied by a few faithful and warlike troops. He gave battle, and came off triumphant. The Tartar troops, led by Babar, attacked, with so much impetuosity the innumerable multitude of Indians, badly armed, that they gave way on the first assault, and fell back upon the elephants, putting them in disorder, as well as the Patan troops, who fled without its being possible to rally them. Fear made them take their flight towards the north, and seek refuge in the mountains, where they fixed their abode; and in the fastnesses of which they still exist: sometimes tributary, and in a state of subjection to the Mogul empire; and at others, in a state of rebellion and hostility. In this first engagement, Amwixa lost both life, and crown; and Babar beheld himself master of an empire more considerable than the one he had lost.

The victor nowentered the capital of his new kingdom; and took possession of the palace, and the treasures of Amwixa. Delhi was then a considerable city, situated in a fertile plain, almost at the source of the Gemna. This river, after flowing through a considerable territory, takes a serpentine course round Agra, and at last disembogues itself in the Ganges, near Eleabas. At this time there was no city in all India where there was to be found a greater number of the remains of antiquity, or more illustrious monuments, than at Delhi. It is probable, that it was formerly the capital, or at least one of the principal cities, of the kingdom of Porus, and, that the celebrated battle, which terminated in the defeat of that hero by Alexander, was fought near Delhi. A column is still to be seen, erected in the time of Alexander, with the remains of an inscription in unknown characters.

The kingdom of Delhi had belonged to princes descended from Porus. It is said, that Rana, who was defeated by Tamerlane, traced his origin to that prince. In the year 1085, sultan Alaudin, the first Patan king, he established court at Delhi, and his posterity continued to reign till the year 1519, when Babar made himself master of it.

The first care of the new king was to establish his authority over the people, which he effected partly by intimidation, and partly by conciliation. The counsels of the virtuous Ranguildas did not a little contribute to reconcile them to the conqueror. The native Indians, naturally effeminate, and born to servitude, easily accustomed themselves to the yoke. The Patans, weakened by the defeat of their king, and by the desertion of the bravest part of the nation, which had taken refuge in the mountains, submitted quietly to the government of a prince of their own religion. Thus the Tartars took possession of all the posts, and of all the dignities of the empire.

Babar conceived the plan of a government entirely new. He established laws, at his own pleasure, in a country which was his by conquest. All the Mogul emperors, his successors, followed in the same path; they became the fundamental laws of the kingdom, and are regarded as the work of the good Ranguildas.

The Mogul has the sole propriety of all the lands of the empire. They descend not from father to son; but they return to the sovereign upon the death of him to whom the usufruct was granted. Thus the people are, properly speaking, only the emperor's husbandmen.

The officers of the court are entirely dependant on the generosity of their master; and as no one is by birth possessed of riches, so none can be great but by the munificence of the prince.

The principal nobility, that is to say, the governors of provinces, the first minister, and the secretary of state, are called Omrhas, and hold the first rank in the state. The idolatrous Rajas, or the Indian nobles, who ruled a small state before the conquest of their country, have also at the court the rank of Omhras. There is this distinction; that the children of Rajas succeed to their fathers in the species of sovereignty which is preserved to them; but that the children of Mahometan Omhras lose every thing in losing their fathers. The emperor is sole heir to all the officers of his court.

The Man-Sebdars are Omhras of the second rank, serving at court, and in the armies. They are gradually promoted to the first dignities, according to their services, and their fidelity.

Babar did not commit his laws to writing, either as they respected proceedings, in civil or criminal causes. A written law would have placed limits to that absolute authority, which the emperor assumed over the wealth, and the lives of his subjects. According to circumstances, without any other rule of action than his own good sense, or his caprice, the Mogul emperor decides causes, and pronounces sentences of death, which are executed on the spot, under the eyes of the prince. The guilty person is beheaded, or trampled under the feet of elephants, trained to this species of execution.

The emperor every day in a saloon gives audience to his subjects generally. He listens to their complaints, adjudges their differences, and punishes the guilty. He suffers no other pretext than extreme illness, to dispense him from this duty. In smaller matters, he acts in concert with a Casy, or judge of the people, and leaves the care of the police to the Cotwall, who fills, at the same time, the office of provost, and of civil judge.

A government, in which the authority of the prince was so absolute, and so well maintained, without, nevertheless, violating the ancient rights of the primitive inhabitants, acquired Babar the love and veneration of the people.

The submission to his rule was universal, and his states in a short time became very flourishing.

The Tartars, the former subjects of Babar, arrived in crowds from Samarcand, to enrich themselves under the new monarch. Employments were given them at court. It was then, that the Indians gave the name of Moguls without distinction to all the Tartars, and transferred to the nation generally, a name, which at first was peculiar to the royal family. A great many Persians likewise came to Delhi, to seek their fortune. The employments which were conferred upon them at court attracted others; thus the Mahometan rule soon became the most influential, and the strangers occupied all the governments, and all the great offices in the state. Finally, the Rajas, who, in the beginning were from necessity treated with consideration, fell by degrees into contempt, and the Mahometan became the prevailing religion.

Laws so wisely conceived, and a domination so tranquil, would have secured to Babar the admiration of his age, if the ingratitude, natural to the Moguls, had not tarnished his glory. The only instance of rigour, and injustice, which he exercised, was towards the very author of his elevation. Ranguildas, who had taught him both how to conquer, and how to govern, was disgraced by his master, and in order to escape death, condemned himself to exile. This great man, disguised as a Faquir, retired to an obscure village. The Chronicle reports, that after the departure of this faithful minister, the kingdom fell into disorder. The insurrections, and the scarcity which followed, afflicted the people, and shook the throne of the new monarch. The state appeared in danger of being subverted, unless recourse was had to the counsels of the man, who had first laid its foundations. The emperor became sensible of his fault, and repented of having obliged so virtuous a subject to fly his presence. He made several attempts to discover his retreat, and at last, it is said, made use of the following artifice to bring him back to court:—

Babar issued a singular edict throughout his kingdom, which commanded the inhabitants of the villages to bring to Delhi their bazars, or market places. He wished to ascertain what apology each village would furnish, by way of evading a compliance with an ordinance, which it appeared impossible to obey. He trusted, that the village, in which Ranguildas was concealed, would display some ingenuity in extricating itself from the dilemma; and that his minister would by this means be discovered. In effect, Ranguildas, who passed, in a village at a distance from the court, the life of a sage, and had acquired some reputation in the place in which he resided, suggested to the inhabitants an excuse, which ought doubtless to have contented the emperor. "Go to Delhi," he said, "and presenting yourselves to the king, speak to him in the following manner:—'The bazar of the village, my lord, whence we come, is ready to obey your orders; there is only one difficulty to be removed, which is, that it is ignorant of the road to Delhi. If your majesty will condescend to send the bazar of your capital, to serve as a guide to ours, it will immediately commence its progress, in obedience to your mandate." The emperor thought the reply of the peasants so ingenious, that wishing to know the author, he commanded that he should be brought into his presence. Ranguildas, in spite of any resistance he could make, was thus conducted by the peasants to the court of his master. Babar soon caused him to forget, by his kindness, his former bad treatment. He was restored to all his posts, and his counsels reassumed all their influence.

Ruled by so wise a minister, the state soon recovered its previous lustre. Abundance seemed to return with

Ranguildas, and peace was re-established after long dissentions. It is true, that the kingdom of Cascar, which had fallen by right of succession to Babar, in consequence of the death of one of the descendants of Abouchaid, was invaded by a descendant of one of the princes from whom Tamerlane had usurped it. But Ranguildas judged it unwise to embark his master in a perilous war, at a distance from a country newly conquered. He relinquished a doubtful, for a certain possession. It was in this spirit, that Babar reigned peaceably, and obtained the reputation of a wise prince, who had the talent to conquer a throne more brilliant than the one he had lost. Babar died in the year 1530. He reigned thirty years in India, five years at Samarcand, and passed three years, partly in exile, and partly in making a conquest of the kingdom of Delhi. Fortune, which abandoned him in Tartary, favored him always in Indostan ; but wisdom and justice accompanied him throughout his career, never forsaking him, even in his reverses.

AMAYUM; OR, HOMAYUM.

SIXTH EMPEROR.

Is dethroned by a Patan Prince. Retires to Persia. Returns to India, and re-establishes himself upon the Throne. His Death.

THE great empire, which Babar had conquered with so much labour, had very nearly been lost by his son Amayum. The young king experienced, that a crown, newly acquired, in preserved with difficulty. The authority of Babar, whilst he lived, curbed the revolting spirit of the natives. But the commencement of a new reign, in a monarchy of such recent creation, furnished an opportunity for intrigue, and the setting up of various pretensions. Chira was a Patan prince, of the race of those whom Babar had dethroned. During the preceding reign he had been suffered to reside at court, and was treated with distinction; but the wise policy of Ranguildas excluded from any office or part in the government, a man of shrewd character, and of a race which rendered him obnoxious to suspicion. Amayum, in this respect, neglected the conduct of his father, and the counsels of Ranguildas. He advanced Chira by degrees to the highest honors; confided to him the guard of his person, and the conduct of his armies. The power of Chira became formidable to Amayum, who soon repented of having too much aggrandised a subject, contrary to the dictates of sound policy. In effect, the general, who found himself in a condition to make use of the confidence, and munificence of the prince, for his destruction, changed his name of Chira, which signifies a young lion, to that of Chircha, the royal or the king lion. Amayum made some attempts to repress the insolence of a seditious subject. Chircha had always the advantage of the king's troops. The city of Delhi became the theatre of several combats. Every one took the side which consorted with his inclination, or interests. The Patans and some Indian Rajas embraced the party of Chircha. Amayum had scarcely any support but from his Tartars, of whom he formed in haste an army, inconsiderable in point of numbers. They were no longer those gallant conquerors, of whom a small number had under Babar brought into subjection a great kingdom, and put to flight the largest armies. They were men already enervated by their residence in India, prone through the heat of the climate to indulgence, and the neglect of discipline. However, with this small force, Amayum took the field, no longer daring to confide in the walls of his palace, where he would have subjected himself to the risk of being starved into a surrender. The countenance of the king displayed still marks of the ancient valour of the Tartars; but he was ill seconded. A battle won gave empire to Babar, a battle lost sent his son into exile. Amayum was defeated, and escaped through the assistance only of some brave Persians, who saved the life of the prince, and escorted him into Persia; in which kingdom he took refuge. After a troubled reign of eleven years, always disturbed by civil war, Amayum was thus compelled to seek protection in a foreign court, against a Patan king, who had re-possessed himself of the rights of his nation.

As the Orientals are scrupulous observers of the flight of birds, they drew a favorable augury from an incident which occurred during the flight of Amayum. The fugitive prince had laid himself down to sleep about mid-day, in an open spot, and was exposed to the sun's rays. An eagle, followed by its young ones, appeared over the head of the king, and soaring in the air with extended wings, covered the head of Amayum, defending him from the sun's heat, and preventing his slumbers from being disturbed. So favourable an omen restored courage to the king on his awaking. The small number of courtiers, by whom he was accompanied, predicted from this incident, that he would once more reign in India, and with great glory.

Amayum, having arrived at the court of Persia, maintained his accustomed dignity, which he knew how to support, even in misfortune. The king of Persia received the Mogul in a garden, on his arrival. Either by chance, or design, there was in the place of interview, a sopha so small, that two persons were unable to be seated at the same time. The Mogul was perplexed. Anger and mortification appeared on his countenance; but good sense came to the aid of his mortified feelings. Amayum resumed at once the sentiments which were suitable to his present condition, and worthy of his great mind. He invited the king of Persia to seat himself on the sopha, and placing himself on the left hand of the Persian, (which is the place of honor in the east), he rested himself on his bow-case, which he placed on the ground. He avoided, by this means, the disgrace, of appearing standing in the presence of a king, whose assistance he came to implore. The Persian was astonished at the presence of mind shewn by Amayum, and felt a still stronger disposition to serve him. The conversation of the two kings consisted chiefly in expressions of condolence, on the part of the Persian, and of thanks and protestations of gratitude, on the side of the Mogul. The interview did not terminate in mere compliments; the king of Persia added to them good offices. He assigned to the fugitive emperor a palace and officers, ordered him to be served as a sovereign prince, supplied him with amusements, and furnished his haram. He then exhorted his guest to take patience, until a favorable opportunity should occur to put him once more in possession of his kingdom.

Chircha, on his side, omitted nothing which could conciliate the people, and render him worthy of the throne, of which he had taken possession. Conveniences for facilitating commerce were much wanted in India. Halting places were no where to be found, to give refreshment to the merchant in his tedious travels. The usurper judged, therefore, that it would be necessary, in order to encourage merchants to trade in a country abounding in all sorts of productions, to follow the example of Persia in building caravanseras, or public inns, for the accommodation of travellers. Many were accordingly erected in the cities, and at certain distances from each other, throughout the country. Had no other advantage accrued to India from the usurpation of Chircha, this alone merits a confession of its usefulness. He did more than merely furnish a place of cover for persons travelling; he established a certain number of domestics in each of the inns, whose duty it was to attend gratuitously upon travellers, to prepare the beds, and to take care of the furniture. He taxed, at a moderate sum, the provisions required for the necessities of the traveller, and his beast. In several of the caravanseras, baths and stoves were constructed; and, in their vicinity, beautiful avenues of trees were planted, to serve as an agreeable recreation to the sojourners. The weary traveller was to be lodged, and fed, at the king's expense. In imitation of the example given by Chircha, many devout Mahometans founded caravanseras in different places, upon the great roads, leading to those cities, where a commercial intercourse was particularly desirable. They were generally erected near to a lake, or piece of water; to which small mosques were added by the founders, destined, by the greater part, as a place of burial for themselves and their families.

In these public inns were commonly to be found those who trafficked in jewels, stuffs, and cloths of different patterns, players on instruments, male and female dancers, artisans of every class; but, more especially, saddlers, shoers of horses, and provincial quacks. How consolatory must have been the reflection to the traveller, of having the certain assurance of finding, at the termination of a toilsome journey, an apartment, a couch, and refreshments free from cost.

Chircha effected a reformation in the weights, and measures of the country, which he brought to a fixed standard. Before his time, the use of scales was unknown. All commodities were sold by guess. Measures of an uncertain character, such as that of a hand or an elbow length, were alone in use. In consequence of these regulations, mercantile operations were conducted with greater facility, and more advantageously; and merchants from all quarters flocked to the Indies. Chircha was not less attached to his religion, than to justice, and a desire of enriching his subjects. He freighted every year a vessel at his own expense; and those of his subjects, who, from a principle of devotion, desired to pay a visit to Mecca, were conveyed thither at the charge of the monarch.

This love of peace, and regard to religion, did not prevent Chircha from attending to those precautions which were necessary for the maintenance of his power. He kept, in a state of readiness, large armies, which he reviewed in the plains of Delhi; and, especially, a considerable corps of artillery. He was himself so good a cannoneer, that he could, at his pleasure, hit any mark at which he chose to take aim. One day, amusing himself at this exercise, he met with an accident which cost him his life. A piece of ordnance, of extraordinary size, had been sent him from Bengal, and, in attempting to make an essay of its capacity, the cannon, being too heavily charged, burst, and one of the fragments striking him, he was killed instantaneously. Chircha reigned nine years, and was interred in the centre of a pleasant island, situated in a beautiful piece of water, near to the city of Samahergam.

The death of Chircha gave birth to one of those extraordinary revolutions, which commonly succeed to a reign which has been an usurpation; especially, when the usurper dies without leaving children of an age capable of succeeding him. The whole kingdom was in a flame, in consequence of the diversity of interests, and the number of pretenders to the crown. The Patan nobles flattered themselves with the hopes of retaining possession of a sceptre which had long remained in their nation. The Indian Rajas, on the contrary, prepared to expel their ancient masters, and re-conquer a throne of which they had been despoiled. The number of rival candidates divided the forces of the kingdom, and rendered its subjection the more easy.

In the mean while, Amayum continued to reside in Persia, in that restless state of mind which was produced by uncertainty with respect to the future, and an anxious desire to remount a throne of which he had been despoiled. He paid his court regularly to his benefactor, the King of Persia, and endeavoured by promises to interest him in his re-establishment. Whilst Amayum was sedulously occupied in watching every opportunity, which might present itself, for recovering his rights, he received the news of the death of Chircha, and of the dissensions to which it had given rise in the kingdom of Delhi. One of the chiefs of the Faquirs, who travel the country under the pretext of piety, thought it his duty to inform his former sovereign of the distractions which prevailed in India, and to invite him to return, and take possession of the government of his former kingdom. He assured him that the people would bestow the crown upon him on his arrival. He made him acquainted with the character of the contending factions, and the facility he would experience in destroying rivals, weak through disunion. Chadaula, which was the name of the Faquir, added, that the stars favored the enterprise, and assured him, on the part of heaven, of a fortunate issue.

Intelligence so favorable, and such useful counsel, were not neglected. Amayum had recourse to the King of Persia, and solicited the aid of troops and money, to enable him to re-conquer his kingdom, for which, in the event of being successful, he should be indebted to him alone; and he engaged, in such case, to pay him tribute. He also engaged to remunerate the king for the expenses he had incurred on his account, by ceding to him the province of Candahar, and the city of Sindy, which border upon Persia. The Persian accepted the offers of the Mogul, and supplied him with an army composed of some infantry and of twelve thousand horse. This was a small force for the atchievement of so great an enterprise; but Amayum was well assured, that so soon as he should make his appearance in that country, he would be joined by his ancient subjects, and that his army would go on increasing in strength, in proportion as he approached the city of Delhi. The Mogul took then his leave of Persia. After mutual expressions of regard at their final parting, the Sophi ventured to give him some salutary counsel. He advised him, as soon as he should have re-possessed himself of his kingdom, to encourage the natural animosity, which had always subsisted between the Patans and the Rajepoots, and insensibly to crush the one by the instrumentality of the other. He added, that to enable kings to reign in security, it was necessary to maintain jealousies among subjects of a formidable and intractable character.

Loaded with the favors of the King of Persia, and instructed by his wise counsels, Amayum entered India on the side of Cabul. His army every day became more formidable by the junction of the Mahometans and Indians, whom interest, or fidelity attached to his new fortune. Scarcely any opposition impeded the progress of the conqueror; and the recovery of all the provinces, which extend from the frontiers of Persia to Lahor, was effected at the price of a few slight skirmishes. Lahor itself threatened a more powerful opposition. This was a considerable city, considered in India as a second capital. It was surrounded by good walls, and had a fortress built on a spot which appeared inaccessible. The governor of this place, a Patan by nation, hoped to profit by the divisions of the country, and to secure to himself a species of sovereignty at Lahor, and in the province of Pangiab, or of the five rivers. Amayum purposed to get possession of this city, (the siege of which would have been attended with considerable difficulty), if possible, by stratagem. With this view, he sent forward, by a different road from that through which his army was marching, one hundred resolute young Persians. They were disguised as pilgrims carrying staffs, to assist their weary steps; and in this manner presented themselves in the evening, without the gates of the citadel. Being divided into several small bands, those, who were the first to arrive, entered the place without difficulty; but others, which arrived at a late hour, found the gates closed. These began to utter aloud their complaints, and to exclaim against so little charity being shewn towards devout pilgrims, who were just returning to their homes from Mecca. They begged only a slight alms, and cover for a single night. They added, that if so inconsiderable an aid were refused them, the avenging Deity would know how to punish the insensibility of the inhabitants. Aziscam, (which was the name of the governor), heard their complaints, and was touched with compassion. He commanded, that the gates should be opened to the poor travellers; but his pity increased, when he beheld this last band of wanderers habited as Santons, who are a sort of Mahometan hermits. This charity, which would, in Europe, doubtless, be deemed injudicious, appears excusable in the Indies. The disguised pilgrims, and false hermits, availed themselves of it to get possession of Lahor. Introduced into the palace of the governor, they appeared with a mark of devotion on their countenances, calculated to deceive the most penetrating observer. They, then, drew their poignards from beneath their vests, and attacking the governor and his garrison with the desperate fury of men determined to sell their lives dear, succeeded in making themselves masters of the fortress, which they resolved to maintain till the arrival of the army of the king should enable them to put it in possession of the city. Amayum, advancing by forced marches, took possession of Lahor. He remained there no longer than was necessary to enable him to place as governor over it an officer on whose fidelity he could rely. He then resumed his march towards Delhi. Every thing hostile was subdued by the presence of the conqueror. Amayum experienced but a feeble resistance from the Patans, or the Rajas. A single battle, fought near Panipat, at the distance of three leagues from Delhi, put to flight all the forces of Indostan; and secured to the successors of Tamerlane the empire, of which they have continued in possession to the present day.

The first care of Amayum, as soon as he had remounted his throne, was to conciliate the minds of the people, and to gain the affections of the Indian nobles; as well as to reward the Faquir Chadaula, who had first acquainted him with the death of Chircha. The king assigned to him revenues to be possessed in his own right, and to descend to his posterity, in contradiction to the laws of the kingdom. The descendants of this illustrious Faquir are the only Mahometans in the empire who possess a domain, over which the sovereign has no control. The family of Chadaula, in consequence, holds the first rank in the Mogul empire. The Faquir himself is, to this day, honored as a saint. The people, and even the emperor, at times, pay a visit to his sepulchre from a spirit of devotion. This trait of gratitude, on the part of Amayum, is so extraordinary in the history of the Mogul emperors, that it is recorded in the Chronicle in the most pompous terms.

Amayum would certainly have merited the praises bestowed on him, if he had kept his word to the King of Persia, which a regard to good faith, and a sense of gratitude for such essential aid as enabled him to recover his kingdom, should have taught him sacredly to observe. But, on the contrary, he, on this occasion, acted in direct opposition to the principles of justice, and of honor. No sooner had he remounted the throne, than the Mogul refused to pay tribute to the King of Persia, or to surrender into his hands the provinces of Candahar, and the city of Sindy. How truly has it been observed, that good faith, or an honorable observance of treaties, has seldom, if ever, been known to exist among the Mahometan princes, of whatsoever nation or sect.

Amayum, subsequently, made as good a use of the counsels of the King of Persia, which were to enable him to rule with effect over his newly-recovered states, as he had previously made of his troops, by which he had been enabled te re-conquer them. He was always devising means for humbling the Patans, and for the advancement of the Indians. He gave particular encouragement to the native race of warriors, the brave Rajepoots. He composed his army of this class of his subjects, promoted them to offices and did not scruple to relax something from Mahometan austerity, mixing at times with the idolaters in their temples, and assisting at their ceremonies. It is even said, that he appeared every morning, before break of day, on a balcony, where he waited the rising of the sun, that he might pay his devotion to that splendid luminary. Whether this be true or not, certain it is, that Amayum never passed for a very rigid Mahometan.

It was in views of policy such as these, that the king educated his son Akebar. The lot of this young prince was involved, for a time, in obscurity. The sultaness, his mother, had been disgraced on false suspicion. I shall relate the account as given by the Chronicle. The Portuguese writers, not having had the opportunity of becoming acquainted with this document, have given a false colouring to the adventures of the queen, and the birth of the son.

At the time, when Amayum was forced to quit Delhi, Chircha made himself master of the palace, the treasures, and the haram of the fugitive monarch. The queen became, with the rest of his women, the captive of the conqueror. Although she was possessed of a beauty, which might have captivated his fortunate rival, Chircha, who was a truly great prince, and more a man of honor than comports with the law of Mahomet, treated the queen with distinction and respect. He did more. As soon as he knew that she was with child, he released her from captivity, and sent her to her husband in Persia. The suspicions of the Mogul were the cause of great unhappiness to the queen. Amayum was fully persuaded that an enemy, who had dethroned him, would not scruple to assail the honor of his wife. The princess, repulsed by her husband on solitary conjecture, claimed the protection of the Sultaness of Persia, and made Chircha acquainted with the bad treatment she suffered, from the jealous alarms of Amayum. "I am," she wrote to him, "an unfortunate princess, of whose entire innocence you are not ignorant; it is incumbent upon you to bear testimony to my purity." The Patan, touched with the affliction of the queen, wrote to the Mogul in her favor; rendered testimony to her virtue, and swore upon the Alcoran, that never had the fidelity of the sultaness suffered the slightest taint. Upon receiving such unequivocal evidence of her virtue, Amayum's former affection for the princess revived; he recalled her to his palace, and she became from that time his chief consolation in his exile. To crown his felicity, the prince Akebar was born, a most lovely infant, in whose features were distinctly to be traced a marked resemblance to his father Amayum. This son was the object of the tenderest cares of the king, after his return to the Indies.

However, Amayum, still in the heighth of his prosperity, calling to mind the precariousness of human existence; although in the meridian of life, and in excellent health, applied himself to the preparing of a mausoleum for the interment of his remains. All the Mahometan nobles in India are inclined to this species of devotion. The expense they lavish on such monuments, and the revenues with which they endow them, are scarcely credible. A provision is made for a certain number of Moulas, (doctors of the Mahometan law), who pray continually for the soul of the deceased, and read the Alcoran by the side of the sepulchre.

Whilst Amayum was engaged in constructing a work so agreeable to Mahometan piety, an accident befel him, which occasioned his death. He had caused the plan of the mausoleum, in which his ashes were to repose, to be marked out without the gates of Delhi, at the termination of a large bridge of twelve arches. The work was already far advanced, and the walls were raised to a level with the key stone of the arch. The king, carrying in his hand a measuring rod, was mounted on the wall, and was walking round the edifice, on its cornice, which was very wide, when the rod on which he rested broke in his hand. The king fell with the pieces of the rod, and having rolled for a while on the entablature, to which the architect had given a slope for the purpose of carrying off the waters, he fell to the ground, was dashed to pieces, and found his death on the very spot intended for the place of his burial. This fine monument of the piety of Amayum was afterwards finished, and his body was interred in it. The sepulchre is still to be seen, ornamented on the inside with the most beautiful marbles; and on the outside surmounted with a magnificent dome, the gilding of which, in a country where the sun shines with a lustre unknown in Europe, is almost too dazzling for the sight. An establishment of Moulas have the charge of keeping the edifice in repair; they scatter continually fresh flowers upon the grave, taking care to cover it with a magnificent cloth of gold brocade.

Amayum lived only two years, nine months, and fourteen days, after the recovery of his kingdom, and twenty-two years from his first accession to it. He died in the year 1552.

AKEBAR,

SEVENTH EMPEROR.

His birth in Persia. Establishes himself firmly upon the Throne. Adds the Kingdom of Guzzerat to his Empire. Undertakes the Conquest of the Kingdom of the Decan. Builds the City of Agra. Besieges Chitor in order to carry off the Princess Padmani. Punishes his Son Iehan Guir for his revolt. Causes some Jesuit Missionaries to arrive at his Court. Becomes the Founder of a new Religion. The Missionaries leave him. Recalls them. Loses his second Son. His Death.

THE successor of Amayum was the true heir of the ability, and valour of Tamerlane. All the good qualities of the Mogul princes seemed to be re-united in the person of this prince, with scarcely any of the alloy of those defects, which occasion the people of Europe to look upon them as barbarians. A prince has rarely been known possessed of more natural sagacity, or a more comprehensive mind; of a nobler or more valiant nature, and, at the same time, so tender, so compassionate, and so sensible to obligation. In a word, Akebar was equally a great king, and a truly honest man. The historians of Europe have done justice to his merit. His glory has been celebrated in their works; but I am able to aver, that they have merely furnished a sketch of the transactions of this celebrated reign. It will be here attempted, with the assistance of the Mogul Chronicle, to trace with fidelity the life of this illustrious prince. The transactions, which will be related, will all have been extracted from the most approved historians, and documents of the country. At times, some use will be made of the historians of Europe, when they are found in accordance with these original records.

The political edifice, constructed by Akebar, was built

upon the foundations laid by his father. He was convinced, that it would not be possible to reign in security without crushing the power of the Patans, a nation which had exceedingly multiplied in India. Such as derived their origin from the Tartars were too few in number to be capable of making head against the incredible multitude of this people, who had been seated in the country four hundred years. He, therefore, resolved to retain in his service those Persian soldiers, whom Amayum had brought with him to India, and of whose assistance he had availed himself to establish and to maintain himself on the throne. In order to attach them the more to the country, and to his service, he encouraged them to form matrimonial alliances at Delhi. Thus it happens, that the greater number of those who are called, in Indostan, the fair men, and sometimes Moguls, is rather composed of the descendants of Persians, than of Tartars. It is not till the third generation, that their complexion changes, together with their native vigour, and courage. In course of time, they become sallow, and effeminate.

Akebar, besides the Persians, of whose valour he availed himself to sustain his power, attached also to his service those brave Rajepoots, who are the flower of the Indians. They were of great use to the Mogul in extending his dominion. The idolatrous Rajas no longer felt any repugnance to acknowledge him as their superior lord. From all parts they collected around his person, and became his principal courtiers. Akebar no longer experienced any difficulty in levying the tributes, the exaction of which had always been attended with so much trouble to his predecessors. A policy which he employed to fix the Indians in his interests, was, to receive into the number of his wives their daughters, and to contract in marriage with the Rajas princesses of the Mogul blood. By means of these

Mahometan women, he embroiled the Rajas in perpetual jars among one another. They had been taught in the haram, in which they were educated, to divert the hostile designs of their future spouses from the Mogul, and direct them towards the Rajas their neighbours. "Your laws," they said to their husbands, "allow you to make war only with the Rajepoots, a people to whose cast you owe your origin; to them only the spirit of rivalry should be confined." It was by language of this nature, that Akebar sowed discord between the native chiefs; through their divisions, Akebar was enabled to reign unmolested, and to pursue his conquests. If these idolatrous princes had considered their own strength, and had combined together against the Mahometan Patans and Tartars, who sought to destroy each other, they might, doubtless, have expelled them the country, and have emancipated themselves from the yoke of foreigners.

When Akebar entered upon his reign, the kingdom of Delhi was much confined on its southern frontier. Some kingdoms of Western India, beyond the river Indus, were in the power of the Moguls. On the side of Persia, Candahar, Cabul, Moultan, the Pangiab and Delhi, of which provinces Akebar was master, composed a considerable empire. The southern part of Indostan, which remained unsubjected, at the present day, forms the chief source of that immense wealth, which renders the Mogul the richest and most powerful monarch in the universe. Although the river Indus partly held its course through the states possessed by Akebar, still, not being possessed of a sea port, his empire was unable to enjoy the advantages of a free commerce; its operations being much shackled, in consequence of their being restricted to land-carriage. Akebar, therefore, undertook to push his conquests to the Southern Ocean, to a great distance beyond the lands, which had been rendered tributary by Tamerlane. The subjection of the kingdom of Guzzerat was the first enterprize undertaken by the young monarch.

Guzzerat is one of the most fertile countries of India, and the best situated for commerce. It extends from the river Tapté on the east, on which is situated the city of Surat, to the mouth of the river Indus on the West. This coast, abounding in all kinds of wealth, was at this time frequented by a concourse of all the nations of Europe, and Asia. The Portuguese had been long established upon the coast, and had made some conquests.

Sultan Bahadur, or Badur, reigned in Guzzerat. He was a descendant of one of those Mahometan adventurers, who, having originally emigrated from Arabia with the Patans, had, with views of participating in the wealth of the country, taken up their abode in India, and from being at first only simple traders, availed themselves afterwards of the weakness and effeminacy of the Indian kings to acquire sovereignties on the southern coast of India. Badur had been engaged in a series of hostilities with the Portuguese, who had recently dispossessed him of the city of Diu, situated in the vicinity of Surat and Cambaye. However, when the Mogul advanced towards the kingdom of Guzzerat, Badur and the Portuguese joined their forces, in order to arrest the progress of the conqueror. The viceroy of Goa, and his council in the Indies, considered that it would be bad policy to remain idle spectators, and suffer the Mogul emperor to extend his dominion throughout the maritime coast of Indostan: and that his power, already become so formidable in the northern parts of India, unless resisted, might eventually prove fatal to their interests. With these views, they furnished assistance to Badur. This prince marched to encounter Akebar, with an army composed of Indians and Portuguese. The Mogul, then, became sensible, how necessary it was for a king to command his armies in India in person, that he might be able by his presence to inspire the weak and timid with confidence, and by his example engage them to bear cheerfully those duties and fatigues, which the heat of the climate renders almost insupportable. The sight of the Portuguese, whose reputation and valour had spread to Delhi, discouraged the troops of Akebar. They had very nearly abandoned the enterprize. Akebar had caused his army to precede him, and followed it by easy journeys. He was at the distance of forty leagues, when the news reached him, that his enterprize was on the point of miscarrying, through the terror which had seized his troops. Their imagination represented the Portuguese as men dropped from the skies, or risen from the bosom of the ocean. They were, especially, terrified at their floating machines, (the name by which their vessels of war were known at Delhi), unaware of their utter uselessness in a battle on land. Akebar made so much haste, that his sudden presence restored confidence to his army. He put himself at the head of his troops, and falling with rapidity upon his enemies, he taught his followers that the Portuguese were by no means invincible. In effect, the army of Badur was completely routed. The Indians then, who fought under his orders, abandoned their chief. Badur fled; his children fell into the hands of the conqueror, and were by his orders put to death. This single victory gave the Mogul entire possession of the rich kingdom of Guzzerat. All the cities opened their gates to the conqueror; the places occupied by the Portuguese, on the coast, alone remained unassailed. They were fortified agreeably to the tactics of Europe, and the Mogul was not yet acquainted with the art of laying siege to places according to scientific rules.

The kingdom of the Decan experienced the same fate as that of Guzzerat. The young conqueror reduced it under his yoke. Brampour, Acer, Amadanagar, and Doltubad are the chief cities of this kingdom. The two first obeyed a Mahometan prince, named Mostafa. The flattery of his subjects had given him the title of Melec, or King, although the state which he ruled was but a province of very limited extent. Amadanagar and its territory were subject to the Princess Candé, who took the title of Queen, or Bibi. Ambar possessed the lordship of Doltabad, which he ruled despotically. These two princes, and the princess, who divided between them the sovereignty of the Decan, forgot their former animosities, made a league against Akebar, and assembled an army of forty thousand horse to combat the common enemy. Mostafa, a prince as sagacious as brave, commanded in chief the army; Ambar commanded one of the wings; and the Princess Candé, animated with a courage superior to her sex, led the other wing, entirely composed of her own subjects. It was not difficult for the Mogul emperor, at the head of a victorious army, to put to the rout a tumultuary force, composed of the troops of three confederate powers, too often found to be inefficient in action; but the besieging them, separately, in their cities, was a task of greater difficulty. The citadel of Acer made the most resistance. Mostafa, who defended it in person, performed all that could be expected from the skill of a great captain. A more powerful artillery had never been known in Indostan. Some ancient culverins in the fortress of Acer, of a most formidable construction, were particularly admired; for, long before the use of powder and cannon was known in Europe, these destructive inventions had been discovered in India. The troops of Akebar suffered incredible fatigue from the frequent sorties made by the troops of Mostafa. Oppressed by the labours of a long siege, and by the heats, which, in this southern latitude, are almost insupportable in the month of May, they were upon the point of relinquishing the siege, when they received intelligence from deserters that water began to fail in the citadel. The renewed hope of a successful issue put an end to their discouragement. Akebar pressed the place more closely; Mostafa, distressed by the want of water, and perceiving that the rainy season was yet at a distance, despaired of being able to fill his cisterns. Under this apprehension, he resolved to abandon, secretly, and alone, a fortress, which it was no longer in his power to defend, and to endeavour to reach Brampour, that he might be enabled, by fortifying himself in that place, to defend what remained of his state. He, then, quitted the place by night, unattended, taking an unfrequented road, but fell, notwithstanding, into the hands of the scouts of the army. Mostafa was by no means disconcerted when brought into the presence of the emperor; he displayed a presence of mind which never forsook him in the greatest dangers. The Mogul demanded who he was, and if he expected any favor at his hands. "I am king Mostafa," replied the prisoner, "who have come out of the place you are besieging, for the express purpose of seeking to obtain from my enemy the counsel and assistance, of which I stand in need, in my difficulties. It will not become so great a prince as you are, to refuse a salutary counsel to one who has need of it; or to give such as will be pernicious to him. The place, which I defend, begins to suffer from a scarcity of water. What does it become me to do, that I may be enabled to escape that state of servitude, with which I am menaced?" Akebar was surprised at the discourse of Mostafa; and as he piqued himself upon a generous bearing, he made him an answer, which was both obliging, and advantageous to Mostafa. "You are free," he replied, "to return to the citadel, which you have so ably defended. Should heaven be disposed in your favor, and will your preservation, you will be furnished abundantly with water, when your occasions require it." Akebar did not suspect the good fortune, which providence prepared for his enemy. Although the rainy season seldom commences in India before the middle of June, when it lasts generally three months, almost without intermission, it now preceded the usual period of its opening. On the following night it rained so abundantly, that the cisterns of Acer were filled. Akebar, who had lost the opportunity of atchieving a conquest, through a principle of generosity alone, changed the siege into a blockade; and marched with his army to the attack of Brampour. As this city was not defended by Mostafa in person, it was soon surrendered to the besiegers. The taking of the capital, was soon followed by tho surrender of Acer. Mostafa, yielding to his unhappy fate, capitulated. He accepted a command in the army of his conquerer, and held for a while, at the court of the Mogul, the rank conceded to the Indian Rajas. The princess Candé did not display less spirit in the defence of the city of Amadanagar. Unappalled by the formidable army of Akebar, she beheld with perfect composure the Mogul, returned conqueror of Mostafa, surround, and lay siege to the capital of her dominions. Akebar was detained more than two months at the foot of her ramparts. Obliged at last to yield to the perseverance of the besiegers, she conceived a singular mode of taking revenge on her enemy. All the gold and silver of which she was possessed, the princess caused to be melted, and made into bullets, on which were engraved in the characters of the country, words, expressive of maledictions against the usurper. With these some culverins where loaded, capable of carrying ball to the distance of a league, and the bullets were fired into the copses and lesser woods, by which the place is on every side environed. The princess at last capitulated, after having scattered all the riches of which she purposed to disappoint her conqueror. The princess soon repented of her rage. At the sight of her vanquisher, she ceased to be his enemy. Akebar placed her among the number of his wives, and she was treated as his queen, or rather, perhaps, she was considered for a long time, as his favourite Sultana. Some of these bullets of gold and silver are occasionally found,even at the present day, in the vicinity of Amadanagar. It is but a short time since, that a peasant discovered one of gold, weighing eight pounds. It was seen by M. Manouchy, who was much gratified with reading the inscription.

Ambar did not think proper to confine himself within the walls of Doltubad, but made haste to succour the besieged princess. His army was composed of fifty thousand men, he, having made a levy of nearly all his subjects, throughout his states, capable of bearing arms. But his troops were all native Indians, destitute of courage, and wretchedly armed. Akebar went out to give them battle, and surprised them while marching without order, resembling more a multitude of men, who were upon a journey, than soldiers, who were marching to battle. A confused troop of cowardly Indians was defeated with little difficulty. The Mogul, who lost not a single man of his army, killed the greater part of the fugitives, and dispersed the remainder. Ambar was found at more than three leagues distance from the field of battle, pierced with many wounds. He had, doubtless, found his death at the hands of his own soldiers; for it was afterwards discovered, that he had not been present in the combat, and that he had always kept himself at a considerable distance from the heat of the action. The Mogul, become thus master of the kingdom of the Decan, beheld nearly all the southern coast of Indostan subject to his empire.

The subjection of two kingdoms established the authority of Akebar throughout the Indies. The terror of his name, alone, kept the Rajas to their allegiance, or drew them into the service of the Mogul. Confiding in the greatness of his power, he hazarded the ruin of the city of Delhi, the ancient residence of the Patan sovereigns, and the capital of Indostan. The particular motive, which induced Akebar to overturn the finest city of his states, has never been clearly ascertained, but the prevailing opinion throughout the empire attributed alone to the ambition of immortalising his name, the resolution he took of founding a new Imperial city. The pretext he assigned for abandoning Delhi, was a vow, which he had made to build a mosque in honor of Mahomet, in order to obtain from heaven a son, who might be the heir to his empire. Adjacent to the mosque, the Emperor built a magnificent palace, in which he fixed his residence. The courtiers soon were eagerly occupied in erecting their houses in the vicinity of the new palace; so that in a short time, there was a sufficient number of buildings to compose a moderately-sized city. The place kept its ancient name of Fetipour. The glory of this new establishment was of short duration. In a little time it was discovered, that the air was unwholesome, and that the waters occasioned diseases. The king himself condemned his bad choice, abandoned Fetipour, and returned to the banks of the river Gemna, to erect a new city in the neighbourhood of Delhi. The ruins of the ancient served for the construction of the new capital. For sometime this place was also the residence of the prince; but Akebar was fond of change. He selected the city of Agra, at that time an inconsiderable place, whither to transport his throne and his court.

Agra, at the present day the ordinary residence of the Mogul emperors, is situated in a spacious plain, upon the banks of the same river which passes by Delhi. It extends itself upon the banks of the Gemna, in the form of a crescent. At one of its extremities, the Imperial palace, and the mansions of the principal nobility are erected. The city in length is about nine Italian miles, but is much less in breadth. It was not, indeed, in the time of Akebar, surrounded with walls, but a large trench, into which the water of the river had been introduced, environed it on all sides. In a short time, the inhabitants were estimated to amount to six hundred and sixty thousand persons, including all sexes and ages, without taking into the account strangers, whom the convenience of caravanseras, and the facilities which it afforded for trade, attracted thither from all the countries of Asia.

The palace of the emperor, which serves for a citadel to the city of Agra, may pass for one of the finest in the world, whether considered with respect to its situation, its structure, or its riches. It is situated upon an eminence, and its walls, raised twenty-five cubits from the ground, are constructed of a kind of red free stone, which resembles marble. The masonry is incomparable; this magnificent edifice has the appearance of one single mass, it being impossible to discern the parts where the stones unite. The view of the structure from the river is particularly fine. The windows and balconies, disposed with much symmetry, are very ornamental. It is thence, the emperor views the combat of elephants, upon a strand, which extends from the palace to the river. Upon the opposite bank of the river, a second city is descried, equal in length to the first, but not quite so wide; this is the quarter of the banians, or merchants. The traffic carried on here is immense.

Akebar considered the city of Agra, of which he was the founder, as the brightest monument of his glory; and was desirous that it should bear his name. In his lifetime, it was called Akerabad, or, the city of Akebar. After his death, when the people were no longer constrained to flatter the vanity of the monarch, Akerabad resumed its ancient appellation of Agra, which it still retains.

The emperor's warlike propensities were not forgotten amidst these peaceable occupations. An Indian prince in his neighbourhood, of the race of the famous Rana, who yielded formerly to the arms of Tamerlane, and who preserved still a species of independence, was particularly obnoxious to him. This chief was named like his ancestor Rana, and boasted his origin from the ancient Porus. The states of Rana were only twelve days' journey from Delhi, and the capital of his country was called Chitor. This was more a place of strength, than a busy or populous town. It is situated on a lofty mountain, insulated on all sides, in the centre of a spacious plain. The summit of the mountain, on which the city is built, is a perfect level. The circumference may be about a league and a half, and the breadth, in some places, half a league. At the foot of the mountain, flow the tranquil waters of the Nug, a river of considerable depth, and pretty wide. A brook of the finest water has its source in the city, and after meandering for a while, and forming several natural cascades on the edge of the mountain, its waters are precipitated into the river. Within the circuit of the fortress are contained fine fields planted with rice, and irrigated by the waters of the brook. A sufficient quantity of provisions is raised to supply a moderate garrison. A place which is so difficult of access, and deficient neither in provisions nor water, is considered in India as impregnable. Akebar, nevertheless, undertook the conquest of Chitor. The passion of the young emperor for the Princess Padmani, wife to Rana, the sovereign of Chitor, enabled him, it is said, to overcome difficulties, which would otherwise have appeared insurmountable. Before engaging in so difficult an undertaking, Akebar caused to be announced to the Raja, by his ambassadors, that his enterprise was not one merely of ambition; that the Indian might preserve his states from the misfortunes with which they were menaced, by resigning the most charming princess of all the east, to the most powerful emperor of the universe. A proposition of this kind in India is not so revolting to the mind as it is in Europe; repudiation is permitted by the laws. Rana, however, was too strongly attached to Padmani to deliver her up to his rival. He, therefore, on receiving these propositions, took counsel only from his courage, and the tears of his wife. "Is it possible," said the virtuous princess, "that you can abandon me to a tyrant I abhor. Do we not possess in Chitor the means of successfully resisting the forces of the enemy, and of extinguishing his passion, by the tediousness of a fruitless siege. Let the worst come; if it be necessary to forfeit life, I shall leave it without regret, provided I suffer not the calamity of surviving you." Language so affecting made Rana resolve rather to risk the result of an honourable war, than to submit to a disgraceful peace. He replied to the ambassador of Akebar, that he would counsel his master not to present himself before Chitor; that should his passion be stronger than his reason, Akebar would find in the person of Rana a true Rajepoot, able to maintain his rights, and incapable of betraying his fidelity to Padmani. The emperor was astonished at so bold an answer. He was not accustomed to experience opposition to his desires, and to find himself thwarted in his pleasures. He then assembled, with the greatest celerity, those victorious troops, which had already subjected to his dominion two kingdoms. Rana, on his side, was no less diligent; and made preparations to sustain a long siege in Chitor. He endeavoured, by his ambassadors, to arouse from their indolence the Rajas, his neighbours. He insinuated to them, that through their neglect and inactivity, they would suffer themselves to be tyrannised over by a Mahometan; that the Moguls were a race of men recently arrived in Indostan, and were powerful only through the divisions, which prevailed among the Indians; that if the princes, who were the worshippers of Brama, would unite to oppose the Mahometan sectaries, the destruction of this people would be easily accomplished. Jamal and Tata, the Rajas of two provinces in the neighbourhood of Chitor, joined their troops to those of Rana, and came to wage war in person against Akebar. They presented themselves in the field at the head of their army; but the Mogul, who advanced with the utmost rapidity towards Chitor, easily dispersed their forces. The two Rajas had no other resource, than to retreat into the strong places of their provinces, and to wait the attack of an enemy, whose strength in the field they were unable to resist. Never had there appeared in Indostan a finer or more numerous army, than was this of the Mogul. Akebar spared no expence, that he might appear before Chitor in all the splendour of his glory. His pavillions displayed riches not easily imagined in Europe. Gold shone resplendent in every part. He was flattered, equally, with the hopes of fascinating and dazzling the princess by so great a display of magnificence, and of intimidating Rana by the prodigious multitude of his forces. Akebar had to experience the ascendancy of virtue and valour over the most flattering projects, and their superiority to circumstances the most calculated to inspire apprehension. The gallant Indians beheld without emotion, from the summit of their mountain, the magnificence, and the prodigious extent of the camp of their enemies. In the beginning of the siege, the Mogul made war in the character of a passionate lover. Arrows, it is said, were discharged into the city, to which the emperor had affixed letters for Padmani. The princess was by no means moved by them. Akebar pressed, then, the siege as a man in despair; he caused the place to be assailed by a furious artillery; but his cannon, which were levelled at the fortifications from the lower grounds, had very little effect. The Indians, from the heighth of their walls, insulted the Mahometans, reproaching them with their want of courage, although they were stimulated to the fight by more than one passion. A Portuguese historian says, that the siege of Troy was renewed in the siege of Chitor. He adds, that it lasted twelve years, and that the duration of the war allowed time for Padmani to lose her bloom, whilst these extraordinary efforts were making to get possession of her person. This is an exaggeration, and is at variance with the account given by the Mogul Chronicle. The siege lasted at the utmost not more than two years, and was terminated only by an event, of a very singular nature. It is not intended to vouch for the truth of the narrative.

It is said, that Akebar, wearied by so obstinate a resistance, affected an inclination to relinquish the siege of Chitor; and that he wrote to Rana a letter, expressed in terms of great civility, but, at the same time, of a very artful nature. He paid the Raja many compliments on his valour; but before relinquishing an enterprize, which he could not, he said, abandon without a portion of humiliation and disgrace, he requested that Rana would grant him two favours.—The first was, that he might be permitted to see the princess; and the second, that he might be allowed to enter Chitor, and have the satisfaction of viewing the only place in the world capable of resisting his arms. The Raja granted, willingly, the second of his requests, and refused him the first. He would allow the Mogul to enter Chitor with a suit of fifty attendants, but he did not engage to permit him to see Padmani. Akebar accepted the offer of the Raja; and, after receiving hostages for the security of his person, he entered Chitor, with a suite yet fewer than the number which had been stipulated. The emperor received, at the hands of Rana, all the respect, and distinction, which was due to his rank. The entertainment, which was given in his palace, by Rana, to the emperor, was served up after the Indian manner. The conversation was obliging on both sides; but Akebar, who was eloquent and persuasive, knew how to lead Rana to go beyond the strict letter of his engagement. As soon as he perceived the Indian somewhat warmed by the fumes of the entertainment, he solicited him, earnestly, to allow Padmani to make her appearance, though it were but for an instant. The Raja gave his consent; but there was the greatest difficulty in bringing the princess to a compliance. At last, out of complaisance to her husband, she just shewed herself, and instantaneously disappeared. The indiscretion of Rana cost him dear. The sight of the princess added fuel to the passion of Akebar; but he had sufficient command over himself, to conceal his emotion. He made Rana believe, that he was resolved on raising the siege of a place, which had caused him but too many losses. He even had the skill to avoid interweaving, in his discourse, more than cold and formal praises of Padmani. Rana, deceived by appearances, treated his most cruel enemy with the greatest confidence. He both received, and returned presents. Akebar gave the prince a cimeter, studded with diamonds; and Rana presented the emperor with some jewels of value. However, the time for their separating was now approaching. Akebar took his leave, and proceeded towards the gate of the fortress, followed only by his suite, composed of forty attendants, and accompanied, out of courtesy, by Rana. During their progress, Akebar renewed the most obliging protestations. Having, at last, reached the gate of the city, the Mogul, apparently in testimony of his regard, threw around the neck of Rana one of those large pearl necklaces, with which the men, as well as the women, adorn themselves in India. He had used the precaution of having them strung on a cord of some strength. Assisted by this collar of pearls, he forced the Raja through the gate; whilst his forty resolute followers opposed any movement, which might be attempted by the guard, for the rescue of their prince. The Indian was compelled to mount on horseback; and the party, after sustaining some discharges of musquetry from the ramparts, at last succeeded in conducting Rana into the Mogul's camp.

The noise, in the meanwhile, occasioned by the struggle at the gate of the city, threw all Chitor into consternation. An alarm was spread, that the enemy had taken possession of the place. Indeed, if the Mogul had been provided with an armed force to sustain the enterprise, the Indians, in their present terror, might have been easily subdued. Rumour, which always magnifies an evil, brought to the hearing of Padmani the intelligence of a sudden irruption of the enemy. She was also told, that her husband had disappeared in the confusion. The noble-minded princess did not suffer herself to be subdued by so unlooked-for a calamity. She mounted on horseback, and with lance in hand, appeared at the head of her troops, prepared to vanquish or perish. It was only on the spot, where the scene transpired, that she was made acquainted with the treachery of Akebar, and the carrying off of Rana.

Sensible that she was the cause of the misfortune of her husband, Padmani exerted all her energies to control her agonising emotions. "He is dead!" she exclaimed, with an heroic spirit; "that beloved husband, whom my fatal attachment has destroyed! Let us no longer think of recovering him by a dishonourable treaty; but let us revenge him, by beholding perish around us the authors of his death." Having thus spoken, without shedding tears, although she was penetrated with the liveliest grief, she made the round of the ramparts, administered every where her orders, encouraged the soldiers, and gave animation to the chiefs. She shewed herself, indeed, as much superior to men in spirit, and in courage, as she surpassed the rest of her sex in beauty.

Akebar already flattered himself with soon becoming master of the fortress. He caused it to be announced to the besieged, that if they did not deliver up the place, as well as the princess, he should begin by cutting off the head of Rana; and that he would complete his revenge by sacking the city, and massacreing the inhabitants. The noble Amazon replied, that her husband having fallen into the hands of a treacherous enemy, she could not doubt but he was already dead; yet, that there still remained a sufficient number of brave Rajepoots among her people, to revenge their sovereign. As for herself, she would exert all the authority which heaven had given her over her subjects, to raise up enemies to the Moguls still more formidable than Rana. Further, that the principal chiefs of her army had sworn sooner to lose their lives than to surrender the place.

Akebar was not unacquainted with the constancy of the Rajepoots in their resolutions. He, therefore, came to the determination of raising the siege, and endeavouring to obtain the princess by the means of negociation. An ambassador carried to Padmani presents of great value, accompanied with letters, expressive of the intenseness of his passion. Akebar represented to the princess, that she had given sufficient proofs of the fidelity due to a husband; that it was now time to make some sacrifice to the power of a great monarch, and to her own interest; that her affection for Rana could not be better demonstrated, than in procuring the liberty of her captive husband: and that in withdrawing Rana from captivity, she would become the most powerful queen in the world. She was shewn even letters, which had been extorted from the captive prince, by which he exhorted her to become happy, in restoring him to liberty. The heroine comprehended, that this consent of Rana was forced; and, that her glory, besides, was interested in remaining faithful to her husband. She considered, however, that she was justified in dissembling, and in trying to deceive a perfidious enemy, who had got possession of the person of her husband by surprise and deceit. She, therefore, gave the Mogul to understand, that she began to change her sentiments, and that ambition had shaken her resolutions: that were it not for an oath, which held her indispensably bound to Rana, she should rejoice to become the sultaness of the Mogul; but, that she had vowed to her first husband by his gods, that she would never be another's, without having his consent granted expressly from his own mouth. That she left the choice to the emperor, to give permission to Rana to come into Chitor, or to allow Padmani to visit her husband in the place of his captivity, and obtain from him a personal declaration of repudiation. Akebar did not hesitate to prefer the latter alternative. He gave his consent, that the queen should come with a large escort, and visit her husband.

The place, where Rana was confined, was a fortress in the vicinity of Agra. It is impossible to describe the impatience shewn by Akebar, to behold in his capital a princess, for whose sake he had incurred so much expense, and run so many hazards. Couriers were incessantly employed to invite her not to delay her departure. Every day the Mogul sent to her presents of jewels, fruits, and that species of nosegay, of a mysterious character, made use of in the East to express, by the disposition of the flowers, the sentiments of the heart. The princess caused equipages to be got ready, with the utmost celerity, for her journey. Palanquins were prepared, of the greatest magnificence. In India, the palanquins are a species of sedan, in which persons of quality cause themselves to be conveyed upon the shoulders of ten or twelve slaves. They are sufficiently long to allow of lying at full length, as in a litter. Those of the men are uncovered, and those in which women are carried, are closed, and are more spacious than those of the men. Four persons may be accommodated with convenience, so that slaves to the number of twenty are sometimes employed in carrying those of the princesses.

In the two palanquins, Padmani caused eight of the bravest of her subjects to be seated, and commanded them to maintain the strictest silence during their progress. As for herself, having seen the palanquins take their departure, accompanied by an escort, she remained at Chitor. The project was executed with so much secresy, that every person in the city was deceived. Tears were shed at the pretended departure of the princess. The people, in crowds, accompanied the escort through the gates, imagining they were taking a last leave of the princess. In the meanwhile, Padmani, preserving the strictest retirement in her palace, rejoiced in the affection displayed by her subjects.

The emperor no sooner heard that the Indian princess had set out for Agra, than he sent various persons to compliment her. The chief eunuch of the princess, who conducted the intrigue, and who was shut up in the palanquin, which they imagined contained the princess, gave answers in her name. Among other communications, he gave notice to the emperor under the name of Padmani; that if she were obstructed on her route, or prevented from proceeding direct to her husband without passing through the capital, or, if she were interrupted even in her conference with Rana; she was determined to pierce herself with a poignard, which she had brought on purpose with her, and which she held always in her hand, to be prepared against a surprise. Akebar took great care not to make the slightest opposition to the wishes of the princess. He gave her to understand, that she would be at perfect liberty to see Rana, to converse with him, and to take her last farewell.

In proportion as the palanquins approached the city, the couriers became more frequent. They were found at every village, and the eunuch continued, unintermittingly, to give answers to the letters of Akebar. At the distance of half a day's journey from Agra, about three or four leagues from the fortress in which Rana was confined, they found a magnificent equipage, which the emperor had forwarded for the use of the princess. It was composed of elephants of war, camels, and a numerous escort, which was destined to accompany Padmani to the palace of the Mogul, and to take the place of the Rajepoots of her guard, at the same time that her husband, attended by the same suite which had escorted thence the princess, took the road to Chitor. At last, in the evening, they arrived at the place in which Rana was prisoner. The two palanquins, and some officers of the Indian escort, were alone permitted to enter the fortress. These, having arms concealed under their vests, in conjunction with the band of resolutes, who had been shut up in the palanquins, slew the governor, who was the first to present himself to receive the princess. Having made themselves afterwards masters of the guard, they made haste to deliver Rana from his prison. He was mounted on a horse of extraordinary fleetness, and as relays had been prepared on the whole of his route, the Raja was soon enabled to reach Chitor, and to testify to Padmani the gratitude which was due to her as his liberatress. Akebar, in the meanwhile, was waiting in a garden the arrival of the princess, when he was informed that the Raja had escaped; armed men, concealed in the palanquins, having appeared instead of Padmani. In the first moment of surprise, and irritation, Akebar ordered the man who was the bearer of the intelligence to be beheaded; but soon recollecting himself, he was contented with banishing him for ever from his presence. "Let Rana be instantly pursued," he exclaimed. But Rana had gained an advance, which precluded the possibility of his being overtaken. With respect to the Rajepoots, who had served as escort to the palanquins; after journeying all night with the utmost expedition, they found themselves, in the morning, in the territory of a friendly Raja, allied to the Prince of Chitor, and returned to their country in safety. No sooner was Rana returned to his city, than he wrote taunting letters to Akebar. He reproached him with his treachery, and rallied him on the ill success of his enterprises. He challenged him to make a second essay of the fortune of his arms by besieging the citadel. He added, in conclusion, that after having been vanquished, and overreached by a woman, he might justly expect a more complete discomfiture from an army of Rajepoots, who waited for him impatiently. Rana did more than insult his enemy by letters. He erected a column in the great square of Chitor, on which he had engraved these words in the language of the country:— "Never more place confidence in the Moguls, of whose faith you have had bitter experience."

The conduct of Rana, and the contempt of Padmani, kindled a rage in the breast of Akebar, which he could no longer master. He assembled a second time his troops; he augmented his artillery; he caused machines to be constructed; finally, he gave such good directions for recommencing the siege of Chitor, that he deemed his success infallible. In this confidence, he surrounded the place on all sides; he caused cavaliers to be raised, upon which he planted his machines. The attack and defence was destructive on both sides. It was no longer an enamoured monarch, who spared the subjects of his princess; it was a vindictive prince, who revenged his personal injuries. The two chiefs were continually occupied; the one in pressing the siege, the other in seeking to counteract the efforts of his rival. Rana was almost continually on the ramparts, where he encouraged his soldiers, and caused the breaches to be repaired. Akebar, on his side, took his station often on the cavaliers which he had constructed, and gave his orders for forming the attacks. One day, that the emperor had mounted on one of those terraces, which nearly equalled in heighth the walls of Chitor, he perceived on the ramparts an officer of the enemy who was pacing slowly to and fro; he took aim at him with a carabine, which brought the Raja to the ground. Akebar learnt, two days afterwards, that the random shot, which he had fired, had caused the death of his rival. The body of Rana was consumed on a funeral pile, accompanied with every display of affection, and all the honors due to his rank and merit; and the noble Padmani, agreeably to the usage of the Rajepoot princesses, threw herself into the flames, and mixed her ashes with those of her husband. Chitor continued to make some resistance, but it became necessary, at last, to yield to the valour and fortune of Akebar.—This history, which is found, says M. Manouchi, both in the works of European writers, and in those of the native historians of India, has the air of a romance. Nevertheless, apparently, there is nothing in it of the manner of those fables, which are so common in the productions of the native writers. They are almost all taken up with dialogues of apes, tales of animals, of the miracles of the gods of the country, and similar matter, the whole entirely destitute of probability. However, as the adventures of Akebar and Padmani are not found in the Chronicle of the empire, the reader is at liberty to place confidence in it to whatever extent he pleases. The capture of Chitor, and the death of Rana, are incontestible facts.

Akebar, after the fatigues of the siege of Chitor, thought proper to allow himself some repose. The Mogul emperors have always possessed the advantage in the Indies, of having it in their power to make war, or taste the sweets of peace, at their option. The Indians defend themselves, sometimes, when they are attacked, but they are never the aggressors. The emperor now employed his leisure, in embellishing his city of Agra, completing the building of his palace, and adorning his gardens. He formed indeed, a chimerical enterprise. It is said, that he entertained the idea of building a palace, to be entirely constructed of brass. This would be the true mean, he said, of obtaining a defence from the heats, which are very inconvenient in the Indies. It is added, that he did not abandon his design, until he found that materials could not be procured in sufficient quantity to carry the project into execution. He was more happy in the execution of another scheme. From Agra to Lahor, the distance is computed to be one hundred and fifty leagues. Akebar caused the whole road, from one city to the other, to be planted with an alley of trees, which, for its length, and its perpetual verdure, is the most beautiful, and the most extraordinary monument in the whole empire. It still subsists, and is a convenience of incredible advantage to those who travel, who are thereby enabled to take so long a journey, defended always by the shade.

All the amusements of the emperor partook of a martial character. He had retained from the Tartars, his ancestors, a fondness for archery, and for the taming of fiery steeds. The exercise, which he more especially delighted in, was to mount on the war elephants, and to serve as their conductor, whilst they engaged in combat. This is a species of exercise so extremely dangerous, that the wives of those, whose duty it becomes, tear their vestments, and pluck the pendants from their ears, when they behold their husbands expose themselves to these kind of combats. Nevertheless, what to others was a terrific occupation, served Akebar as an amusement. An adventure is related of him, which displays the intrepidity of the gallant Mogul. Some rebellious peasants had fled for refuge to a city indifferently fortified, but of which it was difficult to force the gates. Akebar gave orders to employ the war elephants in breaking down the gates, and forcing a passage into the place. The conductors of these animals, which are trained to these kind of conflicts, failed in resolution. The monarch was exasperated. Having that day assumed the dress of a simple soldier, that he might not be known in an inglorious war, undertaken against peasants, he took the place of one of the conductors; mounting on the neck of the elephant, and guiding him with an iron hook, he made the animal, with so much address, go through the manœuvres used on those occasions, that the gate was burst open. This was a perilous attempt. Arrows were discharged at the elephant, and at him who guided it, but the emperor escaped without injury. The conductor of the second elephant, charmed with the valour of the man whom he believed a simple soldier, demanded of Akebar his name, that he might, he said, report his bravery to the emperor. "I am called," replied Akebar, "the Smasher of Gates, do not forget to bear a good testimony in my favor." In effect, his faithful companion did not fail the next morning, at the audience which the king permits generally to all his subjects, to give a recital of the valour and address of the man, named the Smasher of Gates. The emperor, recollected at these words, what had passed, and avowed himself. He then gave the reward, which was due to his own intrepidity, to him who had borne his testimony to it. The man was presented with a complete serpaon, that is, with a dress, a turban, and a horse. His pay was augmented, and he was promoted to a higher rank.

This war, against the rebellious peasants, gave Akebar more trouble, than all his successes over the Rajas. These unfortunate beings were intrenched in inaccessible forests, whose paths were familiar to them, whence they issued in bands, to burn or pillage the villages. When surprised, they fled to, and fortified themselves in the midst of ruined habitations, and if compelled to defend themselves, they discharged their pieces, when the enemy had approached within half musquet shot distance. Their carabines were then re-loaded by their wives; they, afterwards, made use in their defence, of the bow and the javelin. It was in the reign of Akebar, that this war of the peasants began. It may be said, that it is not yet terminated; at the present day, these unhappy wretches are beheaded, whenever they are found in the villages carrying arms. Nothing is more common than for travellers to find heads hung upon the trees, or fixed upon poles, along the great roads. These robbers are to be known by their shaven chins, and long mustachios, which extend to the ears, and are dispersed in all the hamlets which lie between Agra and Delhi.

The astrologers of the country pretend that the planet Mars rules over this part of India. They say, that even the waters, which are drank throughout the country, have the quality of inspiring courage, and warlike inclinations. Travellers have also remarked, in passing through this province, that the bulls which are natives of it, though in size small, have their horns more pointed than is common to those animals, and that they contend together often with a fury, which is rarely seen elsewhere.

Whilst thus occupied in purging his states from robbers, Jehan Guir, the eldest son of the emperor, was entering upon the state of manhood. This young prince had been hitherto educated in the retirement of the haram, and, being destitute of experience, appeared likely to become a prey to the counsels of designing men. Some discontented persons made use of the facility of Jehan Guir's disposition, to inspire him with an inclination to revolt. "Sufficiently long," they said to him, "has a father, jealous of your glory, suffered you to languish in inaction. The first years of a prince, destined to wear so many crowns, ought to be employed in warlike enterprises. It is thus, that a people, whom, by our birth, we are called one day to rule, are impressed with a favorable opinion of our courage. Since a father, envious of your acquiring distinction, deprives you of all opportunity of combatting by his side, endeavour to acquire renown in fighting against him. Whatever you may undertake, to the injury of a tyrant, who holds in captivity your rising valour, will be applauded by the great officers of the crown. As for us, my lord, we are quite prepared to second your designs. Akebar has reigned sufficiently long for his own glory, and too long for the happiness of his people. It is but just, that he should yield his place to a young prince, whose duty it will be when on the throne, to exert himself to promote the prosperity of his states."

Such pernicious discourse, ensnared the young Jehan Guir into an open revolt; but the discontented were few in number, and the authority of Akebar was too firmly established, to be shaken by such means. Jehan Guir trusted, that the good fortune of his father would pass over to his side. He found that an aged and experienced monarch is a dangerous antagonist for a young prince, who calculates only on his courage. He was made prisoner, and was suffered to languish some months, confined in a fortress, under the constant apprehension of being ordered for execution.

At last, the affection, which Akebar had for a son of such great promise, subdued his resentment, and prevailed against the strict demands of justice. But, the disobedience of the prince did not escape without chastisement. The emperor taught his son, how much he merited punishment for his revolt. The very day, that Akebar liberated Jehan Guir from captivity, he carried him, on the pretext of hunting, into the recesses of a forest. This was with the intention of exhibiting to the guilty prince, a terrific spectacle, which might serve to impress him with an abiding lesson, of the respect and obedience due to a sovereign. Akebar had here caused to be affixed, to the different branches of a tree, the heads of a hundred of the principal conspirators. Jehan Guir recognised them all, as being those of his late friends and advisers, and was terrified at the sight; but he was yet more strongly affected, when his father addressed him in these words:—"You have forgotten, perfidious young man, that I am your father; but I cannot forget that you are my son. The vengeance, which I have taken on your accomplices, instructs you sufficiently in your own deserts. I give you back again the life, which I first gave you at your birth, and of which you meditated depriving me. However, notwithstanding my affection, you will be unable to escape one punishment, which it is incumbent uopn me to visit on your unnatural conduct. In the Chronicles of the empire, it will be recorded: that Jehan Guir was the first of the posterity of Tamerlane, to conspire against the life of his father. See that you avoid the infamy, of suffering to descend to posterity, the record of a second crime, of the like guilt." The young prince profited by advice, given under such affecting circumstances, by so indulgent a parent. He repaired the errors of a few months, by an affection and a duty, which ever afterwards remained unshaken.

As a passion for enterprise had been the principal cause of the revolt of Jehan Guir; that he might not be again tempted to acts of disobedience, from motives of discontent, Akebar resolved to furnish him with an opportunity of displaying his valour. He entertained the design of making war upon a powerful Raja, whose territories interposed between his own states and the kingdom of Bengal; a country, the conquest of which he meditated. The name of this Raja was Carn. Akebar had kept his intention so secret, that he had not confided it to a single person. Nevertheless, a report, that the Raja's territories were about to be attacked, was generally diffused throughout Agra. The emperor was astonished, that his purpose should have been so accurately divined, and wished to ascertain the source whence the report originated. He found, that a slave of the palace, whose business it was to keep off the flies from the Sultan, whilst he slept, had discovered the secret. Akebar wished to know the means by which the slave had penetrated his intentions. The slave made the following confession:—"During the time, that you were sleeping, my lord, at mid-day, I observed that you pointed with your finger to the quarter, in which the lands of Raja Carn are situated. You then assumed the postures of a man, who combats with the bow and the sabre. Lastly, you seized yourself by the beard, and placed yourself in the attitude of a man, who seeks to triumph over an enemy, by his humiliation in his presence. As the Raja is the only person of rank among the Indians, who wears his beard long, according to the fashion of the Mahometans; and, as I know his territory lies very convenient for you, I conjectured, that you were meditating, even in your dreams, to make war upon the Raja Carn. I at first mentioned it merely as a matter of conjecture; but, agreeably to the ordinary course of popular rumours, it came soon to be reported as an established fact." Akebar acknowledged, that the slave had guessed shrewdly, and justly; and from that time, he would no more suffer his person to be approached, during his hours of repose. As his designs had now been made public, he no longer thought of entrusting the execution of them to his son.

It was, however, in the power of the emperor, to have given a direction to the valour of Jehan Guir, by employing it in the north, on the other side of the river Indus. It has been stated, that the Patans, who were defeated by Amayum, had retired iuto inaccessible mountains. They had there formed a species of little state, between Cabul and the Tartars; and, issuing, at times, from their retreats, made inroads upon the Mogul territory. This was an enemy, the more to be dreaded, as he had a feasible right to the kingdom of Delhi, of which he had been dispossessed only a few years. Akebar gave orders for an army of eighty thousand men, to march against them. All Cabulestan was exhausted, to furnish troops for this expedition. Jehan Guir desired passionately to have the command of them. His father did not judge it proper, and the event proved, that the caution of Akebar had been just and prudent. The eighty thousand men, who entered the country of the Patans, all perished by the sword, or from distress, in this warfare, undertaken amidst uncultivated and desert tracts. The entire destruction of this nation was reserved for another emperor.

The military enterprises which Akebar was continually forming, obliged him to found a school for engineers. There was no deficiency of artillery in the Indies. It may be said, that from time immemorial, the Chinese, who doubtless were, at one time, masters of Indostan, had in that country cast pieces of ordnance, the antiquity of which cannot be traced at the present day. Unfortunately, there were but few persons in the Indies, who had the skill to work them, with the same science and precision, which is practised in Europe. Akebar entertained, therefore, the plan, of inviting Europeans into his service, and of inducing them to settle at Agra, by the prospect of great advantages. The English had recently established themselves on the coast of Indostan, and had acquired a great reputation for valour. In their sea engagements, they had almost always the advantage of the Portugese. It was from their new establishment at Surat, where they began to carry on a very advantageous commerce, that Akebar procured English cannoneers, to serve his artillery. One of these cannoneers had an extraordinary reputation for ability among those of his nation: he was noted, besides, for his inebriety. This man was much disconcerted, when he found himself in a country, in which wine shops are prohibited. He made use of the following artifice, to procure the enjoyment of his favorite beverage. One day, that the emperor wished to be a witness to his skill; at a moderate distance, on the opposite side of the river, a large cloth had been fixed, at which the cannoneer was ordered to take aim. The Englishman pointed his gun so badly, that he did not even strike an object, so extremely easy. The monarch was astonished, and made him some reproaches. "My lord," replied the Englishman, "since I have been compelled to the disuse of wine, my sight is grown so weak, that I can no longer discern an object, however conspicuous, even at a moderate distance. Wine is alone capable of restoring, sufficiently, my powers of vision, to enable me to discover objects, agreeably to my ordinary habits." There was no want of wine at the palace. Akebar had always some for his own pleasures, and a certain quantity was given every day to the elephants. A bottle was then brought, which the cannoneer emptied at a single draught. Then causing the mark to be changed, and another substituted, which was very little bigger than the ball, which was to be fired, the Englishman hit it with the greatest precision, and obtained the applauses of the king. From that time, Akebar gave liberty to all his European cannoneers, to plant vineyards in the neighbourhood of Agra. Some excellent wine is produced from these plantations. The decree of the prince was inserted in the Chronicle, in these words:—"The Europeans are born in the element of wine, as fish are produced in that of water; to prohibit them the use of it, is to deprive them of life." This permission to cultivate the vine, which foreigners, in the service of the Mogul, possess, is a great source of profit to them. Wine, which is not common at Agra, is dear, and the cultivator does not run the hazard of injury from frost, as in Europe; it is a certain harvest.

It was not only English cannoneers, whom Akebar took into his service; he had procured, also, from Goa, artisans of every description; lapidaries, enamellers, goldsmiths, surgeons, and European practicioners in medicine. Akebar, by their means, became acquainted with the Christian religion, and entertained thoughts, at this time, of embracing it. The viceroy of Goa, had sent Antony Criminal to the court of the Mogul, in the character of ambassador. He was a truly Christian man, who did honor to his religion, by the purity of his manners. The piety, the good faith, and the irreproachable conduct of the Portuguese, made an impression on the mind of Akebar. He formed his judgment of Christians in general, from the demeanor of an individual of that profession, and became persuaded, that such perfect integrity, could be inspired only by the true religion. The emperor wished to be informed of its peculiar doctrines, which the ambassador only explained to him in substance. He replied, "that it was the part of the priests of his religion, to explain in detail, and to develope its mysteries; that two Jesuits, at that time employed in the kingdom of Bengal, in the conversion of the Indians, would think to render God service, should their instrumentality be required, to instruct the greatest monarch of the east." This discourse induced the prince to procure the visit of a missionary from Bengal. It is probable, that he was a Jesuit, but this is not certain. It was through this priest, that the emperor learnt to contemn the Alcoran, and to esteem the gospel. That he might be able to converse with him the oftener, and the more privately, Akebar applied himself to acquire the Portuguese tongue, in which he succeeded with a facility, which was surprising. At the instigation of the missionary, the Mogul determined to invite into his states, as many Jesuits as he could procure. The letter which he addressed to them at Goa, is as follows :—

"Akebar the Great, Emperor of the world, to the venerable fathers of St. Paul.—I have sent to you, on my behalf, Ebadola, with an interpreter, to testify to you the affection, which I entertain towards you. He will request you, in my name, to send to my court some of your fathers, skilled in the knowledge of the sacred volumes, and able to explain the deep mysteries of your religion. I have equally a desire to learn its true merits, and to embrace it. You may judge from this, that your fathers will be treated honorably, and that every attention will be shewn to their accommodation. Suffer them then to come, and let them be assured, that they will have entire liberty to return to Goa, should they at any time become dissatisfied with the docility of their pupil. Further, that they may rely on my protection."

The letter of the Mogul gave great pleasure to the Jesuits of Goa. Every one prayed, that he might be appointed to a mission, which promised to be so advantageous to the spread of the faith. The lot fell on the Fathers Rodolph Aqauviva, Antony Manserrat, and Francis Henric. The first, who was appointed the superior, was son to the Duke d'Atri, and nephew of Father Claude Aquaviva, who became afterwards General of the Jesuits. Father Rodolph had relinquished high expectations, and the strong ties which bound him to his native land, that he might consecrate his life to the service of the missions in the Indies. The apostleship of the Mogul fell to his lot. It is impossible to conceive the impatience with which Akebar expected the missionaries at Fetipour. Naturally of an ardent disposition, as soon as he knew of their having set out, he informed himself, incessantly, of their progress, while on their route.

The emperor received the fathers with as much kindness, as he had shewn ardour, in inviting them to his court. He passed the whole night in conversation with them; and, on the pretence of furnishing them with the means of procuring necessaries, he offered them a pretty large sum of money. The missionaries represented to the emperor, the vow of poverty, which separated them from the interests of this life. This was a strong hold, from which they never allowed themselves to be diverted, notwithstanding the liberal disposition, and frequent pressing offers, of the prince. A disinterestedness, which was so rare among the ministers of the Mahometan religion, was calculated to give a favourable impression of the superiority of that of Jesus Christ. The fathers made their presents to the Mogul; these were, a fine impression of the Bible, printed in four languages; and two pictures, one representing Jesus Christ, and the other the Virgin Mary. Akebar took the Bible, placed it upon his head, in sign of respect, kissed the images, and made his children kiss them.

The visits, which the missionaries paid, subsequently, to the emperor, did not terminate in mere compliments. Akebar desired to know the grounds, which go to prove, fundamentally, the falsehood of the Alcoran; and the principles which establish the truth of the gospel. Argumentative contests were entered upon, every Saturday, at the palace, with the Moulas. The Jesuits had brought with them an Alcoran, from Goa. Father Henric, by birth a Persian, served his companions as their interpreter. His assistance was of the greatest advantage in refuting the doctors of the Mahometan law. The fathers laid great stress on the species of beatitude, which Mahomet promised, in another life, to Mussulmen. They demonstrated the infamy of the promises, which the impostor has made to carnal men, to gain them over to his false doctrines, by the hope of the full indulgence of their passions. The emperor was convinced of the weakness of the Alcoran on this point; he contrasted the spirit of pride, and of sensuality, exhibited in the Alcoran, with the spirit of humility, and of mortification, taught by the gospel. It is, he said, in shedding their blood, that the Christains have extended their faith throughout the earth; and in shedding the blood of others, that Mahometanism has been established in the east. The emperor appeared to have been staggered by these first impressions.

The fathers were always welcomed at the palace, with the greatest demonstrations of regard; but they were well acquainted with the spirit of the Orientals. With them, the heart is little responsible for the protestations they make. In order, therefore, to bind Akebar to good faith, Father Aquaviva had the boldness to address him, in the following manner:—"Your Majesty cannot be ignorant, of the conditions on which we abandoned an abundant harvest, that we might come to announce to you Jesus Christ. You have given us your assurance, that we shall be allowed to return to the country we have quitted, in the event of the seed of the word of life, preached at your court, proving unfruitful. We are, then, emboldened to solicit your Majesty to fix a season, when it may please your Majesty to declare yourself, openly, as a servant of Mahomet, or of Jesus Christ." The emperor was not disgusted at the the freedom of the missionary. "So serious a change," replied Akebar, "is in the hands of God. As for myself, I shall never cease to implore his illumination and his aid."

So just a reply ought, one would imagine, to have occasioned the conversion of the emperor to be regarded as infallible. The fathers were not blinded by it. They always apprehended, that dissimulation and policy, so natural to the Moguls, had the greatest share in the discourse of the Prince. Nevertheless, they received fresh, and unabated testimonials of the favour of the court. Akebar knew, that the house, inhabited by the fathers, was inconvenient, and exposed them to be disturbed by the noise of the people, that were constantly passing; he, therefore, gave them a lodging within the circuit of the palace. Then, for the first time, was seen an altar set up to

Jesus Christ, in the heart of a Mahometan court. The fathers had even the consolation to have disciples of the royal family. The education of the second son of Akebar was confided to Father Manserrat. He was equally instructed in the sciences of Europe, and in the knowledge of our sacred mysteries. Pahari, which was the name of the young prince, was about thirteen years of age, at the time he was placed under the care of the missionaries. His superior understanding, and the natural sweetness of his disposition, occasioned them to be flattered with the hope, of finding one day, in his person, a protector of the Christian faith in the dominions of the Mogul; but, the natural inconstancy of the Indian character prevailed in this young prince over the steadiness of the Tartar.

Akebar maintained always, in his heart, an indescribable aversion for the eldest of his sons. The great object of his affection was Pahari; in consequence, he spared no pains in the cultivation of his mind. His aim was, to enable him to assume, on the side of intellect, that superiority of which he was deprived by the order of birth. The emperor frequently came to visit the fathers during the time they were occupied in the instruction of his favorite son. The young prince, by chance, began, in the presence of the emperor, to recite his lesson of the day in these words :—" To the glory of Amighty God,"—" add, my son," said Akebar, " and of Jesus Christ, the true Prophet." He entered, afterwards, into the chapel, which the fathers had prepared in their apartment. He adored the Saviour by prostrations; then, seating himself upon cushions, according to the custom of the country, he entered upon a conversation with the missionaries, which enabled him to unburthen his mind to them.

" You are not ignorant," he said, " of the profound veneration, which I entertain for the religion in which you have instructed me. All things tend to inspire me with favorable sentiments towards it. The miracles of the Messiah, acknowledged even by the Alcoran; the purity of the morals inculcated by the gospel; its establishment, by the simple instrumentality of the preaching, and suffering, of individuals; are unconquerable impressions, which lead me to the acknowledgment of Jesus Christ, as a prophet sent from God. But, when you raise my thoughts high above all, which appears founded in reason and nature, in the person of the Messiah, I am bewildered in the sublimity of your mysteries. Explain to me," he added, "the eternal generation of the word, in the bosom of his father, and his miraculous incarnation, in time, and I shall subsribe, without reserve, to all the articles, which you propose for my belief."

The missionaries availed themselves of the principles, of which the emperor appeared to be convinced, and drew from them consequences, favorable to our mysteries, which appear the most incomprehensible. "Jesus Christ," they said, "appears to you to have sufficiently proved his mission, by miracles, acknowledged even by the Alcoran: the sanctity of the morals, he inculcated, bear testimony to the truth of his religion; he is an approved Prophet. He ought, then, to be believed on his own word. He declares to us, that he was before Abraham. All the monuments, which he has left us, tend to confirm the Trinity of persons in God. Doubtless, the miracles, which you believe, confirm the mysteries that he has revealed to us, and which you cannot comprehend." The emperor felt the force of this reasoning, broke up the conversation, with tears in his eyes, and several times repeated—"Turn Christian! Renounce the religion of my fathers! What danger for an emperor! What an undertaking for a man educated in voluptuousness, and in the latitude allowed by the Alcoran!"

However, as Akebar was perfectly convinced of the falsehood of the books of Mahomet, he took a pleasure in refuting the doctors of his religion. "If the books of Moses," he said to them, "as well as the book of Psalms, are inspired, as is confessed by Mahomet, why does he prohibit our reading them? It is said in the Alcoran, that the books of the evangelists of Jesus Christ are true writings. Yet how essentially are their respective doctrines opposed to each other. Can the Almighty be inconsistent with himself, when he speaks by the instrumentality, and by the voice of Jesus? In order to extricate myself from the embarrassment in which I am placed, by the contradictions which I find between the volumes which I ought to regard, if I am to believe Mahomet equally as the word of God, ought I not to reason thus? It is agreed, on both sides, that the books of the evangelists are holy and true. The Christians deny that the Alcoran is the word of God. It will then be wise to adopt the safest course, and to renounce the Alcoran, which the Christians abhor, for the gospel, which the Mahometans acknowledge."

Notwithstanding his private sentiments were so favorable to Christianity, Akebar could not be prevailed upon to embrace it. Liberty, however, was granted for the preaching of it throughout his empire. He even consented that our ceremonies should be practised in public, in all their majesty; and that the interment of a Portuguese should take place attended by all the pomp of the Roman religion. The cross was then carried, for the first time, in the streets of Fetipour. Akebar felt much satisfaction at the triumph which he had procured to the religion of Jesus Christ. The evangelical seed, it may be said, had fallen upon the heart of the prince; but it had been too long disposed to voluptuousness to prove a fruitful soil. The ambition of a doctor of the Mahometan law was very nearly contributing more to bring about the conversion of the emperor, than all the zeal by which the missionaries were actuated.

Abdul Fasil, which was the name of the Moula, was persuaded, that he should succeed in gaining the favor of the emperor by adopting sentiments conformable to that prince's inclinations. He declared himself a convert to the missionaries, and by that complaisance insinuated himself so far into the good graces of Akebar, that he drew upon himself the jealousy of his contemporaries. He spoke to him incessantly of Jesus Christ, and represented to him the absurdities of the Alcoran, which he had studied from his infancy. To induce him to change the religion of his states, he made use of a strain of reasoning, which he knew would touch sensibly the heart of the prince. "The authority of your predecessors," he said, "never attained the heighth at which we behold it in your days. How much greater will be the honor reflected on your memory, in rendering your name illustrious to posterity, by a signal display of the empire which you obtained over the minds of your subjects, than it can be by any ascendancy which you may have gained over your enemies. Speak the word, my lord, and you will find all Indostan renouncing their ancient superstitions, and submitting to be guided by your sentiments; its people, through the veneration they entertain towards you, will embrace them. Doubtless, it will be for their interest, that one religion should alone prevail throughout your states. It is not possible that the Mahometan should become the prevailing religion; the antipathy, which the Indians have conceived for the Alcoran, is hereditary. It is the religion of their conquerors, and their aversion to it may be dated from the moment of their being compelled to wear our chains. Make an experiment, whether Christianity may not be so fortunate as to succeed in taking sole possession of the human mind, and effectually banish from the Indies Mahometanism, and the ancient superstitions."

Akebar, at this time, felt himself disposed to found his own glory, and the happiness of his country, by obeying the convictions of his mind. He declared to the missionaries, that he was prepared to give a striking proof of his sincerity, and of the esteem in which he held the gospel. Matters were in this state, when the budding faith of the prince was tried by adversity. The Patans, a refractory nation, broke out into revolt. The brother of the emperor took up arms in their cause, and stirred up all Cabulestan against Akebar. It was then, that the doctors of the Mahometan law exerted themselves to recover their influence over the mind of the emperor. "Heaven," they said, "has permitted a prince, whom it has so greatly favored, to be afflicted by so many domestic dissentions, only since he has become estranged from the religion of Mussulmen. Let him return to us, and tranquillity will be restored." The emperor had, besides, fears, lest his eldest son should take advantage of a conjuncture favorable to his ambitious views, and acquire an influence with a people already disposed to revolt. Thus, whether influenced by a regard for the religion of his ancestors, or the fear of causing fresh insurrections, or through an abandonment of the divine aid, which resists the proud, Akebar experienced his ardour in favor of the Christian religion much abated. He shunned the conversation of the fathers, and spoke no longer to them with his usual familiarity; or, if he still at times listened to them, it was with an appearance of distraction, which afflicted them: in a public conference, he even seemed, contrary to his usual custom, to take with some vivacity the side of the Moulas.

The missionaries, it is true, might have employed, in the conversion of the people, a zeal, which began to appear fruitless at court. Akebar had removed every obstacle to their preaching, by allowing his subjects to embrace the gospel; but, the fathers had experienced how difficult it is to convert the Mahometans. It was hardly possible for any thing less than the authority of the prince, or a revolution in the state, to eradicate from their minds a religion, which had been established only by violence. The function of the missionaries was, therefore, restricted to a small number of European Christians, whom the emperor had taken into his service. The fathers became at last wearied of the languishing state of their ministry at the court, and in the city. The caprice of Akebar became insupportable; he seemed to have countenanced, for a season, the cause of Christianity from a principle of curiosity only, or for the amusement of hearing disputations on matters of religious faith. They were on the verge of returning to Goa, when they were prevented by Abdul Fasil.

"The emperor," he said, "beholds you with satisfaction in his palace; reasons of state only prevent him from declaring himself openly in favor of a religion which you have promulgated to him. I beheld him, yesterday, place the gospel on his head with reverence, a respect which he never paid to the Alcoran when presented to him. Continue to persevere," he said, "and suffer time to ripen an enterprise, in which your cares have already made such progress." It is probable, that Abdul Fasil had imparted to the emperor the purpose which the missionaries entertained of quitting the states of the Mogul. At least, it is certain, that in appearance, they seemed to have recovered the good graces of Akebar. He frequently visited them, and he sometimes would converse with them on topics of religion. At last, as a mark of his entire confidence, he gave them directions to instruct likewise his eldest son in the sciences of Europe.

Father Aquaviva did not allow himself to be so far flattered by these appearances, as to consent to his evangelical fellow-labourers remaining inactive, whilst the rest of the Indies was so ill supplied with missionaries. He had written to his superiors, that a single missionary would suffice to be present with the Mogul, to watch the moments when the prince might be well disposed, and to attend to the weal of the Christian strangers. In effect, the emperor soon after frankly acknowledged, that the season, which would be crowned by his conversion, was yet remote. "I find myself," he said to the fathers, "bound to Mahometanism by ties, which I am unable to break asunder. The Moulas of the palace, and the sultaness my mother, never cease to inveigh against the new religion which I protect. I have an opposition still more difficult to sustain with the women of my haram. From the apprehension of being all discarded, as soon as Christianity shall have reduced me to make choice of a single companion, they spare no caresses, that they may tear from my heart the religion of Jesus Christ. In a word," he added, "the gospel is too pure, and my manners are too corrupt."

Father Aquaviva seized the opportunity, furnished by the sincerity of this communication, to solicit from Akebar permission to return to Goa. The emperor repented quickly of his frankness. "Do you not perceive, my father," he said, "how much your presence is necessary to me? The chain, by which I am bound, has so powerful a spell, that I need the hand of a master to dissolve its enchantments. Can you resolve to abandon me at a moment when I stand in the greatest need of your aid?" Father Rodolph was unable to resist so affecting an appeal. He suffered the two companions of his labours to take their departure, Father Henric for Goa, and Father Manserrat for the city of Agra, with the prince, his pupil. As for himself, he continued to reside at Fetipour, that he might be near the person of the Mogul.

It is not easy to decide, on which side the sufferings of the father were greater; whether those, which were the consequence of the favor shewn him by the prince, or such as arose from the distress, which the aberrations of Akebar occasioned him in the sequel. The consideration in which the missionary was held by the emperor excited the envy of the court. His life was often in jeopardy. At last, the hatred of his enemies had attained to such a heighth, that the emperor was desirous he should accept of a guard for the protection of his person. "No, my lord," the father replied, "an apostolic character is sufficiently defended by the confidence which it is his duty to repose in God. He ought rather to lay down his life, than reject that trust." It was thus, that this zealous missionary already displayed that courage, which he manifested sometime afterwards, by shedding his blood for the cause of the gospel in the island of Salsette.

The life of Father Aquaviva was agreeable to his professions. He was zealously occupied in his studies, whilst the emperor remained at Fetipour, that he might be enabled to refute the objections of the Moulas. The war, which Akebar had to maintain against his brother on the banks of the Indus, left Father Rodolph very solitary. It was then, that the missionary profited, during an interval of repose, by labouring more particularly for his own perfection. He employed almost the entire day, and the greater part of the night, in prayer. The little repose, in which he indulged, was taken stretched on the bare ground, or lying on a mat. His repast was rice, baked in water. His visits were confined to the necessitous; and his austerities surpassed, apparently, what nature was capable of enduring. He was often found engaged in prayer, at sunrise, in the exact situation he had assumed at the setting of the sun.

Akebar, in the meanwhile, triumphed over his enemies, and compelled the rebellious Patans to seek refuge in their mountains. His brother, often vanquished, was obliged to submit to his conqueror. Elated by success, the emperor was tempted to despise the humility of the cross; and the tumult and distractions of war had in part obliterated the recollection of the satisfaction, which he had formerly experienced in listening to the conversation of Father Aquaviva, and receiving instruction in our mysteries. Akebar, on his return, no longer appeared the same person in the eyes of the missionary. It was easy to perceive, that the chief object which the prince had in view, by inviting to his court Jesuits from Goa, was, by their means, to establish an intercourse of commerce with the Portuguese, and to gratify his eager desire to become acquainted with the sciences of Europe.

It may be said, that curiosity and a thirst for knowledge were the ruling passions of Akebar. His indulgence of these propensities prompted him to a very singular expedient. He was desirous to ascertain the language in which children would express themselves, who had been kept in ignorance of the articulate sounds of any known language. The emperor had been informed, that the Hebrew was the original language of the human race, and the one, which all, who had not been taught any other, would naturally speak. In order to secure a conviction on this point, he ordered twelve children to be taken from the breast, and to be closely confined in a castle, which was situated six leagues from Agra. They had given to them, for nurses, twelve women, who were dumb, with the addition of a man, who was also dumb, to serve as porter. The porter was forbidden, on pain of death, ever to open the gates of the castle. When the children had attained the age of twelve years, Akebar commanded that they should be brought into his presence. He then assembled in his palace persons skilled in various languages. A Jew, who was at Agra, was appointed to the office of deciding, whether the language to which they might give utterance, was Hebrew. The capital furnished Arabians and Chaldeans in abundance. The Indian philosophers, on their side, contended, that the children would speak the Sanscrit, which is the dialect of the learned of the country, and holds among them the same place, as does the Latin among the learned in Europe. The ancient books of philosophy and the Indian theology are written in this language. When these children appeared before the emperor, to the surprise of every one, they were found incapable of expressing themselves in any language, or even of uttering any articulate sounds. They had learnt, from the example of their nurses, to substitute signs for articulate sounds. They used only certain gestures to express their thoughts, and these were all the means which they possessed of conveying their ideas, or a sense of their wants. They were, indeed, so extremely shy, and, at the same time, of an aspect and manners so uncouth and uncultivated, that it required great labour and perseverance to bring them under any discipline, and to enable them to acquire the proper use of their tongues, of which they had previously almost entirely denied themselves the exercise.

To ascertain the source of the Ganges was another object of the curiosity of Akebar. This river, which has its course in the eastern parts of Indostan, flows from north to south, and in those places near to where it discharges its waters into the ocean, in the kingdom of Bengal, produces nearly the same effects as does the Nile in Egypt. At certain times of the year it overflows, in some places, its banks; and the sediment which it deposits on the lands, fertilizes the soil, and produces abundant crops. This is not the only point of resemblance, which this river bears to the Nile. The idolaters of India pay it worship, and consider its waters as able to absolve them of their offences. Its source has always been a subject of dispute among the Brahmins of the present day, as it was with the Gymnosophists of former times. In the time of Akebar, the ignorance respecting its source was as great, as was that of the source of the Nile a century since. The emperor contributed all the expenses necessary for ascertaining, with some precision, the origin of a river, which brought so much wealth to his states. He commissioned several persons, and gave them instructions to proceed in the direction of the banks of the Ganges, and by persevering therein, to ascend ultimately to its fountain head. They were furnished with provisions, horses, and money; and with letters of recommendation, to enable them to pass, without molestation, through the various countries washed by the Ganges, which were independent of the power of the Mogul. Their route lay principally to the north; and the nearer they approached towards its source, the more the channel of the river was found to diminish in breadth. Uninhabited tracts of forest were traversed, through which they were compelled to penetrate, by hewing their way, and forming new routes. At last, they came to a lofty mountain, which seemed to have been formed, by labour and art, into the shape of a cow's head. Thence flow a great abundance of waters. The deputies conceived they had here found the original source of the Ganges, and penetrated no further in quest of the object of their researches. They returned, after encountering many perils, to make a report to the emperor of the result of their labours. The relation of the deputies was inserted in the Chronicle; from which I have extracted it. It may be said, that they added little to former discoveries. Long before the time of Akebar, the persuasion was general in the Indies, that the Ganges takes its source in a mountain, whose shape bears a resemblance to a cow's head. It is for this reason, they say, that these animals have been, for so long a period, the object of the adoration of the Indians. One of the principal grounds of hope, among them, of happiness in a future life, consists in being able to yield up their breath in the waters of the Ganges, in the act of holding a cow by the tail. Since the time of Akebar, further discoveries have been made; and it has been ascertained that the Ganges forms a cascade upon the mountain, from which they supposed it to take its origin; but that its source is at a much greater distance, and far removed thence into the interior parts of Great Tartary.

It is easy to conceive, that a prince, whose mind was so eager for knowledge, should entertain novelties in matters of religion. He had been brought up, by his father, in a contempt of the laws of Mahomet; and had been confirmed in those sentiments by the missionaries. Outwardly, he always made a profession of it. He called himself of the sect of Ali, which the pretended true Mussulmen regard as a heresy. He had not attached himself to this sect, in preference to that of the Sonnis, who boast themselves to be the only orthodox sect, with the view of drawing into his service a great number of Persians, a nation which professes itself of the sect of Ali; but from the pride of singularity, and a desire to be distinguished from the common herd of his Mussulmen subjects in matters of Faith. The Christianity, afterwards preached at court by the Jesuits, had for him all the attractions of novelty. If he refused to embrace it, from motives of policy, and an unconquerable attachment to his pleasures; he trusted, that he might, at least, be able to construct a religion founded on the different professions of faith in his states, which would easily be adopted throughout his empire. "Mahomet," he said, "was but a man, as I am, and much less powerful. He framed a religion compounded of Judaism, Christianity, and the suggestions of his own mind and fancy. By this means, the pretended prophet has immortalized his name, and great sovereigns have professed themselves his disciples. It is equally for my interest, and my glory, to become the head and the author of a new religion. The people of my states," he said, "are a singular medley of Mahometans, idolaters, and Christians. I will reunite them all in one belief. The baptism of one, and the circumcision of the other, shall be blended with the worship of Brama. I will preserve the metempsychosis, the plurality of wives, and the worship of Jesus Christ. Uniting thus together the things which the professors of each of those religions hold most sacred, I shall form one only flock, of which I shall myself be the shepherd."

Akebar entered upon the execution of this great enterprise, and took the name of Cha Geladin, which signifies, "the powerful prince of the sovereign law."

Lahor, an imperial city, in which the Mogul had a palace, appeared to him well situated for the first promulgation of his new religion. The vicinity of the army, which he had assembled in its neighbourhood, for the conquest which he was meditating of the kingdom of Cachemire, was a circumstance not to be neglected by an innovator in matters of religion. It was, then, at Lahor, tha he announced himself first the enemy of Mahometanism. The mosques were shut up, or changed into stables, for the accommodation of the court. The use of those lofty turrets, called Alcorans, whence the Moulas are accustomed to call the Mussulmen to prayers, was forbidden them. The people were all exhorted to conform to the religion of the prince. Akebar instituted laws, practised himself the ceremonies, and invited all the officers of his court to give their sanction to his new modes of worship. He adopted, from the Pagan worship, the adoration of the sun, which he practised three times a day; at the rising of that luminary, when it was at its meridian, and at its setting. He, on certain occasions, paid honors to Jesus and Mary. He carried, suspended from his neck, a relic, which he had received from Father Aquaviva—an Agnus Dei, and an image of the Virgin Mary. This was all he had borrowed from the Christian religion. He reserved, for further consideration, the adoption of the sacrament of baptism. He allowed the circumcision of the Mahometans to be preserved; and he recited, agreeably to the manner of Mussulmen, the praises of God upon a species of large rosary. He filled up the measure of his impiety, by wishing to be himself adored as a god. Every morning he presented himself upon a balcony, to the view of his people, who prostrated themselves on his appearance. He received their petitions, he heard their prayers, and caused to be reported, among a credulous populace, that the requests which they had addressed to him were miraculously fulfilled.

Father Aquaviva was no longer able to support, patiently, the affliction, which this change caused him, in a prince, of whose conversion he had entertained strong hopes. No choice now remained, but that of quitting the territory of the Mogul, and returning to Goa. With tears in his eyes, he appeared in the presence of the emperor, at Lahor. "My lord," he said to him, "the time for my departure is arrived. It is no longer proper, that you should retain me near your person; neither is it allowable for me, to remain at your court. You promised the missionaries, before their departure from Goa, that you would suffer them to return without opposition to the Portuguese territory, whenever their labours could be no longer useful to your states. It even seems, that they are become prejudicial to them. You have made no other use, my lord, of our instructions, and the knowledge of Christianity, which we have been the means of imparting to you, than to profane it, by blending with it idolatry and Mahometan impiety. The scandal, of which you are the cause, recoils partly upon me. It is to me, your people attribute the novelties, which you have introduced into their worship. It becomes me, by the most open disavowal, to acquit myself of a conduct so censurable, and in which I have borne no part. I cannot do this more effectually, than by abandoning the Mogul territory, and impressing the whole empire, by my voluntary departure, with a conviction, that the innovations, which you have begun, have not resulted from my instruction or counsels. No, my lord, my eyes shall no longer be offended by beholding you occupying the place of God, and receiving an adoration, which belongs only to the eternal. My prayers shall, nevertheless, be exerted, to entreat that his judgments over you, may be suspended, and that a season may be granted to your majesty, to return to him."

Akebar was neither affected, nor offended, by the language of Father Aquaviva. He was yet in that first delirium of intoxication, which the incense of the people was calculated to excite. He was well acquainted, besides, with the zeal of the missionary, and accustomed to listen to his exhortations without emotion. Akebar had a sincere affection for Father Aquaviva; all imaginable inducements were, therefore, tried to retain him in his states. Father Rodolph persisted in his resolve, and at last the emperor gave his consent to his departure. At their separation, the Mogul gave the father an interesting proof of his regard. A Polonese slave, and a Muscovite slave, to whom she was married, were in the service of the sultaness, the mother of Akebar. The Polonese possessed particularly the confidence of the princess, and it seemed hardly possible, that the sultaness could be induced to part with her. Nevertheless, Akebar, at the solicitation of Father Aquaviva, succeeded in obtaining of his mother the liberty of the husband and wife, and two of their children. This was all the wealth, which the missionary carried away with him from the most opulent of all the countries of the earth. He took the road to Goa with the spoils he had snatched from an infidel country; which he soon after again quitted, to engage in new missions. In these services, he sacrificed his life, in the year 1583, a few months after his departure from the dominions of the Mogul.

Prosperity, as regards things temporal, may be sometimes considered as a mark of the displeasure of heaven. Certain it is, that Akebar never enjoyed a greater portion of success, than at the time, when he subjected religion and decorum to the worst violations. After having caused himself, at the head of the army, to be honoured as a God, he led it to Cachemire. This fine kingdom submitted to its conqueror, almost without resistance. The Mogul became master of it without the shedding of blood. This circumstance might have furnished to any other man, a new occasion of being elated, and of exalting himself above measure. It was not thus with Akebar; possessed of a solidity of understanding, he reflected deeply on the extravagance of his aims. Remorse, besides, agitated, and would not suffer him to enjoy a moment's repose. He opened his mind to Abdul-Fasil; not a single Jesuit had remained in his states. He had been persuaded by Father Manserrat, that it would be proper to send him, in the character of his envoy, to the king of Spain, Don Philip, who, in consequence of the death of the Cardinal Henry, king of Portugal, was about to succeed to the entire power and possessions of the Portuguese. Abdul-Fasil was by nature supple and ambitious. He had acted agreeably to the habits of courtiers, and in spite of his better understanding, he had paid adoration to the king, and declared in favor of the new religion. He no sooner perceived, that the emperor was disgusted with the impious project he had formed, than he made an effort to bring him back to reason. As the most efficacious remedy for the present distractions of his mind, he counselled him to invite other missionaries, in the place of the former.

An Armenian deacon, who happened at this time to be at the court of the Mogul, was appointed to conduct a negociation with the viceroy of Goa. He was charged as bearer of a letter to the principal of the Jesuits; of which the contents are as follow:—"In the name of the Lord. The most powerful and invincible emperor Akebar, salutes the fathers of St. Paul, who have been admitted to the grace of God; who have tasted of the gift of the Holy Spirit; who are obedient to the laws of the Messiah; and who lead men to the knowledge of salvation. To you, venerable fathers, who have separated yourselves from the world, and who contemn riches and honors, I address myself. I have examined with attention all the religions of the earth. It, nevertheless, appears to me, that I am not yet sufficiently instructed in the mysteries of the Christian religion. It is by the aid of your fathers, whom I esteem, and in whose discourse I take pleasure, that I desire to attain to a more perfect knowledge. The Armenian, Grimon, who will deliver you this letter, has assured me, that I shall find among you, wise and able men, capable of satisfying all my doubts. Come then, and here refute the doctors of the Mahometan law; and be assured, that I shall rejoice in your successes. If the missionaries, you may send me, should feel disposed to fix their abode in my capital, they shall be furnished with a mansion, and privileges superior even to those, which were granted to their predecessors. Should they, at any time, prefer returning to Goa, they will be at full liberty so to do, and I will send them back with testimonies of my favor. This letter, written at the time of the new moon, of the month of June."

The emperor sent with the letter, a pretty considerable sum, to be distributed by the hands of the Armenian, to the poor at Goa. He had been taught by the missionaries, that offences were to be redeemed, and the favors of heaven obtained by works of charity. The conversion of Akebar appeared certain, if the heart could be judged from outward evidences. He had risen superior to the chief difficulty interposed to his conversion; the indulgence of the passions. All the women of his haram had been dismissed: they were given in marriage to the nobles of the court: and the emperor reserved for his society, only a single female. The piety of the prince towards the holy virgin was become public. On the day of the assumption of the Virgin Mary, he had caused a throne to be erected, on which the image of the virgin was placed; the Mogul and his children prostrated themselves before it, and all the persons of his court, who, on this occasion, followed the example given by the princes, received presents from the emperor. Such were the results of the remorse with which Akebar was continually agitated. Perhaps the blood of Father Aquivava was heard in favor of the prince, and obtained of heaven these gifts of grace, in aid of his conversion.

Two missionaries took their departure from Goa in the year 1589, with that rejoicing of heart, which the prospect of accomplishing a great enterprise for the glory of God, is calculated to excite in men of Apostolic character. The fathers were, Edward Leiton and Christophe Vega. Flattered by the hope of finding a catechumen in Akebar, disposed to receive the grace of regeneration; they confidently expected, that they should be witnesses to the establishment of Christianity throughout the empire. The emperor waited for them at Lahor; and received them in the most honourable manner. He gave them permission, immediately, to open a school for instructing the Indians to read and write, in the Portuguese tongue. He often visited the fathers, proposing to them the most specious objections to our sacred mysteries, and appearing satisfied with the answers he received. However, although he apparently entertained no attachment to any particular faith, which was opposed to the religion of Jesus Christ; a secret pride, or rather, perhaps, reasons of policy, suspended the effect of those dispositions, with which he had been inspired from heaven. He admired our religion, yet could not resolve to embrace it. The fathers had been too sanguine in their expectation of the conversion of Akebar, and now experienced a proportionate degree of discouragement. Impatience is a fault, which too often attends on disappointment, particularly when it is the result of an overwrought and injudicious zeal. The two missionaries had been instructed to withdraw from the Mogul states, whenever they should be satisfied that their mission had failed in its object. They relinquished, therefore, the expectation of bringing the prince to a confession of the

Christian faith, and returned to Goa; reaping no other fruit from the field of their labours, than the merit of their good intentions.

At Rome, the precipitation of the two missionaries, in quitting the Mogul states, met with censure. The general of the Jesuits gave orders, that two other missionaries should be sent to the emperor, able, according to the counsel of St. Paul, to advance the work of God by doctrine, and by patience. Father Jerome Xavier, nephew to the apostle of the Indies, and Father Emanuel Pinnero were set apart for so important a ministry. The first was superior of a convent of professed monks at Goa. He had long sighed for the appointment to the Mogul mission, which he sought with the greater earnestness, as with a feeble prospect of a successful issue, it would require superior labours. He, then, set out for his destination, under the protection, and with a zeal, equal to that of his uncle, St. Francis Xavier; and, after encountering great fatigues, the two fathers arrived at Lahor. The emperor, who had felt much displeased at the departure of their predecessors, manifested great satisfaction at their arrival. A lodging near the palace was assigned to them in a commodious situation, on the banks of the river. It was in a place, which enabled the emperor's guard to hinder the people from approaching to the annoyance of the fathers. At the first audience, Akebar produced before the fathers, the images of Jesus Christ and the Virgin Mary. He pressed them to his heart, and kissed them with affection. The fathers prostrated themselves before the image of the Saviour. As children are naturally prone to imitate what they see others do, a young Mogul, grandson of Akebar, and the eldest son of the prince who was the presumptive heir to the crown, bent his knees, and joined his hands, after the example of the missionaries. The emperor, overjoyed to see his grandson, at so early an age, enter into his sentiments; "My son," he said to him, "these European pastors will henceforward be to you as parents. Follow their example, and profit by their instructions. Render yourself worthy by their assistance, of one day ruling the extensive kingdoms, which I have conquered for you."

It was no longer possible to doubt, but that Akebar was in spirit and in belief a Christian. There remained only one further effort to make, which was, to declare his profession publicly, and to receive the mark of regeneration in Jesus Christ. To judge of his heart, by the esteem which he appeared to entertain for the fathers, the preference which he gave to their religion was evident. The missionaries never approached his throne, without being saluted by him with an inclination of the head. They were, also, allowed to be seated in the European manner; a distinction never conceded by him to ambassadors, nor, even to kings, who, at times, frequented his court. These were, perhaps, but superficial evidences; the emperor furnished others more solid of his attachment to the Faith. He was often present at the services, which the fathers celebrated in their chapel; he assisted at their prayers, repeating them in a kneeling posture; he also fixed on a spot for the building of a church, and promised to defray all the charges attending its construction. Nevertheless, some vestiges of his former superstition would escape him at intervals. He was pleased to hear his subjects, possessed with a notion of his sanctity, address to him prayers, which are proper only to the divinity. He listened also to their petitions, and received their gifts. Heaven punished the pride and impiety of the prince in a remarkable manner.

On Easter Sunday in the year 1597, Akebar, with his sons, celebrated a festival in honour of the sun, in the middle of a spacious plain, where he had caused pavilions to be erected. The preparations were magnificent. Upon an altar, raised in the form of a throne, was exposed a representation of the day-star, fashioned of precious stones, of a dazzling lustre. The day was serene, and on every side was heard the tumult of the festal rejoicings, when, suddenly, a thunderbolt fell from the skies. The altar was overthrown; the tent of the emperor was set on fire; and the conflagration communicated to the camp. The damage sustained by the throne, alone, was estimated at one hundred thousand ducats. The flames spread even to the city, and reached the Imperial Palace, which was almost wholly consumed. The immense treasures, which had been collected by the Mogul, became a prey to the flames. Melted gold and silver was seen flowing through the streets of Lahor. The emperor, subsequently, determined on abandoning a place, where every thing tended to remind him of his impiety. He retired to the kingdom of Cachemire, and requested the Father Jerome Xavier to accompany him.

In the meanwhile, Father Pinnero, who remained at Lahor, was usefully employed in the conversion of the Mahometans, and the Idolaters. Akebar, with the view of advancing his own reveries, had debased Mahometanism; and the missionary profited by the ancient religion's partial degradation. The church of the Jesuits was frequented by the deserters from the mosques. It was not judged proper, however, at first, to administer baptism to any other than the sick or the dying. The temper of the people of Indostan was known to the Jesuits. A natural fickleness of disposition is the sure concomitant of a native of the Indies. It sometimes happened, that baptism, in giving health to the soul, restored likewise to the sick the health of the body. Martyrs were not wanting to this infant church. A Mahometan mother solicited, with earnestness. that her son, yet at the breast, might be baptised. She became, in consequence, the object of the scorn, and the persecution, of her neighbours. The mother was deterred from embracing the gospel, and had not the courage to confess Jesus Christ for her son. Regret, for having caused him to receive the external marks of Christianity, induced her to poison her milk; and to convey, by this means, the seeds of death into the bosom of the infant. The intercession of the little martyr was not unprofitable to this infant church. The number of catechumen increased; and the fathers entertained sufficient confidence in their virtue, to administer baptism to them.

The day of Pentecost, in the year 1599, was chosen for the ceremony. It may be said, to have been magnificent, considering the country in which it took place. The Catechumen walked in procession through the streets of Lahor, where, an awning, formed of the branches of trees, defended the spectators from the sun's rays. Tambours, trumpets, and other instruments, according to the custom of the Indies, preceded the Catechumen. They were received by the missionary at the entrance of the church. He made them children of Jesus Christ, in the sight of a numerous people, attracted by the novelty of the spectacle. Whilst water was sprinkling upon the heads of the new converts, a girl, sixteen years of age, declared her faith, in a manner which surprised every one. She demanded, with a loud voice, that the same grace should be conferred upon her which was granted to others. "Baptise me, too," she exclaimed; "suffer me, likewise, to be baptised." She repeated, so long, her importunities, that she was easily distinguished from among the crowd. The missionary explained to the young woman, that no one was admitted to the sacrament, of which the ceremony was then performing, except persons well instructed in our mysteries. "I am instructed in them," she replied; "I have continually been present at your public ministerings, though I have not openly declared myself." She was interrogated, and found capable of being admitted into the number of the faithful; regard was had to her fervour, and baptism was administered to her. The grace, which she received in the sacrament, inspired her with courage. The young Christian resisted the persecution of a Mahometan nobleman, who desired to have her among the women of his haram. He accused the missionary, before the judge, of having baptised the Indian woman by force. The woman gave a good account of her faith, and justified, satisfactorily, the conduct of her spiritual father in Jesus Christ. In fine, the same liberty to choose for herself a husband, was left to the Indian woman, which she had before exercised in the choice of her religion. She was married to a Christian, and her firmness was a triumph for the Ministers of Jesus Christ. Such was the progress of Christianity at Lahor. Father Pinnero gathered, with rejoicing, the harvest of the evangelical seed, which his predecessors had sown, and watered with their tears.

In another quarter, Father Jerome Xavier profited, at Cachemire, from the reflexions and the inquietudes of the the emperor. The mind of Akebar was still agitated at times, by the recollection of the sudden, and almost miraculous conflagration of his palace. He condemned his own aberrations in matters of religion; but could not resolve on the absolute retraction of his first measures. The emperor appeared to consider himself engaged, in honour, to support the sect, of which he was the founder. He blamed his own extravagance, in secret, and supported it in public. God, by his afflictions, either took vengeance on the guilty monarch, or furnished him anew with opportunities for his conversion.

Mostafa, formerly conquered, and despoiled of the share he possessed of the kingdom of the Decan; after having resided some time, tranquilly, at the court of the Mogul, had returned to his ancient dominions, had taken up arms, and re-assumed the name of Melec, or King. Those, who were dissatisfied with the reign of Akebar, and, especially, the zealous Mahometans, took part with the rebel. The emperor opposed to the rising revolt his son Pahari, and caused him to take the name of Morad. The whole empire clearly saw, by his putting arms into the hands of the second of his sons, whilst he kept the eldest in obscurity, that he purposed to declare Morad his successor. A victory, gained by the young prince, would have secured to him the throne of the Moguls. It pleased Providence to frustrate the views of Akebar, and to visit him with a severe infliction, in a quarter where he was most sensible. The Imperial army, and the rebel army joined battle near Cambaia. The army of the young Mogul was much superior in numbers; but Mostafa was a great commander. Every thing gave way to his valour. A frightful carnage was made of the vanquished; and the young Morad was found, after the battle, among the number of the slain.

On receiving the news of the death of his son, the emperor was struck to the heart, by the blow with which it had pleased Heaven to visit him. He acknowledged the hand of the Almighty, and felt that it was his duty to subscribe to his decrees. He no longer adored the sun, or arrogated to himself the worship, which was due only to God. Father Xavier aided by his discourses the impressions which grace had effected on the heart of the prince.

The court now quitted Cachemire, and took the road to Lahor; and after some stay at that city, continued its progress southward, until it arrived in the capital. It was at Agra, that the emperor prepared that formidable army, which he proposed to conduct in person against the rebels. Akebar, during the progress of the preparations, partook of no other amusement than that of the chace. It was in the solitude of the forests, that he sought to forget the death of his favorite son. Having become thoughtful, and melancholy, and being harrassed incessantly by that internal monitor, conscience, the chace was the only amusement, which suited his state of mind; but in following this diversion, he met with an adventure, which was, eventually, the cause of his death.

One day, when the Mogul was hunting, in the environs of Agra, he lost sight of his attendants, and being much fatigued, sat himself down at the foot of a tree, which afforded a welcome shade. Whilst he was trying to compose himself to sleep, he saw approaching him, one of those long caterpillars, of a flame colour, which are to be found only in the Indies. He pierced it through with an arrow, which he drew from his quiver. A little time afterwards, an antelope made its appearance, within bow-shot. The emperor took aim at it, with the same arrow with which he had pierced the caterpillar. Notwithstanding the antelope received the shaft in a part of its body, which was not susceptible of a mortal wound, the animal instantaneously expired. The hunters of the prince, who opened the beast, found the flesh black and corrupted, and all the dogs who eat of it died immediately. The emperor knew, from this circumstance, the extreme venom of the poison of the caterpillar. He commanded one of the officers of his suite, to get it conveyed to his palace. It was, on this occasion, that the emperor created the office of poisoner, an office till then unknown to the Mogul government. By the instrumentality of this new officer, Akebar quietly disposed of the nobles, and the Rajas, whom he believed to be concerned in the conspiracy of Mostafa. Poisoned pills were compounded for him, which he obliged them to take in his presence. The poison was slow in its operation, but no remedies could obviate its mortal effects. This pernicious invention proved fatal to its author. Akebar carried always about him a gold box, which was divided into three compartments. In one was his betel; in another, the cordial pills, which he used after a repast; and in the third, were the poisoned pills. One day, it happened, that he took, inadvertently, one of the poisoned pills, and became himself a victim to its fatal power. He immediately felt himself struck with death. He, in vain, made trial of all the remedies prescribed for him by the Portuguese physicians. As his illness was a lingering one, Father Xavier had both time and opportunity to approach him. Happy, if he but knew how to profit by the moments, which were afforded him by Providence for his conversion. He died in the year 1605.

Akebar followed the custom of his ancestors, and had caused a magnificent sepulchre to be erected in his lifetime. It is rather a large edifice, constructed of marble, and supported with a dome of the same materials. The building is elegant, and the Mosaics, which adorn it, are all composed of those precious stones, which are found in such quantities in the Indies, and are of an extraordinary beauty, and a dazzling lustre. M. Manouchi, by the special permission of the reigning emperor, visited this mausoleum. Aurengzebe had commanded the walls of the mosque to be covered with a piece of gold brocade. The object of this was, to conceal from the eyes of Mahometans a crucifix, in relief, which was perceived by M. Manouchi, on raising the tapestry. He saw there, also, a fine statue of the Holy Virgin, and another of St. Ignatius. This has given rise to a notion, that Akebar died a Christian. It may rather be said, that these statues were used only as European curiosities, to serve as an ornament to the tomb of the emperor, without any regard to the persons represented by them; and without any intention of indicating the religion, which was professed by Akebar. This illustrious Mogul possessed great qualities, and was unequalled by any prince of his race, since the time of Tamerlane. Never monarch better understood how to blend the high spirit, and intrepidity of the Tartar, with the mildness of the Indian character. He secured, by the one, the respect of the nobles; and conciliated, by the other, the love of the people. He had a regard for justice, and administered it always with great care. Twice a day, he gave audience to his subjects, and listened to their complaints, while standing, without giving any signs of impatience, or fatigue. A golden bell had been fixed, by his order, in his apartment, which might be sounded, by pulling a cord of communication from the outside of the palace. Persons, whose occasions for recurring to his justice, were urgent, had the privilege of sounding it, and bringing their complaints before him, at any hour of the day. He was not, generally speaking, disposed to the shedding of blood. The ministers of justice were prohibited from putting in force the sentence of death upon any person, until they had received three times, on three several days, his personal orders to that effect. If he availed himself of the use of poison, it was only against the secret enemies of the state, who merited a more violent death. This prince possessed habits of temperance, of which there are few examples; the reigning emperor, in this point, resembles him. Flesh was never served at his table. Rice, a preparation of milk, and some sweetmeats, comprised his whole diet. He was fond of literature, and cultivated it. His greatest pleasure was in conversing with strangers, and informing himself of the manners, the customs, and the religion of Europeans. With respect to the history of his country, and, especially, that of his own reign, he caused it to be written with care; and had it read to him, agreeably to the custom of Oriental sovereigns.

The buildings, which he caused to be constructed, and the manner in which he adorned different parts of his empire, will be never failing monuments of his glory. The system, which he pursued, in making war, was to take his enemy by surprise, whenever he had the opportunity; and when that failed, to contend with him valiantly. By these means, he succeeded in greatly extending his empire. If the Portuguese, who were secretly the partisans of Mostafa, had not arrested the progress of this Mogul, he would probably have carried the glory of his arms as far as Cape Camorin. To conclude, he well merited the name of Akebar, that is to say, peerless, which his people bestowed upon him from the commencement of his reign.

JEHAN GUIR,

EIGHTH EMPEROR.

His partiality for the Christian Religion. His Debauchery. Marries Nurmahal. The influence of the Sultaness over her Husband. She causes her Daughter to marry into the Imperial Family. Mahobet-Cham makes himself Master of the Person of the Emperor. The eldest Son of Jehan Guir is strangled in Prison. The Emperor's familiar manners with his People. Revolt of his third Son. Defeat of his Son. Peace being established, he resigns himself to the enjoyment of repose. Dies.

IT is still a subject of dispute in the Indies; whether Cha Selim, that is, the pacific prince, who took in the sequel, the name of Jehan Guir, which means, the Sovereign of the Universe, was a legitimate king, or an usurper. Some historians pretend, that his father, Akebar, a few days previous to his death, had declared him his successor to the empire; that he had placed the royal turban upon his head, and had girded him with the sword of Amayum. On the contrary, others write, that Jehan Guir, (for it is by this name that we shall always speak of the successor of Akebar), had been disinherited by his father as a rebel; and that the deceased emperor had appointed by his will, sultan Cosrou, eldest son of Jehan Guir, to succeed him. Whatever may be the truth in this matter, it is certain, that these public rumours afforded a pretext to Cosrou for revolting against his father.

The emperor, whose life is now about to be recorded, possessed none of the good qualities of Akebar, with the exception of his good-will towards the Christians. He was, nevertheless, without any of the dispositions, which are the essentials of Christianity. He was a voluptuous prince, who passed the greater part of his life in the pleasures of the haram; and who abandoned himself to a species of sottishness, which was degrading to human nature. During the lifetime of his father, Jehan Guir had the prudence partly to conceal his vices; but he no sooner found himself in the possession of unlimited power, and at liberty to indulge his propensities, than he set no bounds to his irregularities. The religion of the Christians was agreeable to him, chiefly, on account of the licence, which it affords, for the use of wine, and the flesh of all kinds of animals. This was the only view, which he took of it; that spirit of penitence, humility, charity, and temperance, which is the soul of Christianity, was never a subject on which he reflected. With prepossessions, founded on such impure motives, did he declare himself openly in favor of the Christians; and violate, without scruple, the law of Mahomet. He drank wine in the face of his whole court. The fast, which the Mahometans observe, so scrupulously, for an entire month, was the subject of his derision. He invited to his table, the most conscientious observers of the laws of their religion, and inveigled them into a companionship in his excesses in wine, and in eating prohibited meats. The Casi, and the Imans, who are the doctors of Mahometan law, in vain admonished him, that the use of certain meats was forbidden by the Alcoran. Fatigued with their importunities, he enquired in what religion the use of drinks and food of every species, without distinction, was permitted. The reply was, in that of the Christian religion alone. We must then, he rejoined, all turn Christians. Let there be taylors brought to us, to convert our robes into close coats, and our turbans into hats. At these words, the doctors trembled for their sect. Fear and interest made them hold a less severe language. They all declared, that the sovereign was not bound by the precepts of the Alcoran; and that the monarch might, without scruple, use whatever meats and drinks were most agreeable to him.

This accommodating spirit, of the doctors, only served in a greater degree to invite the contempt, and the hostility of the emperor. He considered, that he was justified in availing himself of the weakness of these false pastors, to insult their religion. With this view, he caused small statues of gold to be cast, with which he ornamented his apartments; and to increase their mortification, he commanded the figures of wild boars, an animal detested above all others by the Mahometans, to be made in every sort of attitude. A governor of Lahor, named Amanet-Chan, well disposed to our religion, told some Europeans, that he had been present, when the Mahometan doctors gave their decision in favor of the prince; and that he knew the spot where the statues of the wild boars had been buried by them. He added, that whoever might obtain permission to disinter so considerable a treasure, would find there a rich booty.

It was more particularly during the night, that the king gave himself up to intoxication, in the society of his friends. All the Franks in Agra, that is, all Europeans of whatsoever nation, were allowed free access to the palace. He continued drinking in their company, till the return of day, and he abandoned himself, especially, to these midnight debaucheries, at the season, which the Mahometans observe as a fast with the most scrupulous exactness. When some of his nation of rather rigid principles happened to be present at these meetings, he compelled them to violate their fast, threatening them in case of disobedience, with being abandoned to the rage of two lions, who were kept always chained under the windows of his apartment. One of his greatest pleasures, was, putting to the test the constancy of the Persians newly arrived at his court. He commonly carried in his girdle, a stile, the point of which was particularly acute, with which he pierced the ear of the new comer, at a moment when he was quite unprepared for such a salutation. By his outcries, or by his silence, that is to say, by the impatience or the tranquil resolution which he manifested under the infliction of pain, he formed his opinion of the courage of the Persian; and he measured his favors, by the result of his experiment. In fact, the Mahometans were generally obnoxious to Jehan Guir; and it was his policy to induce them to fly the court from disgust. In the disputes, which the Jesuits had frequently with the Moulas, the prince, consequently, always gave his voice in favor of the arguments adduced by the former.

The historians of the Indies make mention of a singular occurrence, which added much to the reputation of the Christian religion, at the court of Jehan Guir. Our writers of Europe attribute it to Father Rodolph Aquiviva, and pretend that it took place in the reign of Akebar. The circumstances attending this incident are related with some trifling variations. In this place, the traditions of Asia will be followed. Jehan Guir, one day, they say, assembled in his palace the doctors of his own sect on one part, and on the other Father Acosta. He commanded the missionary to state to the Mahometans his strongest objections to the Alcoran. The Jesuit complied in a manner which gave satisfaction to the emperor, and confounded the Moulas. One among them, bolder than the rest, maintained, that the bible was a spurious book, and that it carried no internal evidence of truth. Father Joseph D'Acosta, then superior of the company in Agra, made a singular proposal to this celebrated Moula, who was esteemed in the Indies as the head of the law. "Let a large fire be lighted," said the father, "and the chief of the Mahometan religion on one side enter it, bearing the Alcoran, whilst on the other side, I will cast myself into it, holding in my hand the gospel. It will then be seen, in whose favor heaven will declare, whether for Jesus Christ or Mahomet." At these words, the emperor cast his eyes upon the Mahometan, who exhibited great symptoms of terror, lest the challenge should be accepted. He took pity on the Moula, and refrained exacting from him so severe a trial. As for the Jesuit, they caused him to change his name; and the emperor no longer called him by any other than that of Father Ataxe, which means, the Fire Father.

If Jehan Guir was not permitted to be the witness of a miracle, which Providence refused, perhaps, to the hardness of his heart, and the corruption of his manners; it was permitted him, at least, to be the spectator of another occurrence sufficiently extraordinary. I should not relate it, but for the warrant of an author, who has never yet been reputed either as over credulous, or a visionary. A certain mountebank had, they say, a monkey, possessing extraordinary sagacity in discovering things secreted. The emperor, who had ordered the monkey to be brought into his presence, concealed his ring in the vest of one of his pages. The monkey singled out the page in the crowd, and forced the ring from him. The following incident likewise occurred. Jehan Guir caused to be written, upon twelve separate billets, the names of the twelve principal legislators; of Moses, of Jesus Christ, of Mahomet, of Brama; finally, of all those who are honored in the Indies. The billets were mixed in a vase, and the monkey was commanded to draw the billet, which contained the name of the legislator, who was the founder of the true religion. The monkey obeyed, and drew that which had the name of Jesus Christ. The emperor was astonished, but he was not convinced. The event was attributed to chance, or the address of the mountebank. Jehan Guir then commanded, that the names of the legislators should be written a second time, in that species of cipher, which he used in giving instructions to his ambassadors. The monkey selected again the name of Jesus Christ, drew it from the vase, and kissed it. The astonishment was still greater, after this second mark of sagacity; but it was converted into admiration, after the third prodigy. The king concealed the billet containing the name of Jesus Christ in the hands of one of his courtiers, and mixed eleven only in the vase. The monkey handled them all without drawing any one of them. Advancing, then, towards the courtier, in whose hands had been placed the billet containing the name of Jesus Christ, he disentangled his fingers, and seized upon the billet. We may think what we please on the subject of this incident; but that it actually took place, says the Protestant author, from whom I have extracted the relation, is a fact which will admit of no dispute.

Faith is the gift of heaven, and this was refused to Jehan Guir. It was not, that this prince did not esteem Christianity above all other religions; but the knowledge, which he had of it, served only to render him more criminal. He suffered, indeed, two of his nephews to get instructed in the Faith, and to embrace it. Some pretend, that his motives, on this occasion, were of a political nature. He purposed by this, they said, to secure a pretext for destroying those young princes, at a convenient opportunity, when he should have rendered them devotees to a religion, different from his own. Others assert, that he was prompted to it from licentious motives. He hoped, they say, to be able to fill his haram with Portuguese women, as soon as it should be believed at Goa, that he was well disposed to Christianity. Whatever might be his motives, it is certain, that Jehan Guir lived without religion, a great enemy to the Mahometans, and always, apparently, entertaining a partiality for the Christian faith.

The great heats of Indostan obliged the emperor to quit the residence of Agra. He considered that capital as the work of his father. The desire to erect a monument to his glory, in his turn, made him give the preference to Lahor. This is a city in a more northern situation than Agra; its site is more healthy, and the climate is more temperate. Some historians say, that the fine avenue of trees, which extends from Agra to Lahor, had been planted by Akebar; and others maintain that it was done by Jehan Guir. It seems most probable, that the father began the work, and that the son continued and completed it. With respect to Lahor, it became, under Jehan Guir, the ordinary residence of the court. This emperor extended it, and caused a palace to be built, which has indeed nothing of the magnificence of that of Agra; but taken altogether, is more convenient, and more healthy. One day, when the king was walking upon the terrace, which commands a view of the river, he perceived a boat, navigated by six rowers. A female, whose beauty struck him with surprise, was being conveyed in the bark, under a canopy in the form of a palanquin. It is probable, that it was without design, that Nur-Mahal (which was the name of the lady) presented herself to the view of the emperor; but it is certain, that the sight of her, on this occasion, made an impression upon the prince which lasted all the remainder of his days. Jehan Guir made himself acquainted with her name, and place of abode. Presents were soon followed by the most splendid offers. But Nur-Mahal possessed a virtue, which was proof against seduction. She caused the emperor to be informed, that she had a husband; that he had the honor to be in the service of his majesty; that he commanded five hundred men in a city on the frontier next to

Bengal; and that she trusted to preserve to her husband, as long as he lived, the most inviolable fidelity. This reply of the lady occasioned the emperor to adopt a cruel expedient. He wrote to Chir-Afgam, (which was the name of the husband) ordering him to go to the governor of the province, and to take from him such orders as he had transmitted him. He sent instructions, in the meantime, to the governor, to put Chir-Afgam to death as soon as he should present himself before him. The orders of the prince were executed, but not without bloodshed. The brave captain sold his life dear, and slew several of the assassins, ere they were able to effect their sanguinary purpose. Jehan Guir trusted, confidently, that after the assassination of the husband, the widow would fall easily into his toils.

He was astonished, when he found, in Nur-Mahal, all the resistance which might be expected from an incensed woman, prompted by the most lively resentment. Whether this was artifice, or passion unfeigned, the widow spoke of the emperor in terms only of contempt and hatred. From the first year of her widowhood, she availed herself, nevertheless, of all the advantages of the freedom which she had acquired by the death of her husband, to draw to her residence a large society. Jehan Guir, who was of a temper, which disposed him to be familiar with his subjects, paid his assiduities to her under a borrowed name: declaring, in the sequel, his quality and his passion, he offered to place her in his haram, and to adopt her as one of his wives. The artful widow put on all the semblance of virtue, and even marks of aversion, the more effectually to inflame the passion of the emperor. At last, when she had succeeded in placing him in the situation of not being able to deny her any thing, she consented to enter his haram, on the following conditions: First, that she should have the rank of first queen; secondly, that her father should have the post of Etmadoulet, or first minister; and, thirdly, that her brothers, as well as her other relations, should fill the first places at court. The emperor consented to all her demands; and celebrated the arrival of the new queen, at the palace, by a feast, which lasted eight days. The name of Nur-Mahal seemed too common for the favorite queen; it was changed to that of Nur-Jaham, which signifies the Light of the World.

The emperor suffered himself to be so much under the influence of this new passion, that all others were supplanted by it. Nevertheless, Nur-Jaham was a woman of low rank. Born in Persia, she had followed her husband, at that time a conductor of camels in the service of some Armenian merchants. She arrived in the Indies in low condition, with Chir Afgam, who subsequently obtained promotion, and made some fortune in the armies of the Mogul. If her birth was ignoble, her beauty and her understanding were not of the common order. In fine, it may be said, that she was worthy of the empire to which fortune had elevated her.

When she found herself in the palace, secure in the possession of the heart of her husband, it was her first care to procure the banishment, or even, perhaps, to rid herself of her rivals by poison. This was the general persuasion, when five queens, the most affectionately beloved by Jehan Guir, were known to expire within the space of one year. It is even said, that this ambitious woman exerted her influence to the extent of obtaining the emperor's permission, to coin money in her own name. The impression, which she caused to be struck upon them, represented the twelve signs of the zodiac. These coins are found even at the present day in the Indies; and some of them have been distributed in Europe. It is, however, certain, notwithstanding what may be related by our travellers, that the famous gold and silver pieces, on which the signs of the zodiac are seen, do not bear the name of Nur-Jaham, but that of Jehan Guir. The sultaness may, indeed, have caused them to be struck, but she had not the temerity to cause her name to be engraved upon them.

There was nothing which excited more astonishment in the Indies, than the empire which Nur-Jaham exercised over the mind of Jehan Guir. She insensibly weaned the emperor from his inordinate love of wine; she put limits to his excesses; and obtained his promise, that he would refrain from drinking more than nine goblets, at those seasons, when he resigned himself to sociality and mirth. This was often a subject of contest between the emperor and the sultaness; but the advantage always remained with Nur-Jaham. Never woman exhibited more skill in preserving her power over a heart of which she had once taken possession. The indefatigable Persian found a hundred modes of fixing her husband's attachment; and least he should break from her chain, she furnished him incessantly with new pleasures, of which she partook. The slight disputes, excited sometimes by subjects of little importance, only served to re-animate their tenderness. One day, that Jehan Guir happened to be recreating himself, attended by the musicians and female dancers of his palace, he exceeded the nine goblets, to which he had been restricted by Nur-Jaham. The queen remonstrated, but the emperor turned a deaf ear to her complaint, and carried his indulgence to the extent of intoxication. The sultaness availed herself, the next morning, of the condition to which Jehan Guir had reduced himself the preceding evening. She shut herself up in her apartment, and refused to make her appearance as usual. Never was distress more lively, than that of Jehan Guir. With the most anxious solicitude, he sought the sultaness, and could take no rest, till he had succeeded in appeasing her. The queen exacted from him a humiliation not a little difficult for the pride of a Mogul to submit to. She rejected all accommodation, until she should behold him on his knees, soliciting her forgiveness for his want of complaisance. The emperor, between the claims of his rank, and the unworthy passion which enslaved him, was a long time held in suspense. He availed himself, at last, of the following expedient, by the advice of one of those ancient governantes of the haram, who act the part of guardians to the queens. One day, that the sultaness was walking in the gardens of the palace, defended by a parasol from the sun's rays, the emperor joined her side, and sought the benefit of its protecting shade. The ancient dame made Jehan Guir comprehend, that he might place himself at the feet of the queen, and participate of the shade, which was afforded to herself. It was in this state of humiliation, which the emperor seemed to have sought for his own accommodation, that he reconciled himself to Nur-Jaham. He made vows of a blind obedience, and was received again into favor.

The queen beheld, with delight, the submissions of the emperor; and to testify her satisfaction, she gave a fête to her spouse, which lasted eight days. None of the diversions were forgotten, which are accustomed to be practised, in this the most delightful country of the universe. One day it was a magnificent repast. Another day, a comedy, intermixed with that species of dance, in which actions are represented by figures and attitudes. In these the Indians excel. Some other time it was a concert, agreeably to the taste in music, which prevails in the country. The ears of Europeans are accustomed to it with difficulty, but, in the course of time, they discover in it a peculiar harmony, and a something of sublime, which is not to be found in

European concerts. Then, it was a display of fireworks, in which they succeed better in the Indies, than with us. One of the most remarkable spectacles appertained to a small canal, the banks of which were ornamented with a beautiful promenade. This canal Nur-Jaham had caused to be entirely filled with rose water. The perfumed water was used for a bath. Roses, which are extremely common in the Indies, became, on this occasion, of an enormous price. The magnificence of the sultaness occasioned a discovery, which afforded great pleasure in a country, in which perfumes are so highly esteemed. Whilst the emperor was walking with Nur-Jaham, on the bank of the canal, they perceived a crust, that had been formed, resembling moss, which floated on the surface of the water. In order to take it off the water, and examine it, they waited till it was near the brink. They, then, perceived, that it was a substance derived from the roses, which had been baked, and collected into a mass by the power of the sun's rays. It appeared to the whole haram the most exquisite perfume, which had ever been produced in the Indies. Attempts were, afterwards, made to imitate by art, that which nature alone had formed.

The influence of Nur-Jaham became more powerful every day; and, finally, attained such a heighth, that no other was capable of competing with it. Relying securely on her authority with her husband, her thoughts were now entirely directed to the contracting of alliances, which might mingle her blood with that of the emperors. The sultaness had, by her first marriage, a daughter only; by Jehan Guir she had no children. It was the establishment of this daughter, that brought dissention into the royal family, and became the source of so many wars and revolts.

The emperor had four sons by different wives. The eldest, born during the life-time of his grandfather, Akebar, was the Sultan Cosrou. The second was the Sultan Perviz, a virtuous and pacific prince, who was sent to take charge of the government of the kingdom of Bengal, which he ruled a long time in so much tranquillity, that several historians are even ignorant that such a person has existed. The third was the Sultan Chorrom, a prince of great promise; and who was able, in the sequel, to place himself upon the throne, to the exclusion of his two elder brothers. The fourth, and last, was Sultan Scheriar, a prince of little courage, and of slender capacity. The object of Nur-Jaham was to procure the marriage of her daughter with Sultan Cosrou, the heir presumptive to the empire; but this prince, who was of a haughty spirit, and indignant at the ascendancy, which an obscure stranger had assumed over the mind of his father, refused to dishonor himself by so unsuitable an alliance. He had, besides, for his wife, the daughter of a Raja, a princess of an heroic spirit, and for whom the young sultan had all possible attachment and affection. The rejection of the daughter of Nur-Jaham, by Cosrou, cost him dear :—the loss of his liberty, of the crown, and of his life, quickly succeeded the contempt with which he treated the sultaness, and her proffered alliance. She then cast her eyes upon Prince Scheriar, the youngest of the emperor's sons, as a husband for her daughter. Prince Perviz was overlooked, for reasons, which the history does not explain. Sultan Chorrom had already for his wife the niece of Nur-Jaham, the daughter of her brother, Asaph Cham.

As soon as the marriage of the daughter of Nur-Jaham with the Sultan Scheriar had been concluded, the chief favors were showered upon this youngest of the princes. The three elder princes were sent to take charge of governments at a distance from the court, agreeably to the bad policy of the Moguls. The viceroyalty of Bengal was given to Perviz, and that of the Decan fell to the lot of Sultan Chorrom. The government of Guzurat was intended for the elder of the princes, before he revolted against his sovereign. Never a son had a more specious pretext for making war upon his father, than Sultan Cosrou. It was to him, they said, that the kingdom had been left by the destination of Akebar; and that the reigning emperor had enjoyed the possession of it, entirely by the sufferance of Cosrou, and through the respect, which this prince entertained for him, to whom he was indebted for his birth. Yet it was that very sceptre, which it was in his power to have wielded, that was wrested from him, in order that it might be bestowed upon the youngest of his brothers. What particularly exasperated him, were the intrigues of an ambitious woman, who, for the purpose of establishing her blood upon the throne, violated the rights of nature, and of nations. "I am banished," he said to his confidants, "to a government, which is situated at the greatest distance from the court, whilst Scheriar is retained near the emperor, my father, in order that the people may be accustomed to recognise in him the successor of Jehan Guir. "Let us break silence," he said, "since we have no alternative; and let us not suffer them to deprive us of our rights without complaining, and without contending for them. I shall certainly not become more criminal by taking arms against Jehan Guir, than he himself was in revolting against Akebar. If I offend, it will only be by following the example of my father; besides, I have this argument in my favor, that I reclaim a crown, which belongs to me at this moment, without my being under any obligation to wait for the death of him who wears it." These sentiments, so plausible, occasioned Cosrou to resolve on making war against his father.

Jehan Guir had for his chief ministers, two men, upon

whom devolved the management of the whole affairs of the empire. One was Asaph Cham, the queen's brother, and the other Mahobet-Cham, an adventurer, but a person of superior genius, and of a greatness of soul inaccessible to corruption. That jealousy, so common between two rivals, who divide the confidence of a prince, had embroiled the two ministers. They had taken a part in opposite interests. Asaph Cham was naturally of the same party with the queen, his sister; and Mahobet-Cham had declared in favor of the Sultan Cosrou. The faction of the sultaness had the ascendancy. The Sultan Cosrou received so many provocations, that they forced him, as has been stated, to take up arms, and to put himself at the head of the conspirators. The sultaness, prompted by the advice of Asaph Cham, determined to get possession of the person of Mahobet, at the moment of his leaving the palace. An ambuscade was prepared in the first court of the Mahal, at the entrance of the saloon, in which the king gives audience to his ministers. Mahobet thus found himself on a sudden beseiged, on his quitting the apartment. As he had to contend, at first, with a troop of Indians only, who as yet, respected in his person, the chief of the armies of their master, he got rid of them without difficulty. In the meanwhile, the multitude of the asasssins, which collected around him, increased. He then proceeded to the private entrance of the haram, forced the doors, and found some eunuchs who were devoted to him. With this escort, he entered into the apartment of the emperor, dispersed the timid crowd of women, and eunuchs, by which he was surrounded; compelled the emperor against his inclination to follow him; caused him to be mounted on an elephant, and went forth from the palace, seated by the side of Jehan Guir, under the same canopy. Holding, then, in his hand, a poignard, he announced to the armed assemblage, which had been there planted by Nur-Jaham; that he would plunge it into the heart of the prince, the moment he should perceive any hostile movement to take place among them. So extraordinary a resolution astonished the soldiers.

The emperor was conducted by Mahobet to his own residence; where, the troops, of whom he was the chief, ranged themselves around him. Jehan Guir was thus detained by his minister, in a species of captivity.

The whole city was in a state of anxiety, in expectation of what might be the result of this event to the emperor. The greater part believed, that Mahobet would deliver up Jehan Guir, and the crown, to Cosrou, whose declared friend he was. But the generous Mahobet, knew how to preserve for his master and benefactor, all the respect and consideration, which were his due. He engaged in the most profuse expences, in order to supply him every day with new pleasures. In the meanwhile, Jehan Guir's detention became insupportable to him, on account of his separation from the queen. Mahobet gave his prisoner reason to expect, that Nur-Jaham, provided she were willing to confide in his honor, might come and bear him company. "As for the rest," he said to the king, with an air of submission and respect, which inspired him with confidence; "do not imagine, my lord, that I have violated the sacred asylum of your palace, for the purpose of delivering you into the hands of a rebellious son. I was attached to the cause of the Sultan Cosrou, whilst it was in my power to assist him with my counsels, and with the credit which I derived from your favor. I protected his rights, while labouring under oppression, from the injustice of a woman. Equity, then, required a counterpoise to the faction of the ambitious Nur-Jaham; and it was to labour for your glory, to hinder it from being tarnished, by the unjust preference, which you give to the youngest of your sons, to the prejudice of the elder. But, since Cosrou has been guilty of the impiety of taking arms against his father, I am ready to employ the power, which you have given me over your armies, to combat a rebel. Put my fidelity to the test, and judge me by the conduct, which I maintain towards my sovereign, whom I hold in my power. If I have dared to carry you off from your palace; be persuaded, my lord, that it was with the intention, only, of preserving my life, which was attempted by the ambushes of Asaph Cham, and by the orders of your imperious Nur-Jaham. Yes, my lord, it is this woman who lights up the torch of discord in your family; it is she, who banishes your children from your presence; who tears them from your bosom in spite of yourself; who forces them to renounce the sentiments of nature, and to arm themselves against a father, they love. Expel from your palace that fury, who is the cause of all this dissention; recall your children to your presence; cause their arms to fall from their hands, and by such conduct, you will release yourself from captivity, and restore tranquillity to your kingdom." Jehan Guir, moved by these arguments of his minister, and fearing least his confinement might eventually have some fatal conclusion, promised every thing which was required; but his disposition was light and frivolous. The very day, which he had appointed for dismissing the queen, Mahobet enquired what he could do to afford him pleasure.—" Give me the sultaness, and wine," replied the emperor. The generous minister refused him both. Wine, on account of his attachment to the law of Mahomet; and the sultaness, least she should succeed in destroying that returning reason, with which he had began to inspire the Mogul.

The heart, however, of this faithful subject, suffered itself to be moved by the entreaties of his master. He soon restored Jehan Guir to his liberty. But, that he might escape the persecutions of Nur-Jaham, he immediately took the field at the head of the Imperial army, for the purpose of combatting the Sultan Cosrou, agreeably to his promise. The war was not of long duration. After a single battle, Mahobet returned victorious, bringing back the son in chains to his father. So generous an action, and one, so serviceable to the interests of the emperor, and the sultaness, obliterated all recollection of the violation of that respect, which was due from a subject to his sovereign. The credit of this minister seemed to have increased at court, and the suspicions which had been entertained of his fidelity, to have been forgotten. It was, doubtless, through his influential intercession, that the consent of Jehan Guir was obtained, to the preservation of the life of Sultan Cosrou. They were contented to shut him up in the citadel of Guallier, along with his wife and children.

The captive sultan was passing a melancholy existence in his prison, when the queen sultaness caused a proposition to be made to him, capable of shaking a heart endued with less constancy. He was exhorted to purchase his liberty, by a criminal infidelity towards the princess his wife. They offered to procure a divorce of the daughter of Nur-Jaham from prince Scheriar, and to secure to Cosrou the succession to the crown, as soon as he should have accepted of Scheriar's wife for his sultaness. The law of Mahomet, resembling in this point the law of Moses, permits a brother to contract marriage with the wife of a brother, provided she has not born to him any children. They little doubted, but, that a prince, fallen into a state of captivity, would gladly obey the injunctions of his father, by which he would again be acknowledged as heir presumptive to the crown, in partaking it with the daughter of the sultaness. They were deceived. Sultan Cosrou was not a prince to be easily moulded to their purpose, and his attachment to his wife was an insurmountable difficulty.

Asaph Cham, on the other hand, secretly conducted an intrigue, opposed to the views of the sultaness, his sister. It has been, already, said, that Chorrom, third son of Jehan Guir, had taken for his wife one of the daughters of Asaph Cham. All the views of this ambitious minister were directed to the placing of his son-in-law upon the throne; and the death of Cosrou was considered by him, as an infallible means of securing the success of his project. Asaph Cham, therefore, made use of some of his creatures, whom he had placed near the person of the captive sultan, to encourage him in the resolution of contemning the daughter of the sultaness. They represented to him, that it was an alliance unworthy of his birth. They entreated him to reflect on the injustice, which it would cause him to commit towards the virtuous princess his wife. They added, that the new spouse would not fail, through the credit of her mother, to procure the banishment of the princess. They endeavoured to inspire him with religious scruples. "The law allows," they said, "the marrying of the widow of a brother, but it does not permit a person to marry the wife of a brother, who is yet living." They often gave him deceitful intelligence relative to the approaching disgrace of Nur-Jaham, and, by such means, inspired him with the hope of a speedy cessation to his captivity, without the ignominy of having suffered his honor to have been tarnished, by base compliances. Prepossesed with these ideas, Cosrou refused to the emperor and the sultaness this instance of submission, which they exacted from him. In the meanwhile, Asaph Cham, always attentive to his projects for placing his daughter on the throne of the Moguls, had engaged his son-in-law, Sultan Chorrom, to quit the territory of the Decan, and to appear at court and shew himself to the people of the capital. This prince was ambitious; Sultan Cosrou (though a prisoner taken with his arms in his hands against his king, and father) appeared to him the only obstacle to his future greatness. As for Sultan Scheriar, he regarded him as a prince devoid of merit, despised by the people, and unworthy of reigning. Perviz appeared content in his viceroyalty of Bengal. Chorrom, therefore, conceived the barbarous design, of securing the throne by a deed of fratricide. Every one believed, at the time, that he had been instigated to commit this crime by the counsels of Asaph Cham. It was admitted, that Nur-Jaham had no concern in it.

At the time, that Sultan Cosrou was put to death in his prison, he had began to give the sultaness some grounds for expecting, that he would finally submit to her wishes, and espouse her daughter. At least, the princess, the wife of Cosrou, never ceased exhorting her husband, to be swayed no longer by his tenderness for her; but to embrace such measures, as would best accord with his interest, though they were in opposition to his inclinations. Fearing, least, the heir presumptive to the crown should secure to himself the throne, by rendering obedience to the orders of the court; Sultan Chorrom made haste to accomplish his fratricidal design. Asaph Cham had taken care to place, in the service of the captive prince, persons entirely devoted to his interests, and wretches ready to undertake any office, however odious, for the advancement of their fortunes. Sultan Chorrom engaged these men to assist him in his designs upon the life of his brother. They were instructed to mix poison, in the meats, which were served up to him. The sultan had suspicions, that treachery was at work, and resolved to eat only of such things, as the princess, his wife, prepared for him, with her own hands. As the destruction of the prince lingered, much to the mortification of the ambitious Chorrom, he sent orders to have him dispatched, by the most expeditious means. The captain of the fortress, in which the poor sultan was confined, without the knowledge of the emperor, or the queen-sultaness, executed the orders of Chorrom. He caused him to be strangled with the bow-string. There are historians, who represent the assassination of the sultan in a different manner; but the relation, just given, is the least suspicious, and the most conformable to the Chronicle.

The death of the heir presumptive of the crown secured, to all appearance, the succession of the throne to the murderer of Cosrou; but the conspiracy, which Chorrom imagined to have been enveloped in the profoundest secrecy, was discovered by Jehan Guir, and by the sultaness. The emperor changed the affection, which he had for this unnatural son, into the deepest disgust. Even Asaph Cham, in spite of the protection of the queen, his sister, was near losing his favour at court. The fratricide was sent back to his government.

Cosrou left behind him a son, the heir of all the virtues of his father; this was, the Sultan Bolaqui, a prince, at that time, of the age of seventeen. In the character of his countenance, there was blended the fire of the Mogul, which he inherited from his father, with the mildness of the Indian character, which he derived from his mother. As he had been brought up in the society of an unhappy and captive father, he had learnt from him those virtues, which the great seldom fail to acquire in a season of adversity. He was mild, affable, generous, a little mistrustful; but, knowing how to correct, by consulting his reason, the suspicions, which the miseries of his family had accustomed him to entertain of the courtiers, who approached him. With these happy dispositions, Bolaqui soon became the favorite of the court. Even the sultaness took him into favour; and as he represented the person of the eldest son of the emperor, whose grandson he was, already he was regarded in the Indies as the successor of Jehan Guir. Asaph Cham, alone, in conjunction with his daughter, contemplated getting rid of the son, after having caused the father to be strangled. Bolaqui, in the meanwhile, lived at court in a state of security, under the protection of the emperor, of the sultaness, and the guard of Mahobet-Cham, who was always attached to his duties, and never, during his ministry, took any other side than that of equity.

Whilst Sultan Chorrom, banished to the Decan, was employed in securing to himself partisans, and strengthening his interests, by secret treaties with the Rajas, his neighbours; the emperor thought, only, of enjoying the apparent tranquillity, which now reigned in his empire. It has been said, that he was fond of making himself familiar with his people. Instances of this familiarity are related, which would appear extravagant, even in the West, where kings are more accessible, than in the East. He entered, they say, one day, towards the evening, in disguise, into a tavern. Wine houses, since the days of Akebar, had been tolerated in the capital. The emperor took a seat near an artisan, who was drinking with great gaiety, and, inspired with the wine, was disposed to indulge his vocal talents. Jehan Guir was delighted to find himself in such pleasant society. A familiarity was soon established between them, and the artisan was particularly charmed with the liberality of the new guest, who paid the entire score, and made him drink deep. In their conversation, they treated of the affairs of government; the emperor was blamed for his weakness, in submitting to be governed by a woman, and suffering one of his younger sons to assassinate the elder. They took leave of the tavern most excellent friends, promising to see each other often in the same place. The emperor simply enquired of the artisan his trade, where he lodged, and his name. "I am called," he said, "Secander; I am a weaver, and my home is in a quarter of the city," which he indicated. "Comrade," said the emperor, "I will come to-morrow and dine with you; we will renew our acquaintance, and we will swear a lasting friendship." The two topers separated, highly satisfied with each other; and each, on his part, impatiently expected the ensuing morning. Some hours after sunrise, nearly about the same time the artisans are accustomed to dine; the emperor left his palace, attended by the most magnificent escort, with which he had ever made his appearance in Lahor. He was surrounded by his whole guard, and preceded by twenty war elephants, with their splendid harness of crimson velvet, ornamented with large gold plates. Jehan Guir was himself seated on a throne, burnished with precious stones, borne by an elephant of state; and, in this equipage, he gave orders to be conducted to the weaver's quarters. The cavalry, and the elephants, passed before the shop of Secander. But, he, occupied in preparing the regale, which he was about to give his friend, did not even give himself the trouble to take a peep at the royal cavalcade. Whilst all the people were at the doors of their houses, or dispersed in the streets, a soldier of the king's suite enquired for the house of Secander. The weaver, who heard himself named, came into his shop, holding in his hand a pestle, with which he had just been pounding some rice. "I am Secander," he said, "and you will hardly find better cloth at any other shop in all Lahor."—"You are, also, a jovial toper," said the soldier; "the emperor has, in consequence, come to dine with you, in performance of the engagement he contracted with you yesterday." Secander could not doubt, but that it was the emperor himself, with whom he had been drinking the preceding evening; and, as he recollected the seditious language, which he had held to Jehan Guir, while they were carousing, the poor man gave himself up for lost. In the meanwhile, the emperor approached, and, as soon as Secander recognised him: "Might it please heaven," he cried, "that all those, who put their trust in drunkards, had this pestle thrown thrown at their heads." The king, who heard the poor weaver's exclamation, laughed most heartily. He tasted the good man's wine; and bestowed upon him employments at court, sufficiently considerable, to enable him to dispense with following any longer his profession.

That he might enjoy with greater tranquillity the pleasures, in which peace permitted him to indulge, Jehan Guir often went to pass the summer in the kingdom of Cachemire. This is the most northern province of the Mogul empire. It is situated at the foot of Mount Caucasus. Cachemire, in fact, is only a large valley, surrounded by mountains. Some pretend, that the river Indus has here its source. This is an error, and is not supported by any geographer. It is true, that a great number of small rivers pass out of Cachemire, and empty themselves into the Indus. This river, enlarged by these tributary streams, becomes navigable; and after having fertilised, and diffused abundance throughout extensive regions, continues its course till its junction with the ocean.

The kingdom of Cachemire passes for the terrestrial paradise of the Indies. Neither is there, perhaps, any country in the world, where the air is more temperate, the climate more salubrious, and in which, whatsoever can contribute to the enjoyment of life, is to be found in greater abundance. When the mountains, which separate Indostan from Cachemire have been passed, on a sudden we seem transported, from the most burning climates of Asia, into the most temperate zones of Europe. The trees and the fruits of India are no longer seen. They are pear, apple, and apricot trees, and others which are common to France. The inhabitants of this delightful country are strangers to the effeminacy and indolence of the Indians. They are vigorous and industrious cultivators of the soil, and make brave soldiers. It is an ancient tradition, that the Jews, who were carried away captive in the days of Salmanazar, were settled as a colony in Cachemire; and that the Cachemirians are the descendants of these ancient Jews. It is true, that no vestiges of the Jewish religion subsist at present in Cachemire, all the inhabitants being Pagans or Mahometans; yet, traces are to be found, of a nation descended from the Israelites. The countenances of these people possess much of that peculiar character, which distinguishes the Jews, in whatever part of the earth they may be found. The name of Moses is very common amongst them, and ancient monuments are still to be seen, indicating a people derived from Israel. The remains of an edifice, built upon a lofty mountain, is called to this day the throne of Solomon.

It was in this fine kingdom, that Jehan Guir seldom failed to pass the season of the year, when the heats are the most oppressive. He so much esteemed this province, that he would rather, he said, lose all the rest of his states, than this single one. The Mogul, and the sultaness Nur-Jaham, have, in consequence, left behind them in Cachemire evidences of their munificence. A palace was here built by Jehan Guir, which is, perhaps, more commodious than magnificent. The gardens, which are intersected with canals, and embellished with fountains, have an agreeableness rarely to be found in any other spot. As for the sultaness, her chief amusement consisted in stocking the canals with tame fish. Many are seen at this day, having gold rings, which this queen had caused to be attached to them.

The diversions of Jehan Guir were commonly confined during the summer months, within the precincts of Cachemire; but in the winter, which the continual rains render a melancholy season in the Indies; the emperor supplied himself with domestic amusements, in his palace at Lahor. One of the most agreeable was a species of fair, which was held for eight successive days, in a gallery of the haram. Shops were fitted up, and the wives of the principal Omrhas, or great lords of the empire, acted the part of merchant's wives. Seated at their counters, and decked with all the art common to Asiatic women, some sold rich gold brocades; others, pearls and diamonds: others, again, European curiosities. The emperor, the sultans his sons, the queens, and their daughters were the only purchasers. They went from shop to shop; the merchandise was exposed to their prying curiosity; they haggled about the price; a querulous tone was assumed; jests were bandied; and the remuneration on the part of the king was more or less liberal, in proportion to the wit and ingenuity displayed in this species of contests, and the entertainment furnished thereby to the court. This fete, of which the women were passionately fond, was not at all pleasing to the Omrhas. The jealousy, so natural to Mahometans, kept them in a state of restlessness all the time the fete lasted at the palace. But it was necessary to be patient. The emperor was obeyed in this, as in every thing else.

The tranquillity enjoyed by Jehan Guir was sometimes interrupted by foreign and domestic wars. Schah Abbas, king of Persia, whose name and reputation will live for ever in the memory of his people, demanded of the Mogul the surrender of the city of Candahar, which Amayum had engaged to resign to the Persian monarch, when he aided him in recovering possession of his throne. Amayum refused to keep his promise. Akebar was able to maintain possession of so fine a country; but Jehan Guir was obliged to acquit the debt incurred by his grandfather. The Persians laid siege to Candahar. The governor of this important and frontier city of the Mogul states, on the side of Persia, gave the court intelligence of the irruption of the Persians, and of the siege with which he was menaced. Orders were sent to Siahan-Cham, viceroy of Multan, to march with the utmost diligence to the assistance of the besieged; but neither troops nor arms were to be found in condition for immediate service. The pacific Jehan Guir had neglected to place his frontiers in a state of defence. In the meanwhile, the city and the citadel were battered night and day. The siege had lasted six months, when the emperor, despairing of saving the place, sent the governor orders to deliver it up in the form of a restitution, rather than as compelled to surrender by force of arms. The governor, who received the letter of Jehan Guir, would not believe it to be genuine, and surrendered only at the last extremity, when a bastion had been destroyed by mining. Schah Abbas would have pushed his conquests further; but the powerful army, which the Mogul sent towards the frontiers of Persia, arrested the progress of the conqueror, and obliged him to return to Ispahan.

The state was in much greater danger from the revolt of Sultan Chorrom. This ambitious prince, exiled to his government of Guzurat, received intelligence from his father-in-law, Asaph-Cham, that the emperor was about to transfer the treasure of the empire, kept in the citadel of Agra, to Lahor. The charge of conducting this treasure had been committed to Asaph-Cham. He was in the disposition to deliver it up to the husband of his daughter, provided the Sultan would use due diligence, and present himself with an army upon the road which forms the communication between the two capitals. The possession, of this treasure, was a certain means of enabling the prince to invade the throne, even in the lifetime of his father. Chorrom, then, mustered without delay all the creatures and partisans he had been able to secure to his interests, throughout the vast countries, which the bad policy of Jehan Guir had subjected to his rule. He had taken upon himself to dispose of governments, and lands, without the concurrence of the court. The prince had, in consequence, no difficulty in assembling persons devoted to his service, in sufficient numbers to compose a formidable army. He then advanced at the head of sixty thousand men, and in a few day arrived at Fetipour, about twenty leagues distant from Agra. The eunuch, who had the guard of the treasures of the king, wisely considered, that it would be imprudent to deliver them to the father-in-law of Sultan Chorrom, and expose them to be pillaged by a rebel prince. He gave notice to the court of the march of Chorrom, and sent back Asaph-Cham without the treasure. This news obliged Jehan Guir to come himself to Agra, in order to oppose the designs of his son. He found the city entirely ravaged by the troops of the rebel, and the palaces of the great lords pillaged; but as the fortress was in faithful keeping, the treasure of the empire was saved from a similar fate.

The declaration of revolt, which Sultan Chorrom had just made, was too open and avowed, not to be attended with further consequences. Positive hostilities had become now absolutely necessary; and Chorrom was obliged to prepare for encountering the formidable army, which Jehan Guir had placed under the command of the gallant Mahobet-Cham. Even Sultan Perviz quitted the repose of his government of Bengal, and came at the head of his troops, to combat for his father against a refractory brother. There appeared to be no interested motives, at this time, in the conduct of this good prince; no views towards raising himself to the throne, on the ruin of his brother's fortunes. Motives of duty alone seemed to regulate his motions.

In the meanwhile, Sultan Chorrom was encamped some leagues below Delhi. The army of the king, strengthened by that of Sultan Perviz, advanced against the rebels. It was commanded in person by Jehan Guir. Asaph-Cham conducted the right wing, and Mahobet-Cham the left. As in civil broils, it almost always happens, that there are many traitors on both sides, whom the chiefs have taken care to corrupt before the action; the emperor, suspecting the fidelity of Abdul-Cham, one of the principal captains of his army, sent to him before the battle, by one of his officers, a quiver full of arrows, to give him notice that fidelity was expected from him. The officer, who, on his arrival, perceived that Abdul-Cham was just then making a movement for the purpose of passing over to the side of the enemy, took aim at the traitor with one of the arrows. Abdul-Cham escaped unhurt, and retired to Sultan Chorrom, whose minister and favorite he became. It was this officer, who first commenced the attack, and who penetrated even to the tent of Jehan Guir. After an obstinate conflict, the rebels were put to the rout. Sultan Chorrom retired into inaccessible mountains, and endeavoured to negociate a peace with his father.

During the action, the young Sultan Bolaqui fought under the direction of Mahobet-Cham, and in sight of the emperor his grandfather. He displayed prodigies of valour. Not content with having gained over the enemy an incomplete victory; he penetrated at the head of some troops, into the heart of the kingdom of Guzurat, and sat down before Amadabat, the capital of the government, of which Sultan Chorrom had, in a measure, usurped the sovereignty. He caused the gates to be broken down by the elephants, and took possession of the city. The treasures of Sultan Chorrom were pillaged, his golden throne broken in pieces, and the diamonds with which it was adorned were distributed to the officers. The Imperial army, after taking some days repose, again entered the field, for the purpose of opposing Abdul-Cham, who was conducting against Bolaqui the remains of the army of Chorrom. The two armies were already in each other's presence; the signal for the engagement had been given; when a sudden panic spread through the army of Abdul-Cham. The whole of his infantry was cut in pieces by the soldiers of Bolaqui. The peasants of the country massacred the greater part of the cavalry, whom fear had scattered in disorder throughout all the neighbouring hamlets. Abdul-Cham, being aided by the rains, saved himself with great difficulty in Surat, whence he quickly retired to Brampour, to Sultan Chorrom.

Jehan Guir purposed pursuing his rebel son, and forcing him in the mountains, where he had taken refuge. Sultan Perviz and Mahobet-Cham were ordered to give him battle, and to bring him to his father, dead or alive. The haughty Chorrom was not discouraged. Having assembled an army, capable of opposing that of his brother, he again presented himself in the field, to make head against his adversaries. The rebels, at first, had the advantage in some slight skirmishes; and elevated by these trifling successes, they hazarded a general action, which occasioned them to meet with a great reverse. The forces of Chorrom were vanquished. The unhappy prince, abandoned by his troops, saw himself obliged to have recourse to flight, to place the river Nerbda between himself and the conqueror, and to retire to Brampour. The two principal officers of his army, his chief favorites, escaped with Chorrom. These were, Cham-Canna, and Abdul-Cham. The first had always been attached to the fortune of his master; and had been entrusted with the control of his affairs, and the conduct of his armies, without dividing the administration with another. The second had embraced the service of Sultan Chorrom, since the commencement of the war; and began now to take the ascendancy over the mind of the prince. These competitors, whom the favor of Chorrom had rendered rivals, were always of opposite sentiments in the council. Cham-Canna leaned ordinarily on the side of peace, and was of opinion, that the most eligible course to pursue would be, to endeavour to soften the heart of Jehan Guir, and lead him to be reconciled to his son. Abdul-Cham, who was apprehensive of meeting the just reward of his treason, advised the continuance of the war, and the incurring of all risks for securing the empire. This dissention, between the two ministers, was injurious to Sultan Chorrom. Cham-Canna resolved to betray a prince, who began to neglect him. Under the pretext, therefore, of bringing about a peace between the two brothers, he retired to Sultan Perviz; and discovered to the chief of the Imperial army the destitute condition to which his master was reduced. He even counselled Perviz and Mahobet-Cham to prepare a number of barks for passing the river; and further assured them, that they would find the prince abandoned, destitute of an army, and without provisions. On his side, Abdul-Cham, who suspected the treason of his rival, persuaded Sultan Chorrum to quit Brampour, and seek an asylum in the states of his ancient friend, Melek-Ambar. The counsel of Abdul-Cham proved salutary to Chorrom. A few hours after his departure from Brampour, Sultan Perviz made his appearance, after having crossed the river; but not finding his rival, he began, at the suggestion of Mahobet-Cham, to suspect the good faith of Cham-Canna, and to cause him to be observed. Such were the beginnings of that dissention between Cham-Canna and Mahobet-Cham, which menaced the greatest minister, and the greatest captain, which the Mogul emperors ever possessed, with the loss of his life.

The intelligence of the victory of Sultan Perviz and of the flight of Chorrom was as agreeable to Jehan Guir, as that, which he received from the northern countries, was calculated to give him uneasiness. The Usbec Tartars had passed their frontiers, and had dispersed themselves throughout Cabulestan with thirty thousand horse. They had committed great ravages, and entertained thoughts of besieging Cabul. This capital of a fine kingdom would have become the prey of the Tartars, had not Zaed Cham, son of Mahobet-Cham, made the utmost haste to its succour, and compelled the enemy, weakened by his losses, to confine himself within his ancient bounds. The glory of Mahobet-Cham, thus increased every day, by the services which himself and his children rendered the empire. Jehan Guir availed himself of this season of tranquillity, to go and pass the summer at Cachemire.

The absence of the emperor, in a distant point of his dominions, furnished Sultan Chorrom with a convenient opportunity for putting himself again in motion, and recommencing a war, which it was his interest to keep alive till the death of his father. He entered, therefore, with an army into the kingdom of Bengal. After having ravaged the principal places of that rich country, passed the Ganges, and defeated in a battle Ibrahim-Cham, governor of the kingdom of Bengal under Sultan Perviz;

he took the road to Patna, in order to surprise his brother. But this prince was yet at Brampour; whence he hastened his departure, that he might return and defend his own province. Chorrom had no sooner learnt the arrival of Perviz at Bengal, than he mistrusted his ability to contend with his brother. The valour of Mahobet-Cham, who commanded the army under the Sultan Perviz, further increased his apprehensions. He, therefore, resolved to try what might be effected by artifice, and by sowing discord in the army of his enemies. He wrote letters to Cham-Canna, which he took care should be intercepted. These implied an intelligence as subsisting between himself and Cham-Canna; which was not true. Mahobet-Cham fell into the snare; and judged, that it would be proper to send the children of the traitor, as prisoners, to the citadel of Agra. As to Cham-Canna, he caused him to be narrowly watched.

In the meanwhile, the Imperial army was on its march towards Patna, and had already passed the Ganges. Chorrom had entrenched himself behind the canal of Thonez, which is only a creek of the river, and waited for his brother with confidence. Sultan Perviz at last appeared on the banks of the canal, and there emcamped. During the first days little was done, except keeping up a cannonade with heavy artillery, disposed on both sides of the canal by the respective armies. The army of the emperor suffered much from the cannon of the rebels, which Sultan Chorrom had found time to dispose very advantageously. The chief difficulty was to pass the canal, and give battle to the enemy entrenched on the other bank. The good fortune of Mahobet-Cham enabled him to find a passage, and to join battle with the rebels. Whilst he was making a reconnoissance on the banks of the canal, he perceived a peasant passing a ford, at some leagues from the camp of the enemy. He marked the spot, and during the night caused the canal to be crossed without noise by all his troops; and as soon as the day broke, he found himself near enough to engage the enemy. Never had there been in the Indies, a more desperate or a more sanguinary conflict, and never did the chiefs make a more brilliant display of their valour and experience. The elephants, which composed the vanguard of the army of Sultan Chorrom, charged with fury the ranks of the Imperial army, and threw them into confusion. But as the conductors of the elephants were not supported, the troops of Perviz had time to recover themselves. At last, after great carnage on both sides, Sultan Chorrom was obliged to take to flight, accompanied by only three thousand men. The defeat of the prince was owing principally to the cowardice and the treachery of Abdul-Cham, who left the elephants, in the heat of the action, unsupported. He was suspected, from that time, of intelligence with Mahobet-Cham, who had promised that he should be reinstated in the favor of the emperor. Be this as it may, the battle of Alabassen, for it is by this name that it is known, was one of the most remarkable which was ever fought in the Indies. It was the origin of all the mortifications, with which the old age of the wise and gallant Mahobet-Cham was traversed.

Whilst the emperor was triumphing in Bengal, the sultaness, Nur-Jaham, began to reflect, that the war against Sultan Chorrom, carried on with so much vigour by Sultan Perviz and Mahobet-Cham, was contrary to the interests of her family. She considered, that the rebel prince had married her niece; that, to abandon Chorrom to his evil destiny was to establish Perviz upon the throne; that the great obligations, which this prince had to Mahobet-Cham, would render this minister all powerful in the empire, and that she and her family would be lost, if the party of

Sultan Perviz should happen to prevail. Under these impressions, she obtained of Jehan Guir, that Cham-Canna, the declared enemy of Mahobet-Cham, should be allowed to come to court, under the pretext of giving an account of his conduct. The prisoner appeared, in the presence of the emperor, with all that confidence, which he might be supposed to derive from the protection of the sultaness. He drew an exaggerated picture of the ambition, and of the cruelty of Mahobet-Cham; he laid great stress on the services which he had rendered the empire, in abandoning the party of Chorrom, his ancient master. He added. that the recompense of his fidelity towards the state was to remain a captive in the camp of Perviz, and to behold his children unjustly imprisoned in the citadel of Agra. He insinuated, that the emperor himself had every thing to fear from the victories of Perviz, and the ambition of Mahobet-Cham; that both the one and the other only fought for their own interests, and that duty had a less share in their victories, than a secret desire to reign. "After all, Sultan Chorrom is your son, my lord," he added, "and his past disobedience is less the effect of a bad heart, than the indispensable necessity which he labours under of defending his life from the rage of a jealous brother, and an ambitious minister."

This discourse, which was not devoid of plausibility, supported by the private arguments of Nur-Jaham, who was incessantly irritating the mind of the emperor against Mahobet-Cham, was the cause of that general being recalled, and ordered to come to Lahor without delay, and unattended. Perviz felt no repugnance at suffering the departure of Mahobet-Cham. The artful Cham-Canna had taken care to sow divisions between these two chiefs of the imperial army. Perviz was jealous that Mahobet-Cham shared with him the glory of his victories. Thus, this great captain beheld himself, on a sudden, abandoned by the emperor, and by Sultan Perviz, and delivered up to the rage of his great enemy, Nur-Jaham, his competitor, Asaph-Cham, and his accuser, Cham-Canna. In this extremity, this great man took the wisest course, which was that of submission. He proceeded, by slow journies, to the court, and when he was at Brampour, received a new order to hasten his progress. So much earnestness, on the part of the emperor, gave the accused just suspicions that his life was in danger. Taking his route, therefore, on the side of Ratampour, a city of which the emperor had given him the lordship, he rested at that place, under the pretext of finishing some affairs for the advantage of the state. This delay of the general furnished a pretext to the court to condemn him unheard, and to send him into honorable exile. He received orders to return to Bengal in the capacity of sub-governor under Sultan Perviz, who was commanded to observe him strictly. It was not without mortification, that Mahobet-Cham learnt the news of his disgrace. He wrote to the emperor letters, justifying his conduct; but, as his remonstrances received no attention, he, for the first time, forgot his duty. He then wrote to the emperor, haughtily, that he had found a way to compel him to listen to his defence; and that he would soon come in person to Lahor, and confound his calumniators. The menaces of so great a captain made the court tremble. Nur-Jaham, alone, was not intimidated. Instead of causing the emperor to remain at Agra, where he would have been secure, she persuaded him to take a journey to Cabul; a rash measure, which had nearly proved the destruction of the imperial family.

Whilst the court was on its march, Mahobet-Cham had collected around him some of those brave officers, who, under his command, had for a long period been accustomed to victory. Five thousand Rajepoots, of the very bravest in all the Indies, joined themselves to a chief whom they idolized. With this small body, composed of resolute and warlike soldiers, Mahobet-Cham planned attacking the emperor's escort, making himself once more master of his person, and compelling him to listen to his defence. The design of this great captain succeeded; if he did not extract from it all the advantages which he might have done, it was only through excess of generosity and respect for his master. Mahobet-Cham surprised the emperor, whilst his army was occupied in passing the river Tziunab. The best part of the troops, which served for the emperor's escort, had been conveyed to the other bank in barks before sun-rise. The emperor was still reposing in the tent which had been set up for him on the bank of the river, when Mahobet-Cham arrived unexpectedly, and surrounded the camp of the king. On the first news of his arrival, the whole court was seized with consternation. The bravest of the troops were on the other side of the river. The soldiers of the guard were seized with terror, and took to flight. Thus, almost without shedding blood, the Emperor, the Sultaness, Sultan Bolaqui, Sultan Sceberiar, as well as Asaph-Cham, and Cham-Canna fell into the hands of the gallant Mahobet-Cham.

It is impossible to imagine what changes might have resulted to the empire, from the detention of the whole court. Agra took openly the side of the new conqueror, and delivered up its citadel to one of the friends of Mahobet-Cham. Had this generous chief been ever so little inclined to make a bad use of his success, and been disposed to make an attempt upon the liberty of Jehan Guir, whom he held in his power, he might have set up a new emperor, and selected some one of the sons or grandsons of the Mogul to fill the throne. The profound respect, which he had always felt for his master, caused him to act with moderation. He contented himself with serving the emperor, whom he held in a species of captivity, as his escort; and he led him, in this manner, towards Cabul. Leaving him as much at liberty as if he had been escorted by officers of his own choice, he, nevertheless, did not use the same forbearance towards the other princes and great lords of the court. The Sultans Bolaqui and Sceheriar he sent prisoners to the citadel of Agra. Asaph-Cham and Cham-Canna were loaded with chains, and conducted, under his own eye, by an escort of his brave Rajepoots. He had the complaisance to allow the sultaness the same liberty which was enjoyed by the emperor. This moderation had nearly cost him dear. Nur-Jaham (driven to desperation, by finding herself in the hands of her enemy, and always fearing lest Mahobet-Cham should obtain an ascendancy over the mind of the emperor, to whom this great man regularly paid his court) found an opportunity of surprising him in her turn, by means of the troops which at first attended upon the emperor, and had become dispersed on the arrival of Mahobet-Cham. She caused the chiefs to be informed that the army, before which they had fled, consisted of no more than five thousand men; that delivering the emperor from the captivity in which he was held would be attended with little difficulty; that Mahobet-Cham might easily be surprised at the passage of a river; that on her part, she would take especial care of the emperor during the attack, and so manage, that he should, on the pretext of taking the diversion of the chase, be placed at a distance from his escort. The project of the sultaness was put into execution with great diligence. More than fifty thousand men, collected from all the neighbouring provinces, were placed in ambuscade upon the banks of a river, and there expected the arrival of Mahobet-

Cham. This prudent general, informed of the snare which was prepared for him, soon decided on the measures he should pursue; and thought proper to abandon the sultaness and the emperor to their former guard, to retrace his steps, and to carry away with him Asaph-Cham and Cham-Canna. He resumed, therefore, the road to Agra, and left the emperor to continue his journey to Cabul. In the meanwhile, the sultaness, who, notwithstanding she had recovered her liberty, was exasperated that her brother should be carried off a prisoner, sent instructions to the governors of the neighbouring provinces to stop Mahobet-Cham on his march, and to wrest Asaph-Cham from his hands. The generosity of Mahobet-Cham anticipated the wishes of the queen. He sent back Asaph-Cham to the sultaness, after having made him swear upon the Alcoran, that he never would prove ungrateful for that life and liberty which was now restored to him. The imperious queen could scarcely restrain her indignation at the sight of her brother. "How could you be such a dastard," she said to him, "as to enter into conditions with the most cruel of my enemies? You ought, at least, to have waited until I had either procured your liberation, or your death had filled up the measure of the iniquities of the perfidious man."

Whilst the emperor was proceeding on his journey to Cabul, and Mahobet-Cham was on the road to Agra; Sultan Chorrom, who had taken refuge, after his losses, in the kingdom of the Decan, quitted his retreat, and made his appearance in the field. His march caused a panic among the troops of the emperor, who felt no longer the confidence with which they were accustomed to be inspired by the experience of Mahobet-Cham. It was reported, that certain Rajas, accompanied by their Rajepoots, had joined the rebels. In effect, Sultan Chorrom advanced towards Tatta, for the purpose of undertaking the siege. He was driven from the place by the sallies of the governor, and compelled to retire to Backar. If Sultan Chorrom was not fortunate in the wars, which he waged against his brother, since the recal of Mahobet-Cham; Sultan Perviz enjoyed not, at least, the glory of uninterrupted success against Sultan Chorrom. This prince experienced, that it was better to divide the glory of victories with another, than to cease acquiring them.

The emperor, in the meanwhile, had returned to Lahor from Cabul. The first object of the sultaness was to take vengeance on Mahobet-Cham, from whom she had received such unpardonable insults in the journey to Cabul. She learnt, that a convoy of treasure was on its way from Bengal to Mahobet-Cham. She caused it to be surprised, and conducted to Lahor. Nur-Jaham afterwards placed Cam-Canna, whom Mahobet-Cham had the generosity to restore to his liberty, at the head of an army; of which this dastard took the command, that he might destroy his benefactor. It was then that Mahobet-Cham found himself in a state of destitution greater than he had ever before experienced. His son, who, till that time, had been faithful to him, took the side of the court against his father. The rest of the troops, which had so constantly adhered to him, pillaged his treasures, ravaged his lands, and returned under the obedience of the emperor. To complete his misfortunes, Mahobet learnt that Sultan Perviz, who had resumed for him his former friendship, had died of a malady at Brampour. The Sultans Bolaqui and Sceheriar (whom Mahobet-Cham had imprisoned in Agra, with the view only of causing his own life to be respected, by alarming the sultaness with the apprehension of seeing a son and a grandson of the emperor perish along with him,) had been liberated from their captivity, full of rage against him who had been the author of it. In this universal desertion, Mahobet found only one resource; this was, to retire to Rana, one of the principal Rajas of the empire, and to negotiate from the place of his retreat with Sultan Chorrom. He wrote, then, to this prince, that if he would discontinue carrying arms against his father, his arm and his services should be at his command. That Jehan Guir was already old and infirm; and that after the death of the Emperor, Sultan Bolaqui would not fail to dispute the crown with him; in which case, he would not, perhaps, have cause to repent having engaged on his side an old general, whom a long experience had given some reputation among the troops. That having consulted reason and justice, it appeared to him that his pretensions to the throne were legitimate; but, that it was sacrilegious to enforce them, before the Emperor, his father, had been disposed of by the common lot of mortality; and that he would willingly devote himself to his interests, provided, that in siding with his cause, he should not be obliged to carry arms against his sovereign.

The proposition of Mahobet-Cham appeared reasonable to Sultan Chorrom. He was weary of war and of ill success; and he hoped, that seconded by Mahobet, he should easily bear away the crown from his competitors. However, as he did nothing without the advice of Asaph-Cham, he consulted his father-in-law on the subject of the offers of Mahobet. The opinion of the minister was, that it would be equally advantageous to Chorrom to make peace with the Emperor, and to secure Mahobet-Cham in his interests. Thus, by the wise conduct of the general, faithful even in his disgrace, the whole empire was preserved in peace. The public tranquillity, the work of Mahobet-Cham, was the only revenge which he took of the sovereign who persecuted him.

The Emperor now only thought of enjoying repose. As he was very infirm, he caused himself to be transported to Cachemire, where the air is much more salubrious than in the Indies. The restlessness, so natural to old age and sickness, occasioned him soon to quit so agreeable a residence, and return to his palace of Lahor. The fatigues of the journey, having increased the indisposition of Jehan Guir, he died at Bimber, in the year 1627. He was a prince of an easy disposition, who always allowed the sultaness and his ministers to exercise too great an ascendancy over him. Thence originated the revolts of his children, and his generals. It may be said, that he loved pleasure more than glory; but, it is certain, that he loved justice still more than pleasure. He dispensed it to his subjects with a care, and a disinterestedness, which had never been known before in the Indies, not even in the time of Akebar. He protected the arts, and had a taste in painting.

In his time, there were found, in consequence, in the Indies, native painters, who copied the finest of our European pictures with a fidelity that might vie with the originals. He was partial to the sciences of Europe, and it was this which attached him to the Jesuits. He caused a church and a residence to be built for them at Lahor. This prince, who, towards the close of his days, was persuaded of the truth of our mysteries, found no other obstacle to his conversion, than the fear of a revolution in his empire. As for the plurality of wives, which so much attaches the Mahometans to their sect, this would have proved no obstacle to the salvation of Jehan Guir. For a long time, he had confined himself solely to the Sultaness Nur-Jaham.

After the death of the Emperor, the empire was found to be divided into three distinct factions. The sultaness declared for Prince Sceheriar, the husband of her daughter. Bolaqui had, in his favour, the imperial army, and the whole guard of the palace; but the two ministers, Asaph-Cham and Mahobet-Cham were in the interest of Sultan Chorrom. The influence of the sultaness was confined to the haram. Bolaqui was proclaimed Emperor by the army. The party of Sceheriar, which was confined to women and eunuchs, soon became the weakest. Bolaqui secured the persons of Nur-Jaham and her son-in-law. The first was committed a close prisoner; and the other was deprived of his sight by the application of a red-hot iron.

Bolaqui, who imagined that he was labouring for his own interests, was paving the way by his cruelties, for his uncle, Sultan Chorrom's attainment of the throne. An intrigue, conducted by Mahobet-Cham, and sustained by Asaph-Cham, put him in possession of the crown, without the shedding of blood. As soon as Bolaqui had seated himself upon the throne of his grandfather, by favor of the army, he deputed one of the principal Omrhas of his court to his uncle. The envoy had instructions to exact, from Sultan Chorrom, the accustomed tribute, and to engage him to acknowledge the sovereignty of Bolaqui. He was directed to employ menaces, in the event of finding a spirit of opposition and revolt in the prince. The deputy had no occasion to assume a dictatorial language, or employ, even, the means of negotiation, in order to force from Chorrom the submission, which he affected to require from him. Attacked, apparently, with prodigious vomitings of blood, he found the sultan in a situation to excite compassion. The deputy was affected at the sight, and sent off, immediately, a courier to Bolaqui, to give him intelligence of the extremity to which his uncle was reduced. Sultan Chorrom's malady was nothing but a feint; and the blood, which he vomited, was goat's blood, with which he had filled his mouth, on the arrival of the Omrha.

The report of the sickness of the sultan was quickly succeeded by another, still less true. It was published, every where, that Chorrom was dead. He disappeared, indeed, all of a sudden; and Mahobet-Cham, only, with some other officers, the most attached to the prince, were acquainted with the secret of the intrigue. Every appearance of the deepest mourning took place at the court of the sultan. Mahobet-Cham, especially, appeared inconsolable. The deputy of Bolaqui suffered himself to be deceived. He sent certain intelligence of the death of Chorrom. They even engaged him to solicit, of the new Emperor, permission to convey the body of the deceased sultan, to the sepulchre of his fathers. Bolaqui gave his consent gladly, that all the honors of interment should be paid to a prince of his blood, from whom death, as he believed, had delivered him so opportunely. A convoy was, therefore, prepared, attended with all the magnificence due to a prince of the Mogul blood. The empty bier was conducted by more than a thousand men, chosen from among the principal officers of the deceased. Mahobet-Cham was at their head. Chorrom himself followed, in disguise, his own funeral. Squadrons of Rajepoots, seemingly to do it honor, had been disposed at different stations upon the line of march, which continuing to swell the funeral pomp, accompanied it to Agra. Asaph-Cham, sustaining his part in the intrigue, persuaded the young Emperor, that a just decorum required he should proceed to meet the convoy of his uncle, and conduct to the place of interment, the remains of a prince, from whom he had now nothing to fear. The artifice succeeded. Bolaqui went forth from the gates of Agra, habited in deep mourning, accompanied by a weak escort, and in the equipage of a prince, who is about to pay the last duties to a relative. He was astonished, when he beheld so large an escort, in the suite of a deceased person. He suspected the stratagem, and, retracing his steps, he stole away from the cruelty of a rival, who would not have failed to take away his life, if he had fallen into his power. The place of his retreat was a long time a secret, but it was at last known that he had taken refuge in Persia. In the meanwhile, the trumpets sounded, Sultan Chorrom was proclaimed Emperor, and the mourning chariot was changed into a car of triumph. Chorrom entered the citadel of Agra, amidst the acclamations of the people, and of the army, who transferred, instantaneously, all their affection to the new monarch. It was, then, that this prince took the name of Cha-Jaham, which signifies, "Sovereign of the Universe;" a title which he retained ever afterwards. This was the last exploit of Mahobet-Cham, who, after having placed the crown upon the head of his master, retired to the lands of his government, that he might there terminate, in repose, a life so agitated and so glorious. As for Sultan Scheriar, he had been shut up for three months in an apartment of the palace, with two of his sons. Cha-Jaham caused the door to be walled up, and left all three to perish of hunger. This apartment has never been opened, even to the present time. It is believed in the haram, that certain groans are yet, at times, heard to proceed from it, which has, however, no other foundation, than in the imagination of the women.

CHA-JAHAM.

NINTH EMPEROR.

Seats himself upon the Throne by Intrigue. Condition of the Empire at his Accession. Makes War on the Portuguese. Builds a new City. His love of Justice, and able Administration of it. Becomes addicted to Avarice. Sends Three of his Sons, in quality of Viceroy, into the Provinces. Character of the Princes and Princesses his Children. Confides to the Prince Dara the exercise of his Authority. Aurengzebe, his third Son, governs with Wisdom the Kingdom of the Decan. The Enterprise of Aurengzebe against the Kingdom of Golconda. Cha-Jaham is attacked with a Malady. The second of his Sons takes up Arms to secure to himself Possession of the Empire. Defeat of his Son Cha-Chuia. Aurengzebe and Moradbax, the two younger Sons of Cha-Jaham, confederate, in order to get Possession of the Throne. Cha-Jaham proposes to advance in Person to encounter the two Rebel Princes. Sends an Army, which is defeated, upon the Banks of the River Ugen. Dara takes the Field, to give Battle to his two Brothers. Defeat of Dara. Cha-Jaham is kept in Captivity by his two rebellious Sons. Aurengzebe and Moradbax divide between them the Revenues of the Empire. Aurengzebe causes himself to be proclaimed Emperor. Causes his Elder Brother to be beheaded. Obliges the second of his Brothers to seek an Asylum in the Kingdom of Arracan. Puts to Death the youngest of his Brothers, and reigns in Tranquillity in the place of his Father.

NEVER had the empire been in a more flourishing condition under the administration of the Mogul emperors, than at the accession of Cha-Jaham. The number of provinces, which his predecessors had subjected to their domination, composed one of the greatest monarchies at that time existing. From the frontiers of Candahar, (recently re-conquered by the Persians), the whole country, which extended to the Ganges, was obedient to the Mogul power. The riches of the Emperor were immense. The relation of them would appear a fiction, if a French traveller, of acknowledged integrity, had not rendered a most exact account of them to one of our greatest ministers. Nevertheless, it must be confessed, that the government of the Mogul emperors, however absolute, was subject to great inconveniences. Even at the time, when Cha-Jaham had made himself master of the empire, it did not appear as yet sufficiently rooted to be capable of making a long resistance, had external attacks and intestine broils concurred at the same moment.

As the Emperor has commonly a number of sons, the issue of his numerous wives, they are almost constantly opposed to one another; and the strongest, or the most artful, seeks only to pave his way to the possession of the throne, without waiting till his father shall have ceased to reign by the decree of nature. Hence arise intrigues with the great officers of the state: and the oppression of the people, and the ravage of the provinces are the certain result of these dissentions. The tyranny of the court is another source whence these contests spring. As the Moguls govern their states with the most perfect despotism, the Rajas, who consider themselves as so many petty sovereigns in their respective districts, submit with impatience to that despotic authority, which they, notwithstanding, inflict upon their own subjects. Thus, almost always dissatisfied with the Emperor and his ministers, they are easily led to make a common cause with the parties in opposition to the court; and when the torch of discord has been lighted up in any point of the empire, it is difficult to be extinguished. The country of these Rajas, who consider themselves only as tributaries of the empire, is almost on every side defended by inaccessible mountains and extensive forests; all the native princes, whose states were of more easy access, having been subjected by the Moguls. These tributary Rajas, whose domains are thus locked within the lands belonging to the empire, gladly afford a retreat to the discontented, assist them with troops and arms, and issue themselves from their forests, spreading themselves over the countries subject to the Emperor, where they exercise hostility upon his subjects, interrupt commerce, and pillage the caravans of the merchants.

Religious antipathies was another cause of dissention among the subjects of the Mogul. Akebar and Jehan Guir entertained the design of bringing the different sectaries in Indostan to confess one religion; but they found, by experience, that it was less difficult to usurp a power over men's lives and fortunes, than to subdue their minds, and the prejudices of their early years.

Such was the condition of the empire of the Moguls, when Cha-Jaham commenced his reign, that it would probably have become the prey of its neighbours, had it been then assailed; but Persia, on the west, happened to be governed by an imbecile prince, who was content to pass a voluptuous life in the shades of his haram. On the north, the warlike nation of the Tartars was no longer in a condition to make inroads, or conquests. Those immense colonies, which had issued from Tartary to establish the four greatest empires in Asia, had exhausted that country of men, formerly one of the most populous. The Moguls had no reason to be more apprehensive of danger, from the east. The Indians who inhabit beyond the Ganges, to the frontiers of China, are in general a people destitute of courage, contented with their own uncultivated soil, and inadequate to any great enterprise. It is true, that the Portuguese, and the other nations of Europe, who had possessed themselves of the best sea ports throughout the whole coast of Indostan, were dangerous enemies on the south; but the jealousies, engendered by the conflicting interests of commerce, between the Portuguese, the English, and the Dutch, weakened the force of the Christian colonies.

Cha-Jaham conceived that he should now be able to attack the Portuguese with advantage, and perhaps succeed in exterminating those merchants, formerly so powerful in the Indies, but at this time much fallen in consequence, by the losses they had sustained in their conflicts with the English and the Dutch, and by the rival establishments of these two nations. The war with the Portuguese was the first enterprise of the new Emperor. A zeal for religion, it is asserted, was one of the pretexts; certain, however, it is, that Cha-Jaham evinced as great an aversion to the Christians, as the two kings, his predecessors, had shewn them affection. The refusal of the Portuguese to assist him, during his revolts in the life-time of his father, had exasperated him to such a degree against Christianity, that he made a vow to exterminate it. After the loss of a battle, this prince had retired to a place strongly fortified, a few leagues from Daca. The commander of the Portuguese troops at Ougli, Michel Rodriguez, paid the young sultan a visit, and endeavoured to console him under his misfortune; but the prince desired something more efficient than visits of condolence, and caused it to be intimated to the commander, that he expected the assistance of his artillery and soldiers; giving him assurances of his gratitude for the services of his nation, should he ever attain the throne. The gallant Portuguese haughtily replied, that it would disgrace him to serve the cause of a rebel; that to make war upon his father was fighting against God himself. Rodriguez added deeds to words; he joined the party of Sultan Perviz, and the Portuguese infantry, which fought under the orders of that prince, contributed greatly to the many victories which he gained over his brother.

The Sultaness Taigé-Mahal, wife of Cha-Jaham, is, also, said to have been a principal instrument in exasperating the mind of the Emperor against the Christians in general, and particularly against the Portuguese. The sultaness inherited her hatred to Christianity from her aunt Nur-Jaham, which was further inflamed by an injury she attributed to the Portuguese, who had given an asylum to two of her daughters, converted to Christianity by the missionaries. The hatred of the sultaness, and the oath which the Emperor had formerly sworn were two powerful stimulants, inciting the Mogul to turn his arms against the Portuguese. Orders were accordingly given to Cassam-Cham, to commence the siege of Ougli. This general, in the beginning, employed artifice. Having presented himself before the place with the principal forces of the empire, he threatened to give it up to pillage, unless Rodriguez paid down a certain sum of money, which he named. The Portuguese, after some delay, very reluctantly complied with the demand; there being in the place but a weak garrison, and a want of ammunition, and other necessaries, to enable it to sustain a long siege. An experience of the perfidiousness of the Mahometans was the only result of his compliance. The siege was immediately formed, and a formidable artillery, the principal arm of war used in sieges in Indostan, was brought forward to batter the city. The Christians made a feeble resistance. As soon as a breach had been effected, fearing the consequences of a storm, they surrendered at discretion. Cassam-Cham making them all prisoners of war, sent five or six hundred Portuguese to Agra, and amongst them several jesuits and monks of the Augustine order. The anger of heaven, justly irritated, doubtless was the cause of the disasters of the colony of Ougli. Unfortunately, the Ganges, which is seldom dry, had at this time so little water, that the transports, which might have afforded the means of escape to the Christians, were unable to get out of the harbour. The prisoners were, in consequence, conveyed to the capital. In order to preserve their wives, several embraced Mahometanism. Some of these Portuguese families are still living at Agra, who are Mahometans in name only. A few terminated their days by nobly suffering martyrdom under severe torments. Not one would have escaped the rage of Taigé-Mahal, had she been living at the time of the arrival of the prisoners at the court. The cruel sultaness had vowed to Mahomet to have them cut in pieces; but Providence delivered the Indies from this monster of cruelty and ambition. She died regretted only by the Emperor, who was indebted for his elevation to her arts and influence. Cha-Jaham caused a magnificent mausoleum to be erected for her, which is without its parallel in India. A description of it has passed into Europe, and it has been admired as a monument worthy the greatness, the good taste, and the prodigious wealth of the Mogul. All attempts proved fruitless to persuade or compel the Portuguese missionaries, taken at Ougli, to renounce the faith of Jesus Christ. At last, through the intercession of an Armenian, who possessed, at that time, some credit at court, and of a Venetian much in the favor of the Emperor, they were set at liberty, and sent back to Goa.

The two former emperors had taken a particular pleasure in embellishing, each, his favorite city. The court had been transferred from Delhi to Agra by Akebar; and from Agra to Lahor by Jehan Guir. Cha-Jaham caused it to return from Lahor to Delhi, and re-established that ancient capital in its pristine lustre. The ancient Delhi, it is true, served only as a suburb to the new. The city, which was now built, received the name of Cha-Jahanabad, which means, the city of Cha-Jaham. The expense incurred by the Emperor in constructing and adorning the city is scarcely credible. It is said, that he celebrated the foundation of his new capital by cruelties till then unknown to the Mahometans; and which he must have borrowed, undoubtedly, from the superstitions of the country. He caused several criminals to be slaughtered, and their blood to be shed on the foundations of the city. The circuit was marked out in a great plain, on the banks of the Gemna. Eleven gates were constructed in the walls, which were strengthened with twelve towers; an entrance being left in the centre of each curtain. The largest, and the most magnificent, formed the avenue to the citadel, which served as a palace for the Emperor, and a haram for his wives. The walls are constructed of brick, with great veins of that kind of red freestone, which has a resemblance to marble. The bazars, or public market places of Delhi, are surrounded with arcades, supporting a large terrace, and the shops display an excellent assortment of the various manufactures of Indostan. Although the mansions of the nobles are handsome, well constructed, and adorned with gardens, the houses of the greater part of the citizens are covered with thatch. The apartments, nevertheless, are pleasing and convenient. Two gardens were planted, by the care of Cha-Jaham, contiguous to his new palace at Delhi, of uncommon magnificence. The design was the invention of a Venetian, planned upon the principle of those magnificent vineyards, which contribute so much to the ornament of Italy. As it was difficult to introduce the waters of the Gemna, for the formation of canals, the course of a river was turned, whose bed was distant more than thirty leagues from Delhi. A new channel was dug, which passed through the gardens of the palace. These waters were filled with fish of a prodigious size; and it is said, that gold rings were attached to their nostrils, each of them ornamented with a ruby and two diamonds.

In these delicious retreats, Cha-Jaham forgot the warlike inclinations of his youth, and gave himself up to a voluptuous life. Poetry, music, the dance, the theatre had their prescribed hours; and the entire day was nearly engrossed by these amusements. No one enjoyed greater favor with the monarch, than a poet of the country, whose fertile imagination was continually inventing new entertainments for the haram, and gave a varied form to the pleasures of the Emperor. The grossest farces were the most to his taste. He retained his inclination for the sanguinary exhibitions of the gladiators, who were compelled to combat in his presence, armed with poignards.

Certain days of the week were set apart for the pleasures of the chase. That of the tiger, notwithstanding the peril attending it, was the most esteemed. A brief description of it may not be found without its interest. The evening preceding, the pioneers of the court convey into a neighbouring forest, sheep, goats, and horses, which have been slaughtered for the occasion; the scent of whose dead bodies attract the tigers to a particular spot. The next morning, at break of day, the king, mounted on an elephant, enters the grand routes, which had been formed in the forest. Instead of dogs, wild bulls are led, taught to act a part in this amusement. Rather large, and pointed sword-blades are fastened to the part, where the horns unite to the skull. These animals encircle, at a distance, a tiger, who is discovered intent on devouring the prey, which has been deposited in the forest; the circle contracting in proportion as the bulls advance. As soon as the tiger perceives their approach, he endeavours to fly; the bulls then presenting their horns, and the armed huntsmen prevent the escape of the enfuriated beast; they, at last, succeed in enclosing him in a circle, formed by the bulls closely pressed together. It is then, that the tiger makes those furious efforts to escape, by attempting to leap over the heads of the bulls; but the long swords affixed to their horns, frighten the animal, and sometimes transfix him in the air. If by chance, the beast attempts to make his escape between the legs of the bulls, they drive him off by presenting their horns. At last, the tiger weary of making bounds, and turning so long round the circle, falls exhausted in the midst of the wild bulls. The Emperor, who from the height of his elephant, has enjoyed the pleasure of beholding so animated a combat, finally destroys the tiger by shooting him with his fowling piece.

Had the diversions of Cha-Jaham been confined to sports of this description, they might at least have been considered as harmless; but the Emperor carried his debaucheries, as they regard the sex, to an excess hitherto unexampled among the Moguls, however prone they may be to voluptuousness. Cha-Jaham not contented with the multitude of queens, concubines, and slaves, (the three different orders of women that inhabit the haram,) intrigued with the wives of the principal officers of his court. Those of Jafar-Cham and Calil-Cham gave great scandal to the empire. They went every day to the palace, contrary to the usage of the ladies of the country. As one had her marked hour of assignation for the morning, and the other for the evening, the Faquirs, who are seen always in great numbers in the avenues to the palace, found, on this occasion, a fertile subject for the indulgence of the most malicious reports.

The passion of Cha-Jaham for women made him prodigal in all expences, which might contribute to their amusement; and, especially, in the construction and ornamenting of his apartments. It is said, that he presented the wife of Calil-Cham with a pair of slippers of inestimable value. He rallied the husband upon it, at a public audience, which eventually cost him dear, as will be seen in the sequel. To indulge this passion, Cha-Jaham caused that celebrated gallery to be built and adorned, of which so much has been spoken in Europe; and of which I now give a description, from the report of those, who have been eye-witnesses of its splendor. It is neither very spacious, nor very lofty, but the riches, contained in it, surpass whatever is to be seen in Europe. The light is admitted only from one side, and the windows are neither of great size, nor possessing much symmetry. The wall, opposite to the windows, is covered with so great a number of precious stones, of which some are of inestimable value, that the detail would appear incredible. The wall is covered with jasper; and on this first coating, a vine is seen to climb, entirely composed of precious stones, of shades, analagous to this species of vegetation. The stem is formed of those reddish agate stones, which express the color of the wood. The leaves are emeralds, interlaced with so much art, that the points where they unite cannot be discerned. The grapes, which are pendant from the branches, and seem to come out in relief, are composed, partly of diamonds, and partly of grenats. Materials could not be procured, adequate to the completion of the whole design, and the work remains yet incomplete. The side of the gallery, in which are the windows, is ornamented with large mirrors, whose frames are thickly sown, at intervals, with the largest pearls to be found in the east. Thus, the vine, framed of rich jewels, being multiplied in the mirrors, sheds a surprising lustre, which dazzles by its splendor during the day, and at night has the effect of an illumination. It was reported at the court, that Cha-Jaham destined this magnificent apartment for a female dancer of the lowest rank, and of little merit in her profession. So extraordinary is the estrangement of the human heart; that a prince, who abandons himself to his unlawful appetites, authorised too by his religion, seeks the foulest streams for the indulgence of his thirst of incontinence.

However Cha-Jaham may have been abandoned to his pleasures, he did not cease to have a respect for equity. This seems to have been a virtue, hereditary in the Moguls. It may be said, nevertheless, that Cha-Jaham administered justice, with an exactness, and a care, unequalled by his predecessors. He may be cited as the very Solomon of the Moguls; and some of his decisions are related, which manifest so great a portion of talent, and penetration, that in the Indies, their memory will be indelible. A soldier having stolen away the female slave of a writer, belonging to that class, that copy and distribute the news of the court through the provinces; the complaint was carried before the emperor. The cause had become much involved, as the slave, tired of her first master, maintained that she belonged to the soldier; and the writer produced pretty clear evidence, of the slave being his property. The Emperor, who, at first, affected to be embarrassed, and undecided how to act in so perplexed a case, attended for a time to other complaints; when, on a sudden, calling for ink, he caused the pen, (in the most unaffected manner,) to be given to the slave, that she might assist him to it. The slave gave it back replenished, with so much dexterity, and with so good a grace, that the Emperor judged immediately, that she must have been used to the duty; and said to the slave, angrily: "You cannot belong to the soldier; you must certainly have been in the service of the writer, and in his power you shall remain." The wisdom of the monarch was the admiration of the whole empire.

Cha-Jaham was inexorable towards the lower class of judges, who had allowed themselves to be corrupted by presents, or influenced by improper motives. The Cotwall of Delhi had received from a merchant a sum of money of no great amount, to engage him in his interests. The Emperor was informed of it, and sent to the Cotwall, immediately, by an officer of his court, one of those hood adders, whose bite is mortal. The Cotwall suffered himself to be stung by it, and expired in a few hours.

The Emperor, especially, signalised his regard for justice, in the destruction of robbers. Before his reign, they infested all the roads, and obstructed commerce. He made so fierce a war upon them, that they were exterminated. The means he employed to deliver the kingdom from this scourge, was; to make the officers of justice responsible for all the robberies in their respective districts. Thus, the factory, belonging to the Dutch, having been pillaged by night at Surat, Cha-Jaham compelled the governor to pay the Dutch the sum, at which they estimated their loss.

The impartiality, with which Cha-Jaham caused justice to be administered, without respect to persons, in some measure suspended the contempt, ordinarily inspired by princes of a voluptuous, and imbecile character; though it did not prevent his experiencing, at times, a failure of respect. One of those Omrhas, who serve in the armies, had the audacity, contrary to the custom of the empire, to seat himself in his presence. Cha-Jaham deprived him of all his posts, and took away his pensions. The disgraced officer presented himself, the next morning, at the audience of the Mogul, with the same confidence as the preceding day; and seating himself as before with great insolence; "Now," he said, "my lord, that I am no longer in your pay, I may exercise the privilege becoming an independant man." The Emperor applauded this display of spirit, made additions to his former appointments, and attached him for ever after to his service. The facility of the Emperor in pardoning was often abused by the courtiers, who availed themselves of it, to use a too great freedom of speech in addressing him. An ambassador, of the king of Golconda, followed, in this, the example given by the subjects of the Mogul. Cha-Jaham amusing himself, one day, in questioning the ambassador relative to the person and deportment of his master, suddenly turned towards a slave of a disagreeable figure, who was employed in keeping off the flies from the throne; "Is his majesty of Golconda," he said to him, "as tall as this slave?"—"He must assuredly be wanting considerably," replied the ambassador, "since my master is only taller by the head than your majesty." The ambassador was praised for his spirited reply, and at his departure was loaded with presents.

The defects of the Emperor, so little accompanied by those virtues which gain respect, drew upon him, at last, the contempt of his subjects, and the revolt of his children. The native Indians, especially, failed with impunity in the duty of their stations. It is a custom in the Indies, that the Rajas, in the vicinity of the city which happens to be the residence of the Emperor, should, each, in their turn, mount guard before the palace, and reside under tents with their Rajepoots, to do honor to, and to guard the Mogul. One of these princes, named Amarsin, failed to be present, when his day arrived to attend to the duties of his post. After receiving several notices from his friends, he, at last, presented himself for the discharge of his office. Visir-Cham, one of the secretaries of state, reproached him, in the presence of the Emperor, with his little zeal for the service. The Raja, who imagined himself insulted, drew a poignard, stabbed the minister to the heart, and covered with blood the habit of Cha-Jaham. So great an insolence was instantly revenged. Amarsin was pierced with a thousand wounds; but his Rajepoots revenged the death of their master. In their rage, they massacred whoever they met in the vicinity of the palace, and in the city; and this enormity went unpunished.

So feeble a government gave occasion to the other Rajas to shew their audacity. Champet, one of the haughtiest and most powerful, refused to pay his accustomed tribute. The astrologers, who beset the Emperor, and by their false predictions regulated all his movements, declared, that it was necessary, that Cha-Jaham should appear in person at the head of his army, and combat the rebel. They added, that the residence of Delhi would be fatal, for the space of a month, to whoever should hold there the highest rank. The Emperor marched out, therefore, at the head of his army, leaving the Cotwall, governor of Delhi in his absence. Sadul-Cham commanded the troops under the Mogul. They advanced towards the territory of the Raja, who made his appearance in the field, and marched to encounter his enemy. The general, rendered timid by the presence of the emperor, deemed it better to negotiate with Champet, than to attack him. He was promised pardon for his revolt, and assured of an increase to his territory and government, provided he would retire to his own lands, without drawing his sword against his sovereign. The object, of Sadul-Cham, was; to induce the Raja to abandon an advantageous post which he occupied, and in which it would have been difficult to force him. Champet believed the general's word, and retired. He was pursued, notwithstanding, in violation of the faith promised; and his troops would have been cut to pieces in their retreat, if, by good fortune, some inaccessible forests had not offered an asylum to his army, till it was able to gain certain heighths, and there place itself in security from the perfidy of the Emperor. Cha-Jaham returned to Delhi, covered with disgrace, for having uselessly broken his faith to an enemy; who again, immediately, took the field, and pillaged, without resistance, the lands of the empire. On his return, the Emperor found the Cotwall of Delhi dead. The Emperor's astrologers had caused him to be poisoned, secretly, by his own physician. Cha-Jaham, who believed that he was indebted for his life to their science, became more than ever the slave of astrology.

As the Emperor grew old, his passions changed with his years. Avarice took the place of prodigality. It may be said, that this passion equalled, or even surpassed, all his other vices. He rewarded the principal officers of his court, and of the armies, by permitting them to plunder the people with impunity; and as soon as the Omrhas had become enriched by their extortions, the emperor seized on their wealth, and appropriated to himself the spoil. In order to preserve, with greater security, the immense wealth, which tributes and extortions augmented every year, he caused to be constructed, under his palace of Delhi, two deep caves, supported by vast marble pillars. Piles of gold were stored in the one, and of silver in the other; and to render more difficult any attempt to convey away his treasure, he caused, of both metals, pieces to be made, of so prodigious a size, as to be rendered useless to the purposes of commerce. In these caves, Cha-Jaham passed a great part of the day, under the pretence of enjoying their refreshing coolness; but, in reality, for the purpose of feasting his eyes on the prodigious wealth he had accumulated.

A passion, so little worthy of a great king, caused him to commit an error in policy, which, eventually, brought ruin on him; and caused the desolation of his dominions.

In order to avoid the expense, which the maintenance of the young princes might have entailed upon his treasure; he sent them to a distance, charging them with the administration of different governments; and leaving them at liberty to extort what they could from the people, for the support of their dignity. Had he reflected upon the consequences, which had resulted from the like policy of his father, he might have escaped the danger attendant upon it. Never would Jehan Guir have experienced so many domestic wars, had he not sent his sons to a distance from him, distributing to them, in his lifetime, provinces, which the princes affected to govern independently. In vain was he admonished by paternal example.

Cha-Jaham had only seven children by all his wives; for the Moguls make no scruple of placing limits, by the most culpable practices, to the fecundity of their women. Thus the Emperor's progeny was confined to four princes, and three princesses. The eldest of the children of Cha-Jaham was Begom-Saeb, and the Sultan Dara was the eldest of the sons. The Prince Cha-Chuia was the third, and Aurengzebe, the reigning emperor was the fourth. The fifth, was the Princess Roxanara Begom. Moradbax was the sixth, and the Princess Merniza-Begom was the youngest. As the intrigues of the haram, and the domestic wars, which distracted the reign of Cha-Jaham, relate, chiefly, to these princes and princesses, it will be proper, here, to give some idea of these personages, which may serve to throw a light upon the history of a revolution, that terminated the reign of Cha-Jaham, and placed Aurengzebe upon the throne.

To a great share of beauty, Begom-Saeb united a mind endued with much artifice. The attachment she always had for her father, and the profusion of the avaricious Cha-Jaham towards his daughter, caused a suspicion, that crime might be blended with their mutual affection. This was a popular rumour, which never had any other foundation than in the malice of the courtiers. If there was a guilty passion, on the part of Cha-Jaham, towards Begom-Saeb, they ought certainly to have admitted, that it was not one accompanied with much delicacy. He permitted to his daughter, whom the policy of the empire would not suffer to form a matrimonial alliance, a liberty, in which her father, doubtless, never would have acquiesced, if he had taken an interest of an irregular nature in her conduct. He permitted a musician of the palace to enjoy her favor; and was not ignorant of the assignations given him by the princess. This musician was, nevertheless, highly in the favor of the Emperor. It may easily be imagined, that the influence which Begom-Saeb had over the mind of her father, might be procured by her complaisance, and by the charms of her mind. This princess was always attached to the party of Dara. The hope, which her brother gave her, of marrying her, if he should succeed to the empire, fixed her for ever in his interests.

Joined to a fine person, and regular features, Dara possessed sincerity of mind, and noble inclinations. Never prince, perhaps, of his rank, had a greater share of understanding, or took more pains to cultivate it. He had acquired a knowledge of all our sciences,and almost of all the languages of Europe. So great was his attachment to Europeans, that it gave umbrage to the great lords of his court. They foresaw, that under his reign, the Franks would enjoy the greatest share of favor. His study of philosophy, and of the different religions of the universe, made him contemn that of Mahomet. Had he reigned, the Christian religion would, doubtless, have found in him, a bolder, and more efficient protector, than it had experienced in Jehan Guir, his grandfather. His liberality had drawn into his service the most skilful engineers, and the most expert cannoneers, belonging to all the nations of Europe. So many fine qualities, which might have procured him the favor of the people, rendered him haughty, and full of confidence in his own merit. To give him advice was to offend him mortally, and to have seen further into an affair than himself, was insulting his penetration. Hence sprung the contempt which he had for his ministers, and the little confidence, that his ministers reposed in him. As he never communicated his sentiments to his council; his council, on their part, never dared to give him salutary advice. He imagined himself, in the meanwhile, beloved by all who approached him, and the conceit he had of his own merit, made him accept flattery as the voice of truth. In a word, he was too sensible to his own merit, to be able to make all the advantageous use of it, which he, otherwise, might have done. This prince had two sons, the eldest of whom was called Sultan Soliman-Chacu, and the second Sultan Super-Chacu.

Cha-Chuia was the third of the children of Cha-Jaham. He was not deficient in courage, or in capacity for great enterprises; but art marked his character still stronger, than these qualities. He maintained emissaries at the court of his father, for the purpose of discóvering all his secrets. He kept spies about his brother Dara, who gave him intelligence of all his movements; and who debauched his best officers, and the most expert cannoneers of his army. Cha-Chuia had a secret understanding with the principal Rajas of the empire; and Jacont-Sing, the most formidable of them, was his declared friend. It is said, that this prince had a correspondence even with the king of Persia; it is, at least, certain,, that in order to attract a greater number of Persians into his service, he had embraced the sect of Ali; and that he contemned the species of Mahometanism, which is professed in the Indies, and in Turkey, to attach himself to the heresy of Persia.

The fourth of the children of Cha-Jaham was Aurengzebe. Nature seemed to have taken a pleasure to combine, in the person of this prince, the perfections of mind and body. His figure was good, and he had a turn of countenance naturally mild. A spare habit gave him an air of penitence, which he knew how to accompany with pious discourses. He was always seen, pale, of a livid complexion, and with eyes sunk in his head. He appeared thoughtful, and taciturn, seldom speaking, unless it was with zeal for the religion of Mahomet, and the observation of his law. He almost always carried the Alcoran under his arm. His prayers were frequent, and in public. He recited every day a certain string of the praises of God, in a most impressive manner. It was, also, said, that he had caused himself to be inscribed in the number of the Faquirs; and, that as soon as he might be enabled to escape from the cares of the world, he proposed passing his days in penitence, near the tomb of Mahomet. The better to deceive the multitude, he never appeared in public in any other than a white habit, very plain, and almost entirely unadorned with those rich jewels, which glitter so resplendently, upon the habits of the Mogul princes. His nourishment was conformable to the simplicity of his vestments. A little rice and some roots composed all the provisions, which were served upon his table. He was a stranger to the use of wine, and his abstinence from so essential an article of enjoyment, was constant. From his tenderest years, he was observed to have a turn for policy and dissimulation. Though affecting in his discourse the most retired sentiments, Aurengzebe concealed an ambitious mind; he took, at least, by this method, a certain means of preserving his life, in the event of any sudden revolution. He was convinced, that after the death of his father, Cha-Jaham, there would be no alternative but to reign, or to perish. With this view, he took the resolution, either to mount the throne, in case a fair opportunity should present itself, or to place his life in security, by an appearance of renouncing the world, and sacrificing all his pretentions to it, in consecrating himself to penitence. Slander, in the meanwhile, was busy in publishing, that the prince in private plunged into the most unauthorised debaucheries; the Faquirs, they said, with whom Aurengzebe often associated, were the confidants of, and the ministers to his pleasures.

Roxanara-Begom, the fifth of the children of Cha-Jaham, was inferior in beauty to her elder sister; but she possessed more suppleness and artifice. Begom-Saeb, in regard to disposition and understanding, most resembled Dara, and Roxanara had more of the character of her brother Aurengzebe. She possessed the same dissimulation and artifice. She was joined in interest with this prince, and served him for a spy in the haram, to give him intelligence of whatsoever occurred, of an important nature.

The youngest of the sons of Cha-Jaham was named Moradbax. This prince was brave, but possessed of little prudence. The chase and shooting with the bow were almost his sole amusements. He hunted lions and wild boars, and prided himself more on a fierce and rash courage, than on an exact and circumspect policy. He despised the uses of negociation, and placed no confidence except in his strength, and courage. He was, however, a true Mahometan, and the piety which he manifested in the mosques was sincere.

Mernisa-Begom, the youngest of the daughters of Cha-Jaham, was a princess of a weak mind, and moderate beauty. Childish amusements were her sole occupation. A jewel, a dress, bounded all her desires; and she never took the least interest in the different factions, which distracted the haram, and the empire.

Cha-Jaham entertained, then, the purpose, of sending his sons to a distance from the capital; and confined his daughters, within the bounds of the haram. The viceroyalty of Bengal was given to Cha-Chuia. Aurengzebe was sent to the Decan in quality of viceroy, and the viceroyalty of Guzurat fell to the lot of Moradbax. Dara, only, was retained near the person of the Emperor. As he was destined by the order of his birth, and by the inclination of Cha-Jaham, to succeed him in the empire of Indostan; he remained under the eyes of his father, and became the soul of his councils. Happy would it have been for him, if he had not, so early, allowed the people to perceive, what they were to expect from his administration.

No sooner had Dara began to possess authority, than he became disdainful, and inaccessible. A small number of Europeans, alone shared his confidence. The Jesuits, especially, were in the highest consideration with him. These, were the Fathers Stanislaus Malpica, a Neapolitan, Pedro Juzarte, a Portuguese, and Henry Busée, a Fleming. This last had much influence over the mind of the prince, and had his counsels been followed, it is probable that Christianity would have mounted the throne with Dara. However, whatever influence this father might have over him, he was unable to banish the astrologers from his court. They had so infatuated the prince, that he could not extricate himself from their toils. One of them, having ventured to predict, at the peril of his head, that Dara would be emperor; and being interrogated by one of his friends, to account for the confidence, with which, with so much peril to himself, he could make himself responsible for an event invelopped in obscurity. "I risk less than you may imagine," replied the astrologer, "if the prince attains the throne, I shall have guessed right, and my fortune is made; if he fails, his death is infallible. In that case, I shall have nothing to apprehend from his resentment."

The influence of Dara grew to an astonishing height, during the absence of his brothers. Cha-Jaham, who was advanced in years, was king only of his treasures. His eldest son ruled the empire with absolute power. A sopha had been prepared for him, lower, indeed, than the throne of his father; but he is the only instance of a prince of the Mogul race being allowed to be seated in the presence of the Emperor. He had the power to command a combat of elephants, whenever he pleased; a distinction reserved only for the sovereign. In fine, with the exception of the control of the revenues of the empire, of which Cha-Jaham was always jealous; Dara possessed all the advantages, and all the authority of royalty.

So much power increased the pride of a prince, naturally haughty. His discourse was arrogant, and his air was disdainful. An officer of Mahobet-Cham, who still lived in a retired manner in his government, had insulted a soldier of the prince. Dara gave orders that Mahobet-Cham should be forcibly conveyed to the citadel of Delhi. This old general had still sufficient influence among the troops, to create employment for Dara; and courage capable of making resistance, if he was attacked. Cha-Jaham counselled his son to push the affair no further.

All the ministers of the Emperor, and all the generals of the army were objects of jealousy to the prince, and the sport of his caprices. He was accused of having caused Sadul-Cham to be poisoned, whom the Emperor had raised to the dignity of first minister. Jasing, the famous Raja, whose power and valour were formidable to the Mogul, was insulted by the prince. He called him musician; a term of contempt in the Indies. The Raja dissembled his mortification, and delayed his revenge till a convenient opportunity. Mirza Mula, who was sent to command in a war against the king of Golconda, was despoiled by Dara of his best European cannoneers. "I shall know how to spoil him in his turn," said the general, in taking his departure; and this prediction was but too truly verified in the sequel. All those, whom the prince suspected of not being sufficiently attached to his interests, were imprisoned or condemned to exile. One of the secretaries of state was found strangled in his bed. Suspicion did not fail to fall upon Dara. What aggravated more particularly the noblemen of the court, was; the odious comparison, which the prince made, incessantly, between them and a wretched slave, whom he employed in the most degrading services. A minister of state, or a general of the army, was never praised in the presence of Dara, that he did not enlarge, immediately, upon the merits of Abercan, which was the name of the favorite slave.

So many faults, tending to excite hatred, caused the prince to lose all the fruit of the advantages he possessed on the side of capacity, person, and birth, over the other sons of Cha-Jaham.

Whilst Dara was making himself enemies in the empire by a haughty and imperious carriage, Cha-Chuia led a tranquil life in Bengal. Moradbax, in his government of Guzurat, divided his time between the exercise of arms, the chase, and the pleasures of the haram. Aurengzebe, alone, was deeply employed, in meditating upon the surest means, of snatching the empire from the designs of his two elder brothers; or, at least, of placing in security his life, against the persecution of the prince, whom providence should place upon the throne. Never was justice more vigilantly administered, than in the government of the Decan. He judged, that it was necessary to establish his fortunes, upon a just reputation for probity and disinterestedness. Religion, which served, they say, as a mask for his ambition, seemed to employ all his cares. He built mosques, he mingled with the Faquirs, that he might appear to despise the world, agreeably to their example. It must be acknowledged, however, that through all this dissimulation, there was still to be discerned a certain malignity, even in his actions of piety. He one day collected together all the Faquirs of the country, that he might bestow upon them a considerable benefaction, and have the consolation of eating rice and salt with them; it was, in this manner, that he expressed himself. The place of meeting was a large plain. Aurengzebe caused this vast multitude of poor penitents to partake of a repast conformable to their condition. As soon as they had eaten, the viceroy declared, that he wished to give them all new clothing, and make them change the ragged garments, with which they were so ill accommodated. Aurengzebe was not ignorant, that the greater part of these beggars commonly secrete in their vestments gold rupees, the harvest of their mendicity. In effect, many opposed resigning their old habits, on pretext of the vow of poverty, which is the essential feature of their profession. Their remonstrances were not listened to; the prince was resolute that his charitable intentions should admit of no exception. The Faquirs were despoiled of their old habits; and they were compelled to put on the new, which were distributed to them. A pile was then made of the spoils of the Faquirs, to which fire was applied, and in the cinders so considerable a sum was found, that if some writers of the country may be believed, it became one of the principal aids, of which Aurengzebe availed himself, for making war upon his brothers.

The devotion, of which he made a public profession, did not suppress his warlike inclinations. It is true, that he gave, to all his projects, a colour of piety and zeal. It was under this pretext, that he undertook to dethrone the king of Golconda, a Mahometan by religion; but attached to the sect of the Persians. The occasion, which engaged Aurengzebe to enter upon so great an enterprise, was, as follows: Mirza Mula, (otherwise, Mergi Mola,) by birth a Persian, who had come to the Indies in the capacity only of an attendant upon a merchant of his own nation; after having served for some time in the troops of the Mogul, and arrived by degrees to the first posts in the armies; disgusted, at last, with the contempt of prince Dara, had entered into the service of the king of Golconda. He was, at first, placed as a superintendant over the customs, and the traffic of the king. Mirza Mula profited by so advantageous a post, and trading for his own account, he soon amassed immense wealth. He, at first, made use of it to gain the good graces of his master. Mirza Mula procured rarities from Europe, cabinets from China, elephants from Ceylon, and never ceased making presents to the king. His magnificence caused him to be taken notice of at court, and as soon as he became known, he attained to the first distinctions. What brought him into chief notice was an intrigue of gallantry, which he carried on in private with the mother of the king. She was a princess, who still preserved her beauty, at a rather advanced period of life.

The king's acquaintance with the irregular conduct of his mother served only to advance the fortunes of Mirza Mula. He was sent to a distance from the court, that the queen-mother might be prevented from giving occasion to scandal; and the government of the province of the Carnatic was bestowed upon him. The artful Persian knew how to turn his disgrace to his advantage. The diamond mine, which adds so much to the wealth of the kingdom of Golconda, was within the limits of his government. He, consequently, determined to make the best use of his time. He retained for his own use the largest and the most perfect of the diamonds. One, which he gave, in the sequel, to the Mogul emperor, was unparalleled in its kind. It is still the admiration of all connoisseurs. The governor engaged openly in a commerce of diamonds, and sent little besides the refuse to the king. Don Philip Mascarenhas, viceroy of the Indies for the Portuguese at Goa, was his principal correspondent. The object, of Mirza Mula, was; to secure to himself the protection of the Portuguese, in the event of a change of fortune. The Persian, who found himself supported, no longer placed any limits to his peculations. He plundered the temples of their idols; he seized upon all the precious stones with which the statues were ornamented; he compelled the inhabitants of the Carnatic to surrender to him whatever they possessed of gold and jewels; and he caused those, who, according to the custom of the country, had buried their treasures, to expire under the severity of the lash. So many cruelties rendered him hateful in his province; and such great wealth created him envy at court.

The king, who was informed of the conduct of the governor, contemplated recalling him, and confiscating his property. The purpose of the prince could not be kept so secret, as to escape the knowledge of the queen-mother. She gave her favorite information of the danger which menaced him, and proposed herself a plan of revolt, for the dethronement of her son. The enterprise was concerted in the following manner. Mirza Mula wrote to Aurengzebe, that the time had arrived for conquering the richest kingdom in Indostan; that after having served the Moguls, he had not entered into the service of the King of Golconda, but with the view of facilitating the acquisition of so fine a country to his first masters; that he had, in consequence, maintained a correspondence with certain persons in the haram of the king, and that he was in the possession of all the forces of the kingdom. That Mahamed Amicam, his son, was at the head of the armies of Golconda; and that, in his province of the Carnatic, he himself had a certain number of troops, composed partly of Portuguese devoted to his interests. That if Aurengzebe entered into the kingdom of Golconda with an army, however small in number, all the kingdom would rise in his favor.

Aurengzebe was, at this time, at Orangabad, a city which he had founded in his viceroyalty of the Decan, and to which he had given his name. It is difficult to imagine, how great was his satisfaction, at the moment of receiving such agreeable news. He was sensible, that the conquest of a kingdom would pave the way for the invasion of the empire. In order to ensure success to the project of Mirza-Mula, he judged it inexpedient to begin by attacking the frontiers of Golconda. He resolved to proceed himself, in the character of the ambassador of Aurengzebe, to the court of the king; and to attempt the revolution in person, in the capital. He, in consequence, prepared for himself a suite, composed of the bravest officers of his army, and an escort rather large for an ambassador. Without loss of time, he advanced, by rapid journies, towards Baganagar, the capital of Golconda, spreading a report in his progress, that he was an ambassador sent by Aurengzebe to the king, for the negotiation of affairs of importance. The stratagem succeeded, and the pretended ambassador entered Baganagar without being known.

Upon his arrival, Aurengzebe immediately conferred

with the son of Mirza Mula, general of the troops, and arranged with him, that at the first audience, which he should have of the king, the person of the monarch should be secured at the moment of his presenting his credentials. The treason could not be conducted with so much secresy, as to escape coming to the king's knowledge. This prince learnt, that Aurengzebe was himself in his capital; that his design was to invade his kingdom, and to seize upon his person; in fine, that his own army had conspired against his life. The King of Golconda took the safest measure. He abandoned his capital, Baganagar, and retired into the fortress of Golconda, situated about a league from it, and which gives its name to the kingdom. Aurengzebe could not behold, without mortification, the escape of his prey. He vented his disappointment upon the capital, which he plundered; and upon the palace of the king, from which he carried off the treasure and jewels.

As soon as intelligence was received of the arrival of Aurengzebe, the army of Mirza Mula quitted the Carnatic, and joined itself to that of Mahamed Amicam. It was then resolved to form the siege of Golconda, in which the king had taken refuge. This fortress, which is esteemed in India as impregnable, was already invested by the two armies, of which Aurengzebe took the command; when that prince thought proper to give advice to Cha-Jaham, his father, of the condition of the kingdom of Golconda, and of the conquest he was about to make of it. Machines were raised to commence the siege, and the canals had been cut, which convey water into the citadel. The danger, with which the poor king was menaced, had now obliged him to resolve on making terms with his enemy, and surrendering himself into his hands, upon condition of his life being respected, and the rank of Raja conceded to him at the court of the Mogul. Whilst he was deliberating upon these measures, orders from the Emperor came to Aurengzebe, to raise the siege, and return to the Decan. Cha-Jaham, who mistrusted his son, and was, besides, dissatisfied with an enterprise undertaken without his acquiescence, listened to the representations of Dara, and the suspicions of Begom-Saeb. They insinuated to the Emperor, that the usurpation of the kingdom of Golconda was a step towards ascending the throne of the Moguls; that the artful viceroy of the Decan laboured less for the glory of his father, than for his own interests; that it was better to sacrifice to the public safety a new acquisition, than to suffer Aurengzebe to aggrandize himself, to the great peril of the royal family. Such were the motives which induced Cha-Jaham to force his son to abandon an enterprise already so far advanced. Aurengzebe obeyed; but to conceal the reasons which impelled him to the resolution, he was seen suddenly to take, of abandoning the enterprise against Golconda, false pretexts were put into circulation. He counterfeited the man inspired from above; and caused it to be believed by his soldiers, that scruples of conscience, against oppressing a Mahometan prince, occasioned him to relinquish a war, which he was just upon the point of terminating successfully. He made, therefore, an honorable accommodation with the King of Golconda, and reinstated him in the possession of his states, on the following conditions: First, that the Mogul should be reimbursed all the expenses of the war: Secondly, that the daughter of the king should be given in marriage to Mahamud, the eldest son of Aurengzebe: Thirdly, that the princess should have for her dowry all the revenues of the province of Ranguir: Fourthly, that after the death of the King of Golconda, Mahamud should be his successor in virtue of the rights of his wife: Fifthly, that the coin of Golconda should bear on one side the impress of Cha-Jaham: Sixthly, and lastly, that Mirza Mula, and all his family, should be permitted to quit the territories of Golconda with all their wealth.

It was thus, that Aurengzebe extracted all possible advantages from an enterprise, which he abandoned with regret. After having failed in the conquest of Golconda, he meditated, by secret practices, to pave his way to the possession of the empire. Mirza Mula appeared to him to be a man upon whom he might rely. The enterprise, which they had attempted in concert, as well as the ancient animosity of the general against Dara, rendered him propitious to his designs. Aurengzebe, in order to retain so great a captain in the neighbourhood of his government, solicited of the court, that Mirza Mula might be appointed to command the army destined for the conquest of Visapour. This request was granted to Aurengzebe, upon condition that Mirza Mula should send to the court his wives and children, to serve as hostages for his fidelity. The viceroy, who had thus secured to himself, by his good offices, the gratitude of Mirza Mula, opened himself to him without reserve. He complained of the tyranny of Dara. He added, that the jealousy alone of his brother had prevented him from joining the kingdom of Golconda to the provinces of the empire; that the Emperor himself was a slave to the will of Dara; that Cha-Jaham no longer merited the character of a father, since he had renounced all the paternal tenderness, which he owed to his three younger sons, that his whole care and affection might be lavished upon Dara alone; that in the place of Cha-Jaham, he hoped to find in Mirza Mula, a father, a friend, a protector, and the universal confidant of his secrets. Mirza Mula received with gladness the overtures of friendship from so great a prince, and promised to exert all his power and ability to establish him on the throne. This conversation was kept a profound secret between them. It broke out, however, a little time afterwards into action, as we shall find in the sequel.

Aurengzebe continued, at his city of Orangabad, to make a public display of extraordinary piety, whilst Mirza Mula was capturing towns in the kingdom of Visapour. The famous citadel of Beder resisted him only a few months. No intelligence appeared to subsist between the general and the viceroy of the Decan. All was calm, apparently, in the empire, and every thing bowed to the authority of Dara, when a malady of Cha-Jaham gave rise to a strange revolution.

It was reported, that the Emperor, given up still, at an advanced age, to his debaucheries, was seized with a retention of urine, by which his life was brought into danger, in consequence of the use of a heating medicine, which his incontinence had occasioned him to take. The illness of the king was quickly made known in Delhi with much officiousness by the enemies of Dara, and a report of the death of Cha-Jaham almost immediately followed that of his malady. From the capital it became in a little while current through all the provinces. The three brothers of Dara were informed of it, by the emissaries whom they maintained at the court. It is true, that the danger of the Emperor had been great; but the strength of his constitution saved him. The princes, on the first intelligence of the death of their father, adopted, each, the measures which were most conformable to his genius. Cha-Chuia, the most impetuous of the three, was the first to take the field; and with an army, which he kept prepared for any event which might require its services, commenced his march to Delhi. He had already forty thousand horse in his train. As the wealthiest government had fallen to his lot, he had taken care to furnish himself with camels loaded with gold rupees, to pay his troops, and to purchase the aid of fresh levies. It is said, that as he was upon the point of mounting on horseback, holding in his hand his cimetar, he exclaimed, "Death or the throne!" He took his route by the great road of Agra, at the head of his army, causing a report to be spread during his march, that the Emperor had died of poison, which the perfidious Dara had compelled him to take; and that he hastened to revenge the best of fathers.

Cha-Jaham, who began to find himself recovering, learnt with indignation the news of the step which his son had taken. He trusted, however, that he should be able to keep him at a distance from the capital, by the blandishments of flattery. He wrote to him, therefore, with his own hand, that his indisposition had been followed by no bad consequences; that the ambition of Dara had not been the occasion of it; as for the rest, that he felt obliged for his son's sensibility and fears for his health. Further, he counselled him to return to his government of Bengal, and by an exact obedience, make atonement for the measures into which his too eager affection had precipitated him. Cha-Chuia received the letter of his father, while on his route; but it was accompanied by other letters from some of the emissaries, whom he employed at the court. They gave him assurances, that the malady of the king was mortal; and that his fortune depended upon the promptitude with which he should appear before Delhi. Cha-Chuia communicated, in consequence, to no one, his having received a packet from his father; and hastened his march, that he might not leave Dara time to make preparations. The approach of the rebel obliged Cha-Jaham, notwithstanding his indisposition, to change his abode, and to take refuge in Agra, at a distance of more than twenty-five leagues from Delhi. Dara followed his father, not being willing to be absent from him in circumstances of such extreme peril. In the mean while, he neglected no measures calculated to put a stop to the progress of Cha-Chuia.

Soliman Chacu, the eldest son of Dara, was a prince of great promise. Well made, liberal, conducting himself with moderation, and wise above his years, he possessed all the good qualities of his father, without his defects. It was a prince so accomplished, that the court opposed to the rebel. Two generals were appointed to command under him; the Raja Jasing, esteemed at that time the greatest captain in Indostan, and Dalil Cham, a Patan by birth, who had signalized himself by more than one victory. Secret instructions had been given to Jasing, to moderate the too impetuous courage of the young prince, and to prevent him from engaging in battle before the means of negotiation had been tried.

The two armies were no sooner in the presence of each other, than Soliman Chacu proposed to give battle to his uncle. Jasing, who, till then, had endeavoured to avoid an action, by keeping at a distance from the enemy, wrote to Cha-Chuia nearly in the following terms:—"Your affection for your father, and the marks of valour which you give to all the empire, cannot, my lord, be sufficiently commended. Through tenderness for Cha-Jaham, you come to punish the authors of his death; and your courage has been made manifest by the celerity with which you have come into the presence of an army, more powerful, and more warlike, than the one of which you are the leader. But your father still lives; and it would be dishonorable for you, to attack the most faithful subjects of him, whom from motives of piety you come to avenge. Return to Bengal; and do not imagine that courage is to be esteemed, when it is accompanied by crime."

This letter made some impression on the mind of Cha-Chuia. He deliberated for some time on the measures which it became him to take. At last, the least salutary counsel prevailed. He threw off the mask, and decided upon an open revolt. The apprehensions, however, which he entertained from the experience of Jasing, and the valour of Dalil Cham, induced him to resort to artifice, in order to put these two generals off their guard. He replied to Jasing in these terms:—"The whole empire bears witness, that I have quitted Bengal with no other view, than to seek satisfaction for the poisoning of my father. He lives, and my tenderness is satisfied. I limit my ambition, to continue submissive to his orders, in the territory which he has assigned me. Take your departure, therefore, as soon as possible; and render an account to my father of my unlimited obedience. All which I expect, (in order that I may not appear to fly from you) is, that you will be the first to retire: a compliance with this request I exact as a mark of respect on your own part, as well as on that of my nephew, Soliman Chacu. Save my honor, and you shall find me obedient."

Jasing was sufficiently sensible, that the letter of the prince was only a feint, that he might have an opportunity of surprising the imperial army, and defeating it in its retreat. Nevertheless, that he might not leave the rebel any pretext, he pretended to acquiesce in the conditions of Cha-Chuia; and gave orders that as soon as morning appeared, the retreat should be began. The baggage, in consequence, commenced its march at day-break.

In the meanwhile, the Imperial troops were placed in order of battle; and a few useless foot soldiers, of that class, which follow the Indian armies solely in the hope of sharing in the pillage, were all which were ordered to take the road to Delhi. The spies of Cha-Chuia persuaded themselves, that the cavalry of the Emperor had, in fact, departed. They gave intelligence, to this effect, to the prince. The rash Cha-Chuia commenced, immediately, a hurried attack upon some squadrons, that he thought to be a rear guard, which he should easily dispose of. He was deceived. The whole Imperial cavalry made head against him, and charged that of Cha-Chuia with so much fury, that it was presently thrown into disorder. In spite of all the efforts of Cha-Chuia, he was unable to rally them. His artillery was taken, together with forty elephants, and a number of prisoners, which were sent to Delhi, as a token of victory, Jasing, who might easily have pursued Cha-Chuia and made himself master of his person, preferred allowing him to escape. He judged wisely, that if he brought him a prisoner to the Emperor, the affectionate father would not take away the life of his son, and that he should have at the court an additional enemy. Besides, he felt little inclined to exert himself for the pleasure of Prince Dara. He remembered the contempt with which he had been treated, and the opprobious term of musician, of which the prince had made use, to insult him. Under these impressions, he afforded Cha-Chuia an opportunity of collecting the wreck of his army, and retiring to Bengal.

Whilst the second son of Cha-Jaham had declared open revolt against his father, the two others, each in his government, assembled troops, and deliberated upon taking the field. With respect to Aurengzebe, he thought it best not to avow himself, till he had taken such measures, as might promise him success in the great design he was meditating. He waited till Moradbax, the youngest of his brothers, had taken the road to Delhi. Profiting, then, by the rebellious movements, which the other princes had made before him ; he resolved to exalt himself by their means, and, perhaps, at their expense. He wrote, therefore, a letter to Moradbax, replete with dissimulation; in which he expressed himself as follows:—" You are not ignorant, my dear brother, of the resolution which I have taken, to pass the remainder of my days in retirement, and penitence. The splendors of this world have not the power to tempt me. The only anxiety which I have, is, to establish the worship of the true God, and the law of his prophet, in their utmost purity; I consider, that of all the sons of Cha-Jaham (whose death is but too certain), you, alone, preserve a zeal for the Alcoran. Dara is an impious man, who is attached only to the religions of Europe. Cha-Chuia is a heretic, who has abandoned himself to the sect of Ali; and maintains a correspondence with the schismatics of Persia. God and his prophet be praised! I will not suffer that impiety or heresy shall be seated on the throne. You, alone, my dear brother, whom I honor henceforward as my sovereign; and whom I now salute as my master, merit to wear the crown. You are a true Mussulman, and the only defender of the faithful. Suffer me then to join my troops with yours, and to defend with you the righteous cause, in combating for our religion. As for myself, I ask but one only recompense, for all the services which I propose to render you; that you will permit me, after the victory, to go, and pass the remainder of my life near the tomb of Mahomet, in prayer, and in penitence."

So artful a letter was received with joy by Moradbax. In vain, his faithful eunuch, Cha Abbas, who served him in the place of chief minister, counselled him to enter with great caution into any engagements with Aurengzebe. The overtures of a brother, who flattered his ambition, infatuated him to such a degree, as to render him deaf to advice. He made him the following reply:—" It is but reasonable, my dear brother, that two hearts, whom friendship has always united, should find themselves drawn together still closer by their zeal for the Alcoran. Let us march in concert to defend a religion attacked by two impious men. I swear by the great prophet, that I shall always entertain for you the same respect as for my father; and that if I should ever be seated upon a throne, which you, in the piety and greatness of your soul contemn, I shall preserve for your children all the affection of a parent; and for yourself, all the deference which I owe to an elder brother, and the defender of our religion."

When Moradbax consented to join his troops to those of Aurengzebe, he did not calculate upon those of his brother being superior in number to his own. The government of the Decan, which Aurengzebe had for some time possessed, was much less extensive than his; and, consequently, the forces which it was capable of furnishing could not be so considerable. He flattered himself, besides, that Aurengzebe would be deficient in treasure, and that the troops of his brother, paid by himself, would be devoted to him alone. With this view, he obtained large supplies of money from the merchants of Surat. Moradbax deceived himself. Aurengzebe had been amassing treasure, ever since he had been viceroy of the Decan, to which the spoil of Golconda had added considerably. His frugality, besides, supplied the want of a large revenue, and furnished him with a considerable fund for useful expenses. Aurengzebe made use of the following artifice to augment the force of his army.—Mirza Mula, who made war for the Emperor in Visapour, was attached by interest to the Viceroy of the Decan. Aurengzebe sent to him his son, Prince Mahamud, to propose to him the fulfilment of the engagements, to which they had pledged themselves, after the expedition to Golconda. "The time is arrived," said Mahamud to him, "for placing Aurengzebe upon the throne. You have it in your power, and you have engaged yourself to effect it. By joining your troops to his, you render him superior in strength to his brothers, and you put him in possession of a crown, for which he must acknowledge himself to be indebted to you only." Mirza-Mula was disposed to do all in his power for Aurengzebe; his vows had laid him under an obligation so to do; but he was restrained by his tenderness for his wives and children. Dara had caused them to be conducted to the capital, that they might become guarantees for his fidelity. Aurengzebe, who foresaw the just apprehensions of Mirza Mula, proposed an expedient to him, to which the general agreed. This was, to suffer his troops to be excited to revolt against him; to allow Mahamud to convey him as a prisoner into the citadel of Orangabad; and thus, to abandon the whole of his army to the control of the Viceroy of the Decan. By this means, the subtle Mirza Mula secured the compassion of the court for himself and family, at the very time he betrayed it; as well as both his life and fortune, in the event of the success of Aurengzebe.

The strength of the army of Aurengzebe was thus increased, by the addition of the whole of the troops of Mirza Mula. With this reinforcement, he believed himself in a condition to take the field, and to join Moradbax, who was advancing towards Delhi. With his habitual art, Aurengzebe deemed it necessary, at his departure, to redouble his professions of piety. In order the more effectually to retain in his service the army of Mirza Mula, he called Heaven to witness, that he did not enter upon a war, to which he had the greatest repugnance, but from a zeal for religion. He took the Alcoran in his hand, and and pressed it devoutly to his breast, in view of all the soldiers. Transported, then, with enthusiasm, which he knew so well how to effect; "It is," he cried, "to defend you, sacred law of the great prophet, it is to revenge you of the contempt of the infidel Dara, that I interrupt the peace, which ought to reign among brothers." Aurengzebe did not fail, likewise, to disseminate through his army, the report of the death of the Emperor his father. He procured every day feigned letters from Delhi. All those which might have undeceived the public, were intercepted on the frontiers. In fine, the death of Cha-Jaham was generally credited, before Aurengzebe quitted the Decan.

One of his cares, also, was to prevent Moradbax from entertaining any suspicions. He wrote to him, frequently, during his march, letters couched in the most respectful terms. "If the army of Mirza Mula," he said, "has united itself to mine, it is the sanction of your name alone which has decided it to do so. The conviction, that their services were to be devoted to the purpose of placing you upon the throne, has alone induced them to follow me. They are animated with the same zeal by which we are both governed. They are true Mussulmen, who desire only the triumph of religion, and to fix it with you upon the throne of the Moguls." Ambition so blinded Moradbax, that he did not suspect a snare. He arranged with Aurengzebe the place where the two armies might form a junction; and offered to take the advance, and meet his brother. "It is not proper," answered Aurengzebe, "that the sovereign should anticipate his slave. I will conform myself," he added, "to the direction of your march, and I shall know how to proceed, to the end that an interview, which I passionately desire, may not be delayed." It was near the mountains of Manddo, that Aurengzebe came up with his brother's army.

Never union appeared more affectionate, than that of Moradbax and Aurengzebe. The latter no sooner descryed at a distance his brother, than he descended from his elephant, and hastening on foot to meet the prince, he prostrated himself before him, and honored him as his sovereign. The intoxication of the younger was beyond all bounds, when he beheld the submission of his elder brother. He no longer doubted the sincerity of his protestations. Aurengzebe knew how to accompany them with an air of simplicity, capable of deceiving the most clear-sighted. From that time, he caused Moradbax to take the title of emperor, and treated him both in public and in private, as his superior. He always gave him the precedence; and in the command of the armies, he took his brother's orders, whom he knew how to lead into the adoption of his own measures. Thus, the troops of the two confederate brothers advanced at the same moment towards Delhi.

The defile of Manddo, environed with forests and mountains, would have been a difficult, pass for the rebel army to have forced; by good fortune they found nothing to oppose them. A spirit of infatuation seemed to have taken possession of the council of Cha-Jaham. At tho news of the two brothers having united their forces, the fortifying of the capital engrossed its whole attention; and the propriety of occupying the posts, which might have hindered the enemy from approaching, was never considered. Prince Dara, valiant as he was, and proud of the victory which the government had atchieved over Cha-Chuia, appeared alarmed at the march of the two brothers. He knew the valour of Moradbax, and he mistrusted the artifice and the intrigues of Aurengzebe. He called to mind, besides, some prediction, which promised the throne to the viceroy of the Decan. In this state of alarm, he attempted to sow division between the two brothers, and by that means, to disperse their forces before they could appear before Delhi. He at first wrote to the two chiefs, that Cha-Jaham was yet alive, and that to come to disturb his repose, would be forfeiting the respect due to a father; and a sovereign.

Moradbax, whose heart was sincere, and who had naturally virtuous inclinations, was startled when he beheld himself upon the brink of a crime. Until then, his ambition had stifled his remorse, and had prevented him from investigating the public rumours of the death of his father; but he hesitated, when the approaching hazards, and scandal of his revolt, began to inspire him with doubts of the truth of Cha-Jaham having been poisoned, and of the guilt of Dara. Aurengzebe, who perceived his uneasiness, soon relieved his scruples. "The report which they are so eager to spread, of the Emperor being still living, is," he said, "an artifice of the very person who has taken away his life. Dara, not content with having caused his father's death, is also desirous to spread snares for his brothers. No, my lord, there is no longer any security for us, except in our union. We have to revenge a father; but we have also to preserve our lives, and those of our wives and children. When, through vain fears, we shall have retired to our governments, and left the parricide to establish himself on the throne; we shall experience the effects of his cruelty, and of our imprudence. It will be, then, too late for us, to repent of having relinquished a just enterprise, easy of accomplishment. As for you, my dear brother, your loss will be greater than mine. We shall have the common mortification, it is true, to see impiety reign, and false religions tolerated; but how great for you the despair, when you shall behold a sceptre, which it has depended only upon yourself to bear, in the hands of a brother loaded with crimes. Let us proceed; hesitate no longer, my lord; and since we must perish if we refuse to combat, let us endeavour to conquer, and by conquering to reign. If Cha-Jaham should still be living, which is hardly credible, we will, after our victory, submit ourselves to so good a father; and make him sensible of our affection, by the signal proofs we had given, of the impatience we were under to revenge him."

The ambition of reigning rendered Moradbax once more credulous. He abandoned himself to his destiny, and followed the counsels of Aurengzebe. It is true, that the uncertainty in which they were, in the armies of the two brothers, whether the Emperor was dead or living, was not without foundation. It was doubted even in Delhi. Cha-Jaham, who had retired to Agra, in vain shewed himself to the people upon the great balcony of the palace. "It is nothing," they said, "but a phantom, some mock representation of the king." In the meanwhile, the emissaries of Aurengzebe took care to entertain Indostan with the false notion of his death.

The rebel army kept still advancing towards Delhi. Aurengzebe considered that no time should be lost. He was apprehensive, that Sultan Chacu, occupied in the pursuit of Cha-Chuia, upon the territory of Bengal, would return with his victorious troops, and augment the strength of the Emperor's forces. It was dangerous, besides, to allow time to his own troops, to be undeceived on the subject of the Emperor's death. With these views, he hastened his march. In the meanwhile, Cha-Jaham, indignant at the conduct of his sons, whose daring he had not been able to repress by his letters, proposed in his council, to take himself the field, show himself at the head of his troops, and disarm his children by his presence. This, doubtless, was the expedient which ought to have been tried. It is probable, that Moradbax would not have persisted in his revolt, if he had seen his father. The partisans, whom Aurengzebe had in the council, diverted the Emperor from so prudent a resolution. They represented to him, that it would be exposing to too great danger, the life and the authority of the sovereign. They added, that if their natural daring prompted the rebels to fail in respect to him, he would be without resource; that in case of their disobedience, his army was too weak to make head against the two princes; that his health, besides, was not sufficiently re-established; and that the fatigues of war might produce the most fatal consequences. It was thus, that Calil-Cham, secretly a friend to Aurengzebe, delivered his sentiments. Without doubt, he contemplated, at this very time, the treason, which he afterwards executed; and which proved so fatal to the Emperor. They even say, that he employed the charms of his wife, and the tears of Begom-Saeb, to retain Cha-Jaham in the haram.

Dara, who was unable to resolve to leave his father, neglected to take the field, and to lead in person the army, which was about to face that of the two brothers. Jacont-Sing and Cassam-Cham were the two generals selected to command in his place. Presents and promises were not wanting to attach them to his service. But, Cassam-Cham had brooded a long time over an injury, which had exasperated him against Dara. Under these captains, the Imperial army marched to encounter the forces of the two rebels.

Upon the banks of the river Ugen, a hill rises in the form of an amphitheatre. It was here, that the Imperial army encamped, to dispute the passage of the confederate troops. The army quitted Agra towards the end of the month of April, when the heats are the most felt in the Indies. The waters of the river were at a low ebb, and fordable in more than one place. Aurengzebe, who led the advanced guard of the rebel troops, was the first to appear in the presence of the enemy; but as the rest of the army was not come up, his chief care was to prevent the Imperialists from passing the river, and beginning the action. He disposed some artillery upon the banks of the river, at the spots where it appeared the shallowest, and made a terrible fire upon the enemy, drawn up on the opposite bank. By this means, this able captain gave time for the remainder of the troops to arrive, and to take some repose after the fatigues they had suffered from the heat, and their long marches. If Jacont-Sing had engaged in action on the first appearance of Aurengzebe, his success would have been certain; but he had received orders to remain upon the banks of the river, and to prevent the rebels from passing it.

As soon as his troops had been refreshed, Moradbax, who conducted the rear guard of the two armies, caused his soldiers to approach the shores. His natural courage and impetuosity would not allow him long to deliberate. He threw himself into the river with an intrepidity inspiring to his followers. The cannon, in the meantime, of Aurengzebe protected the soldier, plunged to his middle in the stream, and compelled the enemy to abandon the opposite bank. The bottom of the river Ugen is stony, and the Indian soldiers wounded their feet, which were naked, in treading upon the sharp rocks. Cassam-Cham, who maintained a secret intelligence with Aurengzebe, might have hindered the passage of the two brothers, but he had neglected to secure the aid of his artillery. It is even said, that the preceding night, he had caused the powder and the bullets to be concealed. Jacont-Sing alone performed his duty. He disputed the passage of the river with extraordinary valor; but nothing could resist the impetuosity of Moradbax. The efforts of that prince were further increased, when he beheld Cassam-Cham give ground. He then conceived, that he should have little trouble, in contending only with the troops of the Raja. In effect, this Indian general, who saw himself abandoned by his Mahometan colleague, made his retreat as a brave man, accompanied only by five hundred horse. The gallant prince, after his defeat, retired to his own territories, not daring to appear at court. The loss which he experienced of so many Rajepoots weakened his state. Aurengzebe drew great advantages from so complete a victory. He made himself master of all the baggage, and of the whole artillery of the enemy. There is still to be seen on the banks of the river, where the battle was fought, a mosque and a caravansary erected by Aurengzebe. This Mogul desired, that one should be considered as a monument of his glory, and the other an evidence of his piety.

The news of so deplorable a defeat diffused terror, alike, through the states of Jacont-Sing, and at the court of Cha-Jaham. The wife of the Raja, a princess of the blood of Rana, who called himself a descendant from Porus, was in the greatest despair, when she learnt the defeat of her husband. On his presenting himself at the gates of the citadel, which served him for a haram; the princess caused them to be closed. "It is not possible," she said, "either that Jacont-Sing is vanquished, or that he should present himself again to my sight, after his defeat. If not victorious," she added, "he must be dead; assuredly, he could never have been so dastardly, as to survive his dishonor. If, then, he has lost his life, either in the combat, or by his own hands, what remains for me, but to follow him to the grave." This princess, in a state of desolation, had the funeral pile prepared, on which she purposed to terminate her life, agreeably to the custom of Rajepoot women. Her mother had much difficulty in diverting her from so horrible a resolution. It was not possible to persuade her, even at last, to open the gates of the palace to her husband, till she had been assured, that Jacont-Sing had fought courageously, and that he would not have lost the victory, but through the cowardice of Cassam-Cham.

On hearing of the defeat of the Imperial army, there reigned a still greater desolation in the capital. As soon as Cha-Jaham received the tidings, raising his eyes to Heaven, he cried:—"Thanks be rendered to the Eternal, who disposes me by little and little, and as it were by gentle steps, to the loss of my crown." Then falling into a sort of swoon, "O Lord, thy will be done," he said, "it is for my sins that you afflict me! I have merited much greater punishment, than the losses with which I am visited." Dara had very different sentiments, when he learnt that his two brothers had passed the river Ugen, and that the army of his father had been defeated. Never did passion express itself with more vehemence. He struck his hands together in agony; he stamped with his feet; he broke out into invectives against Cassam-Cham. Turning, afterwards, all his rage against Mirza Mula, "It is that traitor," he said to the Emperor, "whom we ought to regard as the cause of our misfortunes. If he had not delivered up the troops, of which he was the commander, to Aurengzebe, this rebellious son would never have been found to come and insult his father. Let all his wives," he added, "be beheaded, and let the absent father be punished by the death of his children, whom we hold as hostages." The command of the prince would have been obeyed, if it had not been opposed by Cha-Jaham. The Emperor appeased the rage of his son, and changed his purpose of revenging himself, into a salutary determination to defend his rights.

Aurengzebe and Moradbax, elevated by their success, believed themselves invincible. Nothing was heard among the soldiers but discourses full of rash expectations.

"Aurengzebe," they exclaimed, "will lead us into Persia after the conquest of the Mogul empire, and from Persia we shall pass into Turkey." It was by such reports, which the emissaries of this prince disseminated among the troops, that they animated their courage. They even assured the soldiers, that they were sure of a second victory over the parricide Dara; and that Aurengzebe had in the Imperial army more than thirty thousand Musselmen attached to his interests. The propagation of these reports through the two camps, to the advantage of Aurengzebe; and the affectation of giving to him alone all the glory of the victory, occasioned suspicions to arise in the mind of Cha-Abbas, the faithful eunuch of Moradbax. He was persuaded, that the elder of the two brothers laboured only for his own interests, and that he imposed upon the credulity of his master. He came to a resolution, in consequence, without communicating it to Moradbax. He formed the design of assassinating Aurengzebe, when he should come according to custom to pay his court to his brother, for the purpose of saluting him as king. It is not known by what arts, Aurengzebe penetrated the intentions of the eunuch; it is only known, that he did not come according to custom into the tent of his brother; and that he contented himself with sending his son Sultan Mahamud. It was a maxim with Aurengzebe, that it was equally necessary to take precautions against the snares of his enemies, and to dissemble his distrust of them. Without, therefore, appearing to have discovered the conspiracy of Cha-Abbas, he arranged with his brother, that it was necessary the two armies should advance without loss of time to Agra. During their march, those, who were discontented with the court, and almost all the friends of Aurengzebe, came to join the confederate princes. Such as remained with the Emperor only staid behind, to give Aurengzebe intelligence of all the proceedings of his father. Thus Cha-Jaham, on all sides betrayed; abandoned by his bravest generals, just ready to fall a victim to the persecutions of two of his children, took an extraordinary resolution, which, doubtless, must have been suggested to him by some friend of Aurengzebe. He transferred the whole of his authority to Dara. He even commanded his people not to acknowledge, at least for a time, any other sovereign than his son. This step caused the ruin of the father, and eventually deprived the prince of the sceptre. Many of the nobles, that from duty and affection, where yet attached to Cha-Jaham, refused to obey Dara; and the people, discharged by this measure from the fidelity which they had sworn to the old Emperor, appeared to entertain great indifference for the cause of the new. Some historians report, that Dara caused his father to be arrested, as soon as he had entrusted himself to his hands ; but M. Manouchy, who held at that time an employment in the palace of the prince, declares, that he always behaved to Cha-Jaham with that respect and submission, to which he was entitled.

This almost universal desertion of the nobles, and lukewarmness of the people to the party of the court, did not prevent Dara from assembling one hundred thousand horse, and fifty thousand foot. One hundred pieces of artillery were taken from the arsenals of Agra, the smallest of which carried balls of twelve pounds weight. All the officers who served the artillery were Europeans. Sixty elephants were equipped for war, with towers on their backs, each carrying a small piece of field artillery. Five hundred camels were charged with the prince's baggage. With this considerable army, Dara quitted the capital, to take the field. It was on the 14th of May, in the year 1656. In beholding this prodigious number of troops, extending themselves as far as the sight could reach, in the great plains which environ Agra, it might have been imagined, that the prince would inevitably have forced victory to declare in his favor. The more sensible persons did not so judge. In the principal members of this great body, they perceived a certain leaven of hatred against the chief. Dara was the only person who was unsuspicious of his danger. The conceit he entertained of his own merit would not suffer him to imagine, that any one could fail in fidelity to him. However, the time had arrived, when the great men of the empire had it in their power, to take vengeance for the dishonor, with which Cha-Jaham had covered them, in debauching their wives; and for the bitter railleries, with which they had been taunted by the prince. To increase his misfortune, the son of Dara, Sultan Chacu, deceived by the counsels of Jasing, had obstinately continued to pursue Cha-Chuia into Bengal, and was unable to form a timely junction with his father. The young prince had with him the choicest troops of the empire. The army of Dara was, in consequence, almost entirely composed of new raised troops, and of officers of suspicious fidelity.

The feelings of Cha-Jaham, when he embraced his dear son for the last time, are not easily to be described. "I was in hopes," he said, "to have left you, after my death, a kingdom in the full enjoyment of peace. Heaven has not permitted it. Go, my son; go, and crown yourself with your own hands. If the Eternal is favorable to my petitions, he will cause to fall upon rebellious children the maledictions of their father, and he will shower upon an affectionate son all the blessings which he merits." Begom-Saeb accompanied with tears her adieus to her brother. The prince then quitted the fortress of Agra, and proceeded to take the command of his army. Never had warlike preparations appeared on a more magnificent scale in India. The camp, formed on the plan of a great city, had its streets and its bazars. The imperial tents, entirely covered with gold brocade, placed in the centre of the camp, and the magnificent pavilions of the officers and nobles, dispersed by intervals throughout a vast circuit, elevated themselves above the huts of the simple soldier, and presented a picturesque appearance. Dara would have preferred waiting, in this post, for the junction of the troops of his son; but he learnt that the enemy was advancing with a celerity, which would oblige him to break up his camp, and advance to the encounter. Nothing could be more splendid than the march of so formidable an army. As the army advanced simultaneously, one part taking the route of the hills, and the other of the vallies, the steel of the javelins, which shone resplendently in the mid-day's lustre, and were variously agitated, according to the movements of the squadrons, caused it to resemble the waves of the sea, when reflecting the sun's rays. The army marched, for four days, in this fine order; and at last arrived upon the banks of the river Chambal. It was here, that the prince deemed it advisable to wait either for the arrival of his son, or that of the enemy. He fortified the banks of the river with all his artillery, and so strongly entrenched himself, that he could not be attacked with any probability of success. The rebels soon appeared on the opposite bank. Dara did not think proper to pass the river for the purpose of engaging the enemy. The ground, on the opposite side of the Chambal, was observed to be unequal, and mountainous; consequently, his elephants would have been useless, and his numerous army would not have been able to extend itself.

On his side, Aurengzebe (not imagining it would be possible to force the passage of the river, in the presence of an army, more numerous than his own, and intrenched on the opposite bank) considered that it would be better to employ some ingenuity. He, in consequence, assembled his principal officers, and represented to them the danger which might attend delaying the battle. He added, that if Soliman Chacu should join his father, the only course left them would be a retreat. He conjured them, therefore, to be constantly in readiness to follow him to battle; and gave them to understand, that it would be necessary, at every hour of the day, to be in a condition to pass the river, and fall upon the enemy. This intelligence, which was reported in the camp of Dara, kept him constantly upon the alert. In the mean while, the indefatigable Aurengzebe negotiated in secret with the Raja Champet, an ancient enemy of the court, for obtaining a passage through his territory, that he might proceed to cross the river twelve leagues higher up than the camp of his brother, in a spot where it was fordable. The Raja complied with the request of Aurengzebe, who sent a detachment of eight thousand only of his troops, which he caused to take their route through an unfrequented tract of country, in the midst of mountains and forests. As soon as these troops had taken possession of the passage, the whole army of the two brothers decamped during the night, and took its way to the ford, through the states of the Raja. The news of the sudden departure of the enemy astonished Prince Dara. There was still, however, time to have remedied the evil. If due celerity had been employed, they would have found the army of the two brothers upon the banks of the river, fatigued with a long march; and they would easily have defeated half-drowned soldiers, in a state of general confusion. This was the measure, which Dara proposed to take; but Calil-Cham found means to persuade him, to bestow upon him the command of the force, which was to proceed to encounter the two brothers at the place of their passage.

Dara, who, with the highest courage, had no experience in war, and possessed of the best understanding, was too sincere to entertain suspicion, abandoned himself to the pernicious counsels of his most cruel enemy. Calil-Cham acted in all things in concert with Aurengzebe. The traitor gave him time to pass the river, and intrench himself among mountains, till the arrival of Moradbax. It is even said, that Aurengzebe and Calil-Cham had a private conversation in a neighbouring forest, and agreed upon the measures which they had to take, to ruin the party of Dara. At least, it is certain, that there appeared always, afterwards, between the head of the rebels, and the first general of the troops of the Emperor, an intelligence, which could scarcely have been contrived, but by means of an interview.

Ram-Sing, second general in the army of Dara, and chief of those brave Indian Rajepoots, who obey only a Raja of their own nation, was of opinion, that a battle ought to be fought without delay, and that Aurengzebe should be forced in his intrenchments, before he could complete his means of defence. Calil-Cham exaggerated, in a council of war, the difficulties of so hazardous an enterprise. "I have examined," he said, "the enemy's camp, and have found the approaches to it impracticable. Let us wait," he added, "till famine, or imprudence, shall have drawn our enemies from their post; we shall then engage them with advantage." The traitor was believed, and the advice of the faithful Ram-Sing was neglected.

The troops of the two brothers, at length, quitted their defiles, and appeared in the open field; Dara, then, again proposed to attack them immediately. The ardour of this gallant prince was once more restrained, and the vivacity of his soldiers was suffered to abate. He was even advised, to range all his artillery at the head of his army, upon a single line. Calil-Cham had assumed an authority over the chief of the cannoneers, and had prohibited him from obeying any orders that did not emanate from him. Aurengzebe and Moradbax, in the mean time, advanced with a resolute countenance. Before they were within reach of the cannon, Calil-Cham caused his artillery to make a terrible fire, without a single discharge being capable of annoying the enemy. Dara, who was mounted upon his elephant, was unable to perceive, by reason of the smoke and dust, the treason of the general, who had placed himself in the advanced guard, that he might, he said, sustain the first shock of the enemy. After a useless firing, on the side of the imperial troops, there was heard, for the first time, three discharges, which proceeded from the artillery of Aurengzebe. This was the signal agreed upon, for the purpose of conveying intelligence to Calil-Cham, that the rebel army was prepared to enter upon the action. In effect, the traitor, hastening to Dara, who commanded in the centre of the army; "It is now the time, my lord," he said, "to go and destroy an enemy, already nearly put to the rout by the fire of your artillery. The foe is very deficient in cannon," he added; "they have only as yet replied to ours by three discharges. Shew yourself only, my lord, and the victory is yours."

The manner of drawing up armies in India is very different from that practised in Europe. It is not a number of small squadrons, commanded by a great number of officers, or battalions, which may easily be made to change their positions; it is large corps of troops, commanded by a single officer, which remains united in one body, and which can with difficulty be separated or divided during a battle, for the purpose of affording aid, where danger is most pressing. The two armies were placed in array in the following manner. Dara was in the centre of the army, and his division was opposed to that of Aurengzebe, posted in the centre of the rebel army. Ram-Sing, with his Rajepoots, made head against Moradbax, who was posted in the right wing of the confederate army; and Calil-Cham opposed the large force which fought under his orders, to the Sultan Mahamud, to whom his father had given the command of the left wing of the rebel armies. In this order it was that the troops of Dara were the first to give ground. Calil-Cham prohibited the artillery from firing, whilst the Imperialists were advancing to engage the enemy. The corps, in which Dara commanded, was the most active. It presented itself before Aurengzebe with horrible shouts. The soldiers of the Emperor let fly their arrows, upon an enemy, whom they thought already thrown into disorder by their cannon. Aurengzebe suffered them to approach, and without precipitating his discharge, he caused his cannon, his musquetry, and his archers to take aim at so just a distance, and so opportunely, that there were seen to fall around Dara a prodigious number of dead. This carnage did not intimidate the prince. He advanced with fury into the midst of the squadrons of Aurengzebe. He penetrated even to the spot, on which the enemy had planted the batteries, which occasioned the greatest loss to his followers. He put the Portuguese cannoneers to flight, and then directed all his efforts against the great body of troops which surrounded Aurengzebe. Never was greater intrepidity seen on one side, or greater bravery on the other. Dara, by his voice and gestures, recalled to their duty such of his followers, as the pursuit of plunder was carrying away from the action; and Aurengzebe, keeping his battalion always in compact order, waited his brother's attack with the greatest presence of mind, purposing to take advantage of the least fault into which his ardour might betray him. It is even said, that

Aurengzebe, resolved to perish or conquer, on the spot on which he was attacked, caused those sort of chains to be attached to the feet of his elephant, which are used to be affixed when it is necessary to constrain them to proceed only at a short pace. Having thus deprived himself of the means of flight, he directed his petitions to Heaven with that air of piety, which he never relinquished amidst even the greatest dangers. He exhorted the chiefs of his troop, to give up their lives for the interests of their religion. The historians of the country say, that by a miracle evidencing the protection of heaven, Dara changed his purpose, and quitted his attack on his brother, to direct his rage in another quarter. Had the prince persevered in his attack, it is more than probable, that Aurengzebe would have been taken prisoner, and the war terminated.

Calil-Cham, who only made a feint to engage Mahamud, but who caused himself to be informed, every moment, of what was passing between the two brothers, learnt the peril of Aurengzebe. To relieve him from it, he caused Dara to be informed, that his best officers had been killed; that the son of Aurengzebe, fighting like a lion, had destroyed the bravest chiefs of the Imperial army; and that in order to deliver his father from the danger which menaced him, he was about to make an attack on the troops of Dara, with a victorious force. On receiving this false intelligence, Dara let go his hold, suffered Aurengzebe to escape, and hastened to encounter Mahamud, whose soldiers were yet fresh, having only been feebly attacked by Calil-Cham.

Moradbax had not been assailed with less vigour by the gallant Ram-Sing. This Raja, followed by his Rajepoots, had forced the advanced guard of the Mogul prince, and, at last, had arrived sufficiently near to Moradbax, to be able to engage hand to hand with his enemy. Moradbax was mounted upon a war elephant, and seated on a kind of throne, open on all sides, that he might be enabled to issue his orders in every quarter. Already, the Indian who guided the elephant of the prince had been slain by an arrow. Moradbax took his place, and while with one hand he guided his elephant, with the other he threw darts at Ram-Sing, who had attacked him with the greatest resolution. The Mogul prince received no less than three arrows in his face, which, however, raised only the skin. The Raja, whose quiver was empty, and who could not reach his enemy, dismounted from his horse, with the intention of piercing the elephant of the prince under the belly. This rash attempt cost Ram-Sing his life. Moradbax struck him with his javelin, and overthrew him in the dust. The elephant of the Mogul prince crushed the Indian prince with his trunk, dashed his head against the ground, trampled upon him, and ended with depriving him of life. The Rajepoots, who were discouraged, on witnessing the death of their chief, were soon put to flight, and by their desertion contributed to the loss of the battle. Dara endeavoured in vain to rally them. The Indian soldiers never obey any other voice than that of their Rajas. These fugitives spread through the empire a report of the entire defeat of the Imperial army.

There remained to Dara a sufficient number of troops for securing the victory, even after the desertion of the Rajepoots. He continued, therefore, the action, and directed his efforts against Mahamud with success. Calil-Cham, who fought under the eyes of the prince, made at this period some efforts, the better to conceal his treason. The squadron of Mahamud had been penetrated, when Aurengzebe and Moradbax, who had dispersed the troops which had made head against them, having formed a junction, came to make a charge upon Dara. The combined troops of the two brothers were not found sufficiently strong to contend with him; they often lost ground, and were unable to recover it. Moradbax, at last, was put to flight. Aurengzebe himself maintained his ground with difficulty. It was at this moment, the perfidious Calil-Cham succeeded, by a bad counsel, to blast the hopes of Dara, and to render useless all the fruits of his valour. "You are, my lord," said the traitor, humbling himself in the presence of the prince, "victorious; and the first of your campaigns effaces the glory of all the Moguls. In order to complete the work which you have begun, it only remains, that you pursue the two fugitive brothers, and make them serve for your triumph. Dismount from the elephant which bears you. You are too much exposed to the arrows, to be able long to sustain, without danger, the fierceness of the encounter. Mount on horseback, and let us pursue the enemy." The unthinking Dara followed a counsel, the consequences of which he did not foresee. Mounted on one of those Persian horses, which are so much esteemed for their fleetness, he rushed upon, and forced a passage through his enemies. Aurengzebe felt alarmed at a resolution, which menaced him with the destruction of his hopes of empire; but the troops of Dara, who no longer beheld their prince seated on his elephant, in the view of his army, thought him dead; and panic struck with apprehensions of the loss of their chief, there was no longer any thing but disorder in the Imperial army. Like to the clouds, when they are propelled by a strong wind, the soldiers took to flight with a rapidity which astonished the general. The prince then perceived, when it was too late, the treachery of Calil-Cham. "Let him be pursued," he exclaimed, "and cut to pieces!" The traitor had already taken measures for his own security. Followed by a large squadron, devoted to his party, he had passed over to the army of Aurengzebe. The unfortunate Dara, who beheld one of his generals slain, and the other a deserter to the enemy; his two brothers become superior by the desertion of his troops; and the best part of his army routed; no longer thought but of effecting his retreat. He accomplished it in better order than might have been expected, from his slight experience in war. The fight terminated at his departure, after having continued ten hours. It had commenced at seven o'clock in the morning, and was not ended until five in the afternoon.

Aurengzebe, who saw himself no longer with an enemy to oppose, took possession of the tents and baggage of the imperial army. The dissimulation, and deep policy, of this prince, was never more conspicuous, than in the moderation he displayed, after his victory. He reserved the tent of Dara, and the imperial quarter, for his brother Moradbax. As for himself, having retired privately to a hut, he remained a long time in prayer. Afterwards, with the air of a man inspired, holding in his hand the Alcoran, he entered the apartment of his brother, and presented to him Calil-Cham. "It is to Heaven," he said to him, "it is to you, my lord, and to this faithful friend, that we are indebted for the victory. I have returned thanks to the Eternal, who has appeared for the preservation of the law of his prophet, by the defeat of his enemies. I now prostrate myself before my master. It is you, my lord, who, by a valor without example, with troops exhausted from fatigue, have dispersed the numerous army, which was opposed to you by Dara. There only now remains for me to solicit your favor for the gallant and faithful Calil-Cham. It is he, who, by great services, has rendered fortunate the commencement of your reign; it is he, who merits to sustain, under you, the weight of that empire, of which you are about to become the master. As for me, my lord, my destiny is about to be accomplished. As soon as a third victory shall have fixed you on a throne, you so much merit, I shall go and reign over my passions in solitude, whilst you will cause to reign in Indostan the true religion."

It was, in this manner, that Aurengzebe discoursed in public, but, secretly, he exerted himself to procure friends on every side. His design, in bestowing Calil-Cham upon Moradbax, as his minister and confidant, was to get intelligence of the secrets of his brother, and to secure his ascendancy over him. Night and day he was employed in sending off dispatches to his correspondents at the court of his father, to the Viceroys of Indostan, and the governors of the strong places.

The first care of Aurengzebe was to write to the two generals, who commanded under Soliman Chacu, to acquaint them with the victory of Moradbax (it was thus that he expressed himself), and to let them know the defeat of the Imperial army, and the flight of Dara. He commanded them to put their chief to death, or to bring him in chains to his camp. Jasing and Dalil-Cham were the two generals, who, under the son of Dara, had pursued the fugitive Cha-Chuia into his government of Bengal. Jasing was the Raja, whom Dara had formerly insulted, by applying to him the opprobious term of musician. As for Dalil-Cham, he was a man of a venal mind, always inclined to range himself on the side of the strongest. However, neither the one nor the other were so cruel as to dip their hands in the blood of a Mogul prince, or to deliver him up to his enemy. They adopted a more moderate course. They persuaded the unfortunate Chacu to retire to the mountains, if he desired to preserve his life. The prince was compelled to follow the advice of these two cowardly deserters of the royal cause. With a small escort, he took his route towards the territory of the Raja of Sirinagar, a prince always steady in his loyalty to the Emperor. It is even said, that the two generals, through avarice, had the cowardice to cause him to be pillaged in his march. The young sultan, arrived, at last, almost without attendants, in the kingdom of the mountains; and the two generals proposed proceeding to augment the strength of the brothers.

In the mean while, Dara, who had escaped with difficulty from the pursuit of the rebels, appeared at nine o'clock in the evening, at the gates of Agra. He did not dare to remain in this capital, least the conqueror should arrive to form the siege, and endanger his falling into his hands. The shame, besides, of coming into the presence of his father, vanquished, and as a fugitive, overpowered his affection, and prevented him from entering the palace. As he was naturally eloquent, the picture he drew of his misfortune was affecting in the extreme. Sometimes the violence of his grief, too strong for his reason, caused him to say the most extravagant things. He was heard to break out into invectives unworthy of so great a prince. Dara was, therefore, contented with writing to Cha-Jaham, and his affectionate sister Begom-Saeb, two letters, which he meditated at leisure, and which drew tears from the Emperor and the princess. Cha-Jaham was not less affected with the misfortunes of his son, than with the calamity of the empire. He sent to the prince one of his most faithful eunuchs to console him. He was flattered with the hope, which still remained to the empire, in the troops of Chacu; for, as yet, they were ignorant at the court of his misfortune.

The Emperor committed violence upon himself, in favor of his son. In spite of avarice, which was then his ruling passion, he sent to his disconsolate son ten camels loaded with gold and silver rupees, for the purpose of levying fresh troops. He advised him to take the road to Delhi, to remain there till the arrival of Sultan Chacu, and to assemble fresh soldiers. He added, that he would find, in the stables of the fortress, a sufficient number of elephants and horses, for the equipment of a new army. Thus, Dara fled from the court, without having seen his father; and found himself obliged to go a begging to the people for protection; and to endeavour to move the nobles to compassion by his misery; he, who had been accustomed to exasperate them by his contempt, in the days of his prosperity.

The prince perceived, but too plainly, on his arrival at Delhi, how much the change in his fortunes had wrought indifference towards him in all hearts. The governor of the citadel, gained, it is said, by the promises of Aurengzebe, refused him admittance. The rage, and the menaces of Dara only served to render the governor more obstinate. He was in doubt, how far he should be justified in shewing the least deference, towards an enraged and vindictive, though unfortunate prince. The fugitive sultan was, therefore, obliged to seek at Lahor, a retreat, which was denied him at Delhi. It was in that city, that at a distance from the enemy, he collected the wreck of his army. The people, who had more affection for him than the nobles, were sufficiently disposed to volunteer their services; but he was in want of officers. Dara, indeed, might, in his own person, have been equal to the conduct of his armies. The battle, which he had lost, had instructed him in the science of war; and his valor and capacity would have been able to supply what he wanted in experience. In fine, if to conquer in battle had been required only, Dara would have reigned; but it was necessary to contend also against the artifices of Aurengzebe. The prince disdained the employment of intrigue; he was naturally too little suspicious to discern his brother's snares; or had he discerned them, was wanting in the adroitness which might have enabled him to escape his trammels.

On the 8th of June 1656, a few days after the battle, Aurengzebe and Moradbax caused their victorious troops to advance to the environs of Agra; and they pitched their camp within two miles of this capital, near the imperial garden.

The first care of Aurengzebe was to send one of his most faithful eunuchs, to his father Cha-Jaham, to make professions of obedience. The ambassador had special instructions to cast the blame of the measures adopted by the two brothers, upon the bad conduct of Dara, and the abuse he had made, to their prejudice, of the power, which the Emperor had conferred upon him. "Your sons, my lord," said the eunuch to the Emperor, "have not made war through ambition, or a refractory spirit. They know how to respect, in you, their father and their sovereign. The cause of their arming is, that they have found, in their elder brother, a tyrant rather than a brother. This, my lord, is the sole reason why they have taken up arms, on the uncertain rumours of your death. You live, and Heaven, which has restored you to health, subjects to your commands your two sons. They have selected me for their envoy, to give you assurances of their submission, and the acknowledgment of your supremacy, as their lord and Emperor. It was to revenge you that they have conquered; it is at your feet that they come to lay their laurels. Judge, my lord, of the distinction, which justice requires should be made, between two sons worthy of your esteem by their valor and their victories; and a son generally hated by all the nobles, whom Heaven is about to punish for his pride." Cha-Jaham replied to the eunuch with the dignity of a sovereign, but with the moderation of a prince, who finds himself upon the point of being invested by a formidable army, whose chiefs it might be dangerous to irritate. "Assure my children," he said to the eunuch, "of my affection for them. Their past disobedience has not entirely extinguished it. I shall always retain it, provided they render themselves worthy of it. Let them dismiss their armies, and let them come and implore, in my presence, the forgiveness, which I am willing to bestow upon them. They shall experience the clemency of a father, who has a just right to punish them."

The Emperor, in the meanwhile (who knew Aurengzebe too well, he said, to confide in his professions), thought of retiring from Agra. The rebels had an interest in not suffering their prey to escape them. Troops were posted in every direction, and prevented any person from leaving the city. If the people of the Indies had resembled the people of Europe, Agra would have been able to sustain a siege for a sufficient length of time, to afford Dara an opportunity of raising a new army, and hastening to the succour of his father. But the Indians, accustomed to servitude, care little about a change of masters. They are contented with blindly obeying, without feeling any interest, concerning the individual to whom they are to render obedience. The only resource left Cha-Jaham, for extinguishing the rebellion, was to inveigle his two sons, on the pretext of a friendly conference, to enter the citadel without escort, and then to take away their lives. Aurengzebe was too prudent to fall into so gross a snare. He never ceased disseminating, throughout Agra, a report, that he was about to visit his father, to be reconciled to him, and to submit himself to his commands. By this means, the citizens were cajoled, and neglected making any effort to obstruct his designs. In the meanwhile, he deferred, from

from day to day, his visit to the Emperor, and secretly negotiated with the officers of the court, who still preserved some remains of affection for his father. As soon as he had secured his interests in that quarter, he caused his son Mahamud to enter the city of Agra, in order to blockade on that side the citadel, whilst Moradbax surrounded it on the side of the country. The surrender of Agra restored to liberty the wives and children of Mirza-Mula, who had been retained as hostages.

Cha-Jaham, from the loftiest tower of his palace, easily perceived that his citadel was invested. Necessity, as well as a feeling of indignation, roused in him a portion of that warlike disposition, which he had possessed in his youth. He caused his artillery to be planted on the rampart, and fired upon the rebels. The cannon of the haram produced little effect on the side of the country, and destroyed only a few houses in the town. The army of Moradbax, therefore, advanced, almost without loss, to the foot of the wall. A great firing of the artillery lasted for three days, and as many nights. At last, Aurengzebe, who remained in the camp two miles distant from Agra, where he counterfeited sickness, sent the eunuch, whom he had before employed on a similar embassy, to visit his father in his name. He entreated, that the Emperor would pardon the audacity of his troops. It was, he said, against his orders, that they had approached so near the citadel. He begged his father to consent, that the Sultan Mahamud should in his name visit him, and make his submissions to him. He added, that an improved state of health would soon allow him to pay his respects to him in person. Mahamud, in the meanwhile, did not neglect to plant a battery, for the purpose of making a breach in the imperial palace. It was about to be reduced to dust. Cha-Jaham, therefore, consented to the proposal of Aurengzebe, and suffered his grandson to enter the fortress.

The Emperor had prepared the presents, which he destined for Mahamud. It is said, they were of inestimable value. This was a bait to draw Aurengzebe himself into a snare. The young prince, by the instructions of his father, entered the fortress; and as he had gained the soldiers of the first watch, he made himself master of it without difficulty. He caused himself to be followed into the interior of the palace by a considerable troop; and with this escort, he penetrated to the Imperial apartment. Soldiers, women, slaves, and eunuchs; every one without distinction, whom he encountered in his progress, were put to death. Mahamud having, at last, reached the presence of Cha-Jaham; "Your great age, my lord," said Mahamud to him, "has rendered you incapable of reigning. Terminate in tranquillity the remainder of your days; and retire with your wives to those delicious gardens, which you have caused to be adorned at so great cost. We do not envy you the light of day; but it is necessary you should resign to your children, a place, which you dishonor." At these words, a great shout was heard from all the Tartar women, who wait upon the prince in his apartment; and who are instructed like men in the use of arms. Their menaces were vain. It became necessary to yield to force; and to pass into the apartment of the gardens, without the circuit of the fortress.

The unfortunate Cha-Jaham, betrayed by his children, kept in a species of captivity by his grandson, reduced to a country palace, where he was surrounded only by women; bethought himself of a stratagem, which might have cost Aurengzebe the empire. He caused Mahamud to be invited to pay him a second visit. As soon as he saw the young prince approach, he threw himself at his feet, and spoke to him in this manner:—"If I am so unhappy as to be dethroned by rebellious children, assume courage, my son, and suffer not these guilty princes to enjoy the fruits of their crime. I place my crown in your hands, a crown which you appear worthy of wearing. The city of Agra is subject to your orders; your troops have rendered you master of it. Profit by so favorable an opportunity; and revenge me, by withdrawing yourself from servitude under an ungrateful parent, who after having dethroned his father, will not spare his own son." Mahamud was startled at the offers of Cha-Jaham. He considered for a moment; wavering between a passion for empire, and the danger which might attend the attempt to acquire it. As he had good sense, he did not allow himself to be dazzled by illusory hopes. All the officers of his army were attached to Aurengzebe; consequently, had the prince shewn the slightest disposition to be guilty of infidelity to his father, he would have found himself abandoned by his followers. Mahamud contemned, therefore, so brilliant a temptation; and contented himself with obliging the Emperor to deliver up to him the keys of the apartments, and of the treasures of the palace.

The people, in the meanwhile, touched with compassion for the misery of Cha-Jaham, began to complain of the inhumanity of the two brothers, and especially of the proceedings of Aurengzebe. They were unable to reconcile the piety, of which he made profession, with the condition to which he had reduced his father. This able politician put an end to all these murmurs, by a stratagem of which he availed himself, to give some colour to his conduct. He caused, it is said, the hand-writing of Cha-Jaham to be counterfeited; by which means, a letter was supposed to have been written by the Emperor to Dara. He was made to announce to his dear son, that it would be proper he should draw near to Agra with a body of troops; that Aurengzebe and Moradbax would soon be entrapped in a snare, which he had laid for them; that by pretending affection, he had engaged the two rebels to pay him a visit; and that he had men prepared to put to death his two sons, as soon as they should come into his presence. This counterfeited letter was delivered to Aurengzebe in a circle of the principal officers of his army, as if it had been intercepted by his vigilance. All were astonished at the cruelty of the father towards his children. The prudence of Aurengzebe was extolled, who till then had deferred paying a visit to Cha-Jaham; and the indignation, which they had began to feel towards the sons, was turned against the father.

It was at this period, that the two princes disposed of the public employments. All orders were given conjointly by the two brothers. The treasures of Cha-Jaham, and the revenues of the empire, were divided equally between them. The liberality of Aurengzebe became then unlimited. He rewarded his former friends, and procured for himself new partisans. Cha-Stecam, the uncle of the two princes, was made governor of Agra. Every thing was tranquil in the capital; without, therefore, further delay, the two armies began their march in pursuit of Dara. The friends of Moradbax were of opinion, that he had better not accompany Aurengzebe, in the expedition he was entering upon. "Your presence," they said, "is necessary in the neighbourhood of Agra. You will, by this means, be at hand to prevent a rising of the people. Remain here, and do not engage yourself in a hazardous enterprise." This credulous prince listened only to the promises of his brother, and suffered himself to be carried away by his natural impetuosity, and his love of glory. The two armies, in consequence, took the road to Delhi, following always the course of the river. After some days march, they encamped near a town named Matura.

Here, upon a hill, stands a magnificent mosque, an ancient monument of the piety of the first Mogul sovereigns. Aurengzebe had the art to make Moradbax believe, that in a few days, he would be crowned Emperor on this spot. They stopped, therefore, at Matura, one of the most fertile and agreeable situations in Indostan. Never did the caresses of Aurengzebe, and his deference for his brother, appear more unaffected. As the two camps, though separated by the river, communicated with each other by several bridges, Aurengzebe every morning and evening passed into the tent of his brother, and conversed with him upon no other subject, than the magnificence of his approaching coronation. He deferred it, in the meanwhile, from one day to another, upon various pretexts. At one time, the magnificent tents, which were preparing, were not finished; at another, the presents destined for him were not ready; sometimes, it was the dilatoriness in providing the new dresses, with which the whole army was to be clothed; then, the harness for the horses and the elephants had not been completed at the appointed time. Moradbax waited without impatience for a ceremony, which he thought secure. The discipline, in the meanwhile, of the two camps, was very different. On the side of Moradbax, the chief and the soldiers abandoned themselves to pleasure. In the tent of the prince nothing was heard, except concerts and dramatic exhibitions; feasting and dancing were their sole occupation. Notwithstanding the law of Mahomet, wine was not spared on these occasions, but was indulged in to excess. On the side of Aurengzebe, the greatest silence prevailed. Discipline was strictly observed. Prayers were said in the evening, in the morning, and at mid-day, with the same punctuality as in the cities. Councils were frequently held. The principal officers, instructed in the plans of Aurengzebe, discoursed only with their soldiers, on the happiness they would possess; in having for their sovereign, a prince, whose manners were so pure, and whose disposition was so pious, as were those of their chief. At last, the day for the coronation of Moradbax was fixed for the 15th of June of the year 1656.

The spot, chosen for the ceremony, was a plain, which served as a place of exercise, in front of the mosque of Matura. Tents were set up around this place framed of the richest gold brocade. The whole circuit was covered with magnificent painted cloths, forming a sort of canopy, supported by silken cords, which defended the assemblage from the sun's rays. A theatre was prepared, opposite the mosque. It was there, that Moradbax was to receive the turban, and the Imperial sabre, from the hand of the Cazi, or chief of the Mahometan religion. Moradbax was prevented from suspecting the designs of his brother, by all these preparations. The evening that was to precede the ceremony, Aurengzebe feigned a slight indisposition; and caused Moradbax to be invited to his tent, for the purpose of consulting with the astrologers, whether the day fixed for the coronation would be a fortunate one. In vain his faithful eunuch, Cha-Abbas, endeavoured to persuade his master, that every thing was to be apprehended from a brother of so artful a character. The unfortunate prince suffered himself to be led by his evil destiny, and obeyed only his prepossessions. He entered the camp of his brother, followed only by Cha-Abbas, and some officers of his army. He had scarcely crossed the river, when Ebrahim-Cham, touched with the calamity in which this good prince was about to precipitate himself, ventured to seize the reigns of his horse, and said to him:—" Whither are you going, my lord, and what evil star leads you to Aurengzebe?"—"I go to fetch the crown," replied Moradbax, "it is from his hands I shall receive it." At these words, the good Ebrahim let go the head of the prince's horse, and retired, weeping. The daring of the officer offended Moradbax, and intoxicated by ambition, he continued his march towards the quarter occupied by his brother. The Cazi received Moradbax on his arrival in the tent of Aurengzebe, and made him a compliment, calculated to warn him of his danger. "Your entrance is fortunate, my lord," he said to him; "may it please the Almighty that your departure may be equally so." He had scarcely said these words, when Aurengzebe made his appearance, followed by the principal chiefs of his army. Never were his caresses more affectionate, and the respect shewn to Moradbax more marked. Aurengzebe caused his brother to be seated in the place of honor. He chased away himself the flies which molested him; with a piece of linen he wiped off the perspiration which ran down his face. During the conversation, which was long, he repeatedly called Moradbax, his master, his lord, and his sovereign. A bath of rose water was prepared for him, and a grand repast was afterwards served up. This is the first time, they said, that Aurengzebe has permitted the use of wine at his table. The two brothers eat by themselves, whilst the officers of Moradbax were entertained by the generals of Aurengzebe, in tents at some distance. Cha-Abbas, alone, remained near his master, and never quitted him. The joy of the two princes was animated by music and dancing. Aurengzebe, who never put off the air of piety, of which he made a profession, drank nothing but water. As for Moradbax, who was not so scrupulous, he drank wine to excess. A deep sleep succeeded to his intoxication. Cha-Abbas caused the prince to retire to a neighbouring tent, that he might take some repose. The eunuch was seated at the feet of the bed, on which his master was sleeping. Inquietude, through presentiments of danger, occasioned some time to elapse before sleep overtook him. Weariness, at length began to overpower his senses, when he was awoke by Aurengzebe, who appeared suddenly before him. The eunuch was alarmed, and his exclamations were nearly awaking Moradbax; but he recovered himself, when he perceived that Aurengzebe was followed only by a child. This was the young Azam, son of Mahamud, only six years of age. Then, Aurengzebe, as if he intended his brother only a piece of pleasantry while sleeping, promised his grandson a jewel, if he could take away from the prince his sabre and his poignard without awaking him. The child acquitted himself very dexterously of the office, and conveyed the arms of Moradbax into the adjoining tent. At the same instant, six soldiers belonging to the guard of Aurengzebe, holding in their hands chains, which they destined for the prince and his eunuch, by the noise they made around his bed, awoke Moradbax. The gallant Mogul, who, on awaking, beheld himself surrounded by unknown persons, made an effort to sieze his sabre, which he no longer found lying beside him. He uttered, then, a loud shriek, but his voice was stopped by their placing their hands upon his mouth. Aurengzebe, who blended sentiments of piety with every occasion, exclaimed, in raising his hands to heaven:—"Let the law of Mahomet be revenged of the contempt of an intemperate prince; and let a man, who has rendered himself unworthy of a throne by his impiety, be secured." Aurengzebe was obeyed. The prince suffered himself to be loaded with the same chains of silver, which his brother had for a long time caused to be made; and which he often shewed to his son Mahamud, to keep him to his duty. As for the eunuch, he was secured without difficulty, and loaded with irons.

Two elephants were provided, and waited for the two captives. Each was made to occupy one of those litters, which are borne on the back of elephants. It is known that the prince, in departing, made use only of these short words to his brother:—"Are these then the oaths, which you have sworn to me on the Alcoran?" One was now made to take the road to Delhi, and the other that to Agra, under a like escort.

All this was dispatched with so little noise, and with so much secrecy, that nothing of it was known in the camp of Moradbax, or in the tents where the officers, who had accompanied him, were entertained. The music still continued. All the night it was heard in the tent of Aurengzebe, as if the two brothers were still passing their time in it in rejoicing. At break of day, the soldiers of the two armies assembled in the vast circuit which had been adorned for the coronation of Moradbax. An order had been issued, that they should attend without arms, as a measure of precaution, in the event of those broils, to which these sort of spectacles sometimes givebirth. Every one expected, soon, to see arrive the brother of Aurengzebe, to seat himself upon the throne, which had been prepared for him. Their expectation was frustrated. Some squadrons of the troops of Aurengzebe, well armed, surrounded the enclosure on all sides. Certain persons, then, posted for the purpose, cried out with a loud voice, "Long life to the Emperor Aurengzebe." At these cries, the soldiers of the two camps became united in one mass; and as if they had been governed by one sentiment, they repeated in concert, "Long life to the Emperor Aurengzebe." In effect, this prince appeared soon afterwards upon the platform, which had been prepared for his brother; seated himself for a moment upon the throne, and then retired. What is most surprising, is, that so sudden a change did not cause the slightest movement, or the least alteration in the minds of the people. Besides, that the naturally passive disposition of the Indians easily acquiesces in these sort of revolutions, the prudence of Aurengzebe had provided against every contingence. He had attached to himself the greater part of his brother's dependants, and had taken care to prevent those, whom he had not been able to corrupt, from throwing any impediments in his way. The empire became, in consequence, the fruit of an intrigue, the best sustained, and the most ably conducted, of any recorded in history.

When it was time to reign, Aurengzebe threw off the the mask. That Faquir, who a little time before, only aspired to lead a private life near the tomb of Mahomet; after depriving of their liberty an imbecile parent, and an imprudent brother, now proclaimed himself Emperor.

Whilst Moradbax was being conveyed a prisoner to the citadel of Delhi, Aurengzebe prepared for pursuing Dara to his retreat at Lahor. Of the army of Moradbax, and of his own, he composed but one force, in which he caused a uniform discipline to be observed. Dara, on his side, had already assembled more than thirty thousand men, composed of Patans, Persians, and Indians. The Raja Surup-Sing, whose states are at a short distance from Cachemire, brought him the further aid of four thousand Rajepoots. This was a small force for so powerful a Raja. Dara, therefore, in the hope that Surup-Sing would, in due time, reinforce him with all his troops, had placed the daughter of that prince among the number of his wives. Dara's preparations were well known to Aurengzebe. He made it his whole application to thwart the alliances of his brother, and to corrupt his partisans.

Daut-Cham was the most faithful of all the officers, whom Dara had in his service. He commanded a pretty considerable body of cavalry, posted at the passage of the river Bear; which Aurengzebe was necessarily obliged to cross, in order to arrive at Lahor. This was the only obstacle that the new Emperor had to encounter on his march. Aurengzebe despairing of being able to force the post, had recourse to artifice, and endeavoured to gain Daut-Cham by negociation. But this chief was more a man of honor, than Persians are commonly found, when transplanted to the Indies. He resisted the solicitations of Aurengzebe. The Emperor then tried to render the officer suspected, in the hope, that, by such means, a man, he had been unable to corrupt, would be superseded in the command of an impregnable post. He caused a letter to become current in Lahor, by means of his emissaries, as if written by Daut-Cham, wherein a correspondence was implied as subsisting between that general and Aurengzebe. It is the fatality of princes, who have suffered calamity by an overweening confidence, to become afterwards suspicious to a high degree of injustice. Dara, who had ruined his fortunes in the last engagement, by placing too great confidence in Calil-Cham, lost himself a second time, by falsely suspecting a faithful servant. Daut-Cham was withdrawn from his post. The prince with difficulty suffered him to continue in any duty about his person; and at last banished him entirely his presence; after having given him permission under his own hand, to embrace the interests of whichever party he pleased. The passage of the Bear became, in consequence, free, through the cowardice, or the treason of the officer who was appointed in the place of Daut-Cham.

The formidable army, which Aurengzebe marched by hasty journies across the plains which extend from the river Bear to Lahor, terrified the troops of Dara. The prince found himself on a sudden abandoned, both by his Mahometan troops, and by the hope he entertained of being soon assisted by the Indians of Surup-Sing. There appeared to him no alternative, but to seek an asylum in Persia, and to traverse, as a fugitive, the great kingdoms which extend beyond the Indus, as far as Candahar. This was his safest course; but misfortune, which never ceased to persecute Dara, would not permit him to execute his project. The governors of Multan and of Cabul were devoted to Aurengzebe. To pass through their jurisdictions would have been attended with the danger of exposing himself to be surprised, and delivered up to his rival.

In the almost universal desertion, in which the eldest son of Cha-Jaham found himself, there yet remained to him one faithful friend, and a fortress, at his devotion. This friend was a eunuch; his real name history has not preserved, but it has furnished us with that which the friendship of princes in the Indies sometimes confers on their favorites. He was called "The Flower of the Spring." The fortress which remained to the prince is known in the Mogul states by the name of Bakar. It is situated on a spot where the river Sindy, augmented by the junction of five rivers, spreads itself into a wide and deep bed, and forms a species of lake. It was here, that the faithful eunuch placed in security the best troops of his master. He caused to be transported thither, from the arsenals of Lahor, cannon, powder, and provisions; and shutting himself up in it, determined to arrest, by his resistance, all the forces of Aurengzebe, while his master was engaged in making his escape into Persia. The resolution of this faithful servant gave fresh courage to Dara. Followed only by some domestics, he descended the Indus, and, after suffering incredible fatigues, arrived in the kingdom of

Guzurat, where he sought a temporary asylum. It was here that the prince found an interval of repose, and received some assistance, whilst waiting for a favorable opportunity of passing by sea to Ormus. Aurengzebe continued to follow the track of the fugitive, and after some long marches, he arrived at last in the kingdom of Multan. Here it was that unexpected intelligence occasioned him to relinquish his march, and obliged him to abandon the enterprise of Bakar, and return to Agra.

Cha-Chuia, the first of the sons of Cha-Jaham, who left the province of which he was viceroy, (that of Bengal) to make an attempt to possess himself of the throne of his father; having recovered from the fears which his conqueror, Soliman Chacu, had spread throughout his government, had a second time advanced towards Agra, with a considerable force. As the pretext for his first expedition had been to revenge the pretended death of Cha-Jaham; the pretence for his second enterprise, was, to deliver the Emperor, and his brother Moradbax, from the captivity in which they were held by the usurper. Cha-Chuia, who experienced no opposition to his march, advanced with a surprising celerity towards the capital. It was equally important to Aurengzebe, to pursue the track of an enemy who fled before him, and to advance to encounter a new enemy, who was in a condition to act upon the offensive. There was reason to apprehend the assembling of fresh forces on the part of Dara, and that Cha-Chuia might avail himself of a favorable interval to acquire a superiority, and get possession of the capital. In this two-fold difficulty, Aurengzebe hastened where the danger was most pressing. After having confided to Bader-Cham the conduct of the army which was to undertake the siege of Bakar, and afterwards to pursue Dara to his very last place of retreat; he flew towards Agra, attended by a small escort. The peril, in which he found himself upon his route, was the most critical and unexpected of any which he had ever encountered. The Raja Jasing, who, more through the fear of Aurengzebe than any affection he had for him, had abandoned the cause of Sultan Chacu, was advancing towards Multan, at the head of ten thousand Rajepoots. He gave out, that he was about to join his troops to those of the conqueror. But he was much surprised, when he beheld Aurengzebe retracing his steps to Agra, accompanied only by a small number of guards. He felt persuaded, that the new Emperor had been defeated; and that having been put to flight by Dara, he was seeking an asylum in the capital. The sight of a prince, whom he believed vanquished, and a fugitive, caused a sudden revolution in the mind of the Indian. With these impressions, he formed the design of sacrificing Aurengzebe, and of liberating from captivity Cha-Jaham, to whom he had been always much attached. Aurengzebe was sensible of his perilous situation; but it was not by flight that he sought to divert the danger. With an air of intrepidity, which attracted respect, he passed through the midst of the troops of the Raja. Afterwards, addressing himself to their chief: "Our common enemy," he said to him, "is entirely routed. Wandering through the provinces of Indostan, Dara is gone to find, in Guzurat, the death which he seeks to avoid, but which he cannot escape. I have ceased pursuing a wretched man who is no longer worthy of my care; and I hasten to confront another rebel. Vanquished before by your arms, Cha-Chuia is come to make trial of his strength with ours. Follow me, noble Jasing, and the same aid which you have brought for the contest with Dara, lead against your ancient enemy." These words, pronounced with an authoritative air, occasioned Aurengzebe to be treated with respect by the Raja. He reflected, that the death of Aurengzebe would serve the cause of Dara, to whom he was a personal enemy. He came to the resolution, therefore, of obeying; and as an instance, illustrative of the levity of the Indian character, Jasing was then seen to place his Rajepoots in the train of the very prince, whose assassination he was but a few moments before meditating.

The new antagonist of Aurengzebe called forth all his energies. Cha-Chuia possessed, alike, bravery and prudence. He displayed both, in an eminent degree, in his conduct of the war against Aurengzebe. He learnt that his brother, followed by Jasing, whose valour he had but too well experienced, was advancing to meet him, at the head of that formidable army, which the Sultan Mahamud commanded in the neighbourhood of Agra, during the absence of his father. Cha-Chuia determined to intrench himself, and wait for the enemy. The position which he fixed upon was convenient, and naturally fortified. It was a large hamlet called Caiva, environed with mountains and forests. His army was encamped upon the banks of a small lake, which was the only spot where water was to be found within a circuit of four leagues. The whole plain on the side of Agra was covered with a sterile sand, where neither fountains, trees, nor meadows were to be seen. Cha-Chuia waited in this situation for the army of Aurengzebe. He flattered himself that his brother would arrive, and waste his troops to no purpose before a camp he would find to be unassailable. His expectation was realised. Aurengzebe appeared before Caiva, at the season, when the summer heats are the most oppressive. The excessive fatigues, which his army experienced, by the precipitation of their march, and the great privations in which it found itself, when it came into the presence of the enemy, are incredible. Forage and provisions were equally wanting. The greatest suffering to which they were exposed was the want of water, in a soil parched by the devouring heat of the climate. It was found necessary to bring it from the Ganges, upon the backs of camels, and to seek it at a distance of more than six leagues. This was a labour, which it would have been impossible long to sustain, if the propitious stars of Aurengzebe had not favored him on this pressing occasion.

Mirza-Mula, having left his confinement at Orangabad, after the liberation of his wives and children, conducted to Aurengzebe, in his camp at Caiva, the fresh levies which he had made in the Decan. The sight of so great a captain, and so faithful a friend, reanimated the hopes of the new Emperor, at a season, when his embarrassments were at their height. Mirza-Mula gave the prince a counsel worthy of his long experience. He proposed that a report should be spread among the soldiers, that it would no longer be possible to subsist before Caiva; and that it would be necessary to decamp the next morning at the latest. This rumour passed from the camp of Aurengzebe into that of Cha-Chuia. He believed it too hastily, and, without sufficiently investigating it, made preparations to assault the troops of his brother in their retreat. A great silence was maintained at day-break in the intrenchments of Aurengzebe. Orders had been given, that no fires should be lighted, and the tents were commanded to be furled, as if the camp had been abandoned. Finally, troops; camels, and elephants bearing burdens, which commonly compose the rear guard of the armies in the Indies, were made to appear taking the road to Agra. The feint succeeded agreeably to the expectation of Mirza-Mula. Some soldiers of Cha-Chuia quitted their mountains and forests, to pursue, as they imagined, the fugitive Aurengzebe. The rear guard, which was attacked, faced about to the enemy, and repulsed his first squadrons. Assistance was diligently dispatched, on the part of both armies, in support of the attacked, and of the assailants. At last, the whole of both the armies appeared in open field. Aurengzebe came out of his camp, which was supposed to have been abandoned. Cha-Chuia now perceived that he had, at last, imprudently committed himself to a combat, which, till then, he had wisely avoided. However, he did not lose courage. The two brothers fought the most sanguinary battle, India had ever witnessed. Intrigue had no share in the victory, valour alone decided it. It is remarkable, that the followers of Cha-Chuia should have maintained a uniform fidelity towards him; Aurengzebe not having been able to corrupt a single partisan, or officer. The brothers, in consequence, sought to decide their pretensions by a personal conflict. The eldest was mounted upon an elephant, unparalleled for strength. This furious animal overthrew, with his trunk, every thing which was opposed to his passage. Preceded by the squadrons of the prince's guard, an opening was made for him to advance to the spot where Aurengzebe was fighting. It is impossible to describe the fury with which the soldiers of Cha-Chuia joined battle with those who defended the new Emperor. At last, the two princes drew sufficiently near to each other, to be able to combat hand to hand. Each, mounted on his elephant, shot arrows at the other, and emptied his quiver; but, an accident, which occurred, seemed to menace the life of Aurengzebe. It does not appear whether it was by chance, or design, that the girths of his elephant gave way, and that the seat upon which he was placed leaned on one side, and threatened the Emperor with a fall. It is at least certain, that Aurengzebe gave ground, and caused his elephant to retire. The impetuous Cha-Chuia followed his brother with vigour, not being aware of a snare. A wide trench had been purposely excavated, and a surface formed, composed of branches of trees intertwined, and some sand well levelled.

The elephant of the prince plunged, with his enormous weight, into the trench, and was incapable of extricating himself out of it. Cha-Chuia was, therefore, compelled, by necessity, to adopt the same course, which bad counsel had occasioned Prince Dara to follow, in another action. He quitted his elephant, to mount on horseback. Thence followed the disorder of his troops. As soon as the prince was no longer beheld combatting from the tower of his elephant, fear took possession of all hearts. Every one took to flight. Cha-Chuia himself, borne along by the press of the fugitives, fled in his turn, and retired to the city of Eleabas.

A rumour, however, of the defeat of Aurengzebe, was spread throughout Agra. Some deserters from his army, who had seen him in that perilous situation, when on the point of falling from his elephant, hastened to carry the news of his death to the capital. This report, which continued prevalent some days, caused Raja Jacont-Sing to hasten to the deliverance of his master, Cha-Jaham; that he might efface the shame of his former flight, and re-establish himself in the good opinion of the princess, his wife. He made, therefore, all possible diligence, in order to present himself before the citadel of Agra, and release the old Emperor from his captivity. All was fruitless. Aurengzebe, after his victory, gave in charge to Mirza-Mula the care of continuing the pursuit of the vanquished; and took himself the road to Agra. The arrival of Aurengzebe extinguished every project of rebellion. Jacont-Sing then found himself under the necessity of flying a second time, and returning to his own territory, again to endure the reproaches of an imperious woman.

Aurengzebe placed the capital in a state of security, whilst Mirza-Mula, who commanded in chief the victorious troops, compelled Cha-Chuia to fly from one city to another, along the course of the Ganges, and to seek on every side an asylum, which was in every place denied him. At last, after a number of marches, he intrenched himself in an inaccessible position, where he collected what he was able of his former army; and caused himself to be joined by the new levies, which he had procured to be raised in Bengal. It was here, that he practised against Aurengzebe those arts of seduction, of which Aurengzebe had so often availed himself against his brothers. He tried to detach the Sultan Mahamud from his father's interests, and to induce him to favor his own. He was not ignorant of the mortifications to which Aurengzebe had subjected this young prince. Independent of the species of servitude, in which the Emperor had till then kept him; by giving the command of his army to Mirza-Mula, Mahamud was reduced to the rank of a subaltern, and obliged to obey the orders of an inferior. The prince, who, on account of his great merit had become an object of jealousy to his father, suffered some expressions of dissatisfaction to escape him, which came to the knowledge of Cha-Chuia. He availed himself of so favorable a circumstance, tempted the fidelity of his nephew, and gained him to his side. Mahamud quitted the camp of his father, to go and combat under the orders of his uncle. Never did he give greater proofs of bravery than during the period of his revolt. In its consequences it was very injurious to the cause of Aurengzebe. Many of the officers ranged themselves on the side of the nearest heir, whose virtues and whose valour rendered him worthy of the throne. The disobedience of the son would have proved fatal to the father, had not Mirza-Mula taken measures to bring it to a period. He sowed so many jealousies between the uncle and the nephew, that Mahamud growing disgusted, quitted the cause he had inconsiderately embraced. The repentance of Mahamud was not followed by an equal return on the part of his father. Aurengzebe was sufficiently sensible, from the conduct which he had himself observed, how dangerous it is for a sovereign to trust a son of an enterprising disposition, and capable of throwing off the yoke of subjection. He deliberated, whether he should rid himself of a prince, who might find the means of struggling against him with a success equal to that, which had resulted from his own enterprises undertaken against his father, Cha-Jaham. He recalled him to his presence by writing to him letters of the most soothing and affectionate nature; while, at the same time, by others written to Mirza-Mula, he commanded him to take care that the prince took his departure under a strong escort. The young prince was sensible of his situation, when the opportunity for escape was lost. After some fruitless attempts to deceive the vigilance of his guards, and to reach the kingdom of Sirinagar, the ordinary place of refuge for guilty or unfortunate princes, he was shut up in a close litter, placed upon the back of an elephant, and conveyed to the citadel of Guallier; to which fortress they were about, also, to transfer the unfortunate Moradbax. The detention of so great a number of princes, whom Aurengzebe had sacrificed to his ambition; and the defeat of his two most formidable enemies, gave him time to respire. In this interval of tranquillity, he meditated taking the reins of empire in good earnest, and causing himself to be acknowledged Emperor by the people, as he had already been by the armies. He transported himself therefore to Delhi, which he entered in triumph, in the midst of the acclamations of the inhabitants. He here established his court, in the magnificent palace, which had been built by his ancestors. Money was coined in his name, with the following inscription: "I, the King Aurengzebe, conqueror of the world, have caused this money to be struck, resplendent as the sun."

The repose, which the Emperor enjoyed, was not of long duration. Prince Dara had collected new forces in Guzurat. There was reason to apprehend, that his claims to the empire, assisted by the aversion which was beginning to manifest itself towards the new sovereign; and by the compassion which the people ordinarily feel for unfortunate princes; might eventually prevail against the artifices and the good fortune of Aurengzebe. The Raja, Jacont-Sing, always so well affected towards the loyal cause, had promised to lead against the usurper ten thousand Rajepoot soldiers, as soon as Dara should appear in the field, with a force capable of making head against his brother. The designs of the prince, and of the Raja, did not escape the vigilance of Aurengzebe. He gained over Jacont-Sing by negotiation, whilst he proceeded to finish the war against Dara, by a final conflict. The surprise of this unfortunate prince was extreme, when he learnt at the same time, the infidelity of Jacont-Sing, and the approach of Aurengzebe. There was no longer any opportunity for retreat. It was in the hottest season, when it is difficult in the Indies to undertake long marches. He was not certain, besides, of being able to engage with any chance of success, in the open country, an enemy much more numerous, and hitherto victorious. There remained, therefore, no choice, but that of intrenching himself in a fertile country, where he might subsist his troops, and wait for favorable circumstances. The intention was good, but the new Emperor and his followers did not allow the prince time to put it into execution. The army, which Aurengzebe had confided to Bader-Cham, after the first defeat of Dara, quitted the siege of Bakar, and came to attack the prince in the rear, whilst Aurengzebe assailed him in front. It was not possible for Dara, who saw himself placed between two fires, to make head against two armies, the least of which was more numerous than his own. He fled, and with difficulty found refuge for his wives and children, under the walls of Amadabad.

The defeat of Dara spread terror among the governors the best disposed towards him. The gates of all the cities, and of all the fortresses, were closed against him. Bader-Cham continued the pursuit with indefatigable activity. He had orders to bring him, dead or alive, to Aurengzebe. The prince, followed scarcely by two thousand soldiers, traversed the plains of Sindy, marching night and day, and suffering incredible hardships. Abandoned, at last, by his followers; without aid, without an asylum; destitute of provisions, or resource; having been disappointed in his hopes of reaching the Persian territory by sea; he directed his way thither by land. He flattered himself with experiencing facilities in his flight. The governor of the province of the Mogul States, which confines upon Persia, was named Given-Cham. This nobleman was indebted both for his fortune and his life to Dara. He would have been trampled to death under the feet of elephants, by the order of Cha-Jaham, for an atrocious offence of which he was accused, if Prince Dara had not solicited his pardon. This wretch received his benefactor with every demonstration of the sincerest gratitude. He solicited him to accept a hospitable welcome for some days. He gave up the apartment of his women to Normahal, the favorite wife of Dara. The traitor, notwithstanding, gave intelligence to Bader-Cham, that he had Dara in his power; and that he kept a strict watch upon his motions. The prince soon perceived, that under the mask of paying him honor, he was, in fact, retained a prisoner. When he complained, Given-Cham either treated his apprehensions with ridicule, or endeavoured to tranquillize him by futile excuses. Normahal, on her side, sensible that the career of her husband was approaching its termination, sought an opportunity of taking poison. When on the point of swallowing it, (the princesses of the East carrying ordinarily about them poison concealed in their rings, that they may have the power, at any time, of terminating their misfortunes by a voluntary death) Normahal was diverted from her purpose by her chief eunuch, who gave her a ray of hope, by offering to assassinate Given-Cham. In effect, he enclosed in a brocaded sack a pocket pistol, resolved to discharge it at the heart of the traitor. He approached him carrying the sack in his hand, as if it had been a present, which he brought from the princess. The governor received him without suspicion. When the eunuch was sufficiently near, he drew the trigger of the pistol, which missed fire. There are calamities so inveterate in their nature, that nothing, apparently, is able to arrest their course. Of the truth of this, Prince Dara had proof. Every thing conspired to accelerate his fate. After the ineffectual attempt of the eunuch, the governor kept no longer any measures with his prisoners. He prohibited the princess leaving her apartment. The unfortunate Normahal, overwhelmed with grief, deprived of the consolation and counsels which she had been accustomed to receive from her faithful eunuch, who was massacred by Given-Cham, listened only now to her despair. After embracing her children—"I will never," she said, "consent to survive my husband. Never shall the cruel Aurengzebe have the gratification of dealing to me the severest blow which yet awaits me, in exposing to my view the head of Dara. O Heaven, that I should be so dastardly, as to suffer myself to endure a wretched widowhood, shut up in the haram of my enemy! Or rather, what is even more horrible to my imagination; if I should be so miserable as to be placed among the number of his wives!" Having uttered these words, she swallowed the poison, which passing into her veins, put a speedy end to all her sufferings. The cries of her women drew the prince into the apartment of the sultaness. He beheld her expiring, and no longer thought but of following her. Two days after Bader Cham arrived; invested the governor's house, and made himself master of the apartment of the prince. He saluted him with the most profound respect; but these first marks of deference were succeeded by the rudest treatment. Some soldiers seized upon the person of Dara, threw him to the earth, loaded him with chains, and confined him in a litter, preparatory to his being conveyed away upon the back of an elephant. Bader-Cham, conducting his prisoner, resumed the road to Bakar, that he might proseoute the siege.

The remains of the partisans of Dara still maintained in that place the cause of their master. That generous eunuch, named, the Flower of the Spring, when first besieged by Bader-Cham, had displayed greater valor, and more fidelity, than might have been expected from a person of that class. He was still disposed to weary out, by a long resistance, the army of his enemies; but it became necessary to yield. He received an express order from Dara himself, a captive in the besiegers' camp, to deliver up the place to the troops of Aurengzebe. The grief of this faithful adherent cannot easily be expressed, when he learnt the captivity of the prince, and received a command to surrender the only asylum which remained to him. He quitted Bakar, after making an honorable capitulation; and received permission to retire to the kingdom of Cachemire.

Bader-Cham carried in person to the Emperor the news

of his success, and conducted Dara to Delhi, where the court was residing. He entered the city, as it were in triumph, exposing to the view of the people the captive prince, mounted on an elephant, his feet in chains, on an open seat, upon which was placed by his side the youngest of his children. All the people regretted a prince, rather indeed of an imperious temper, but yet possessing many amiable qualities. They drew a comparison between the former government, as administered by Dara, with that of which they had present experience. Aurengzebe was averse to an interview with his brother. He gave orders, that he should be conveyed to a fortress without the walls of the city, and secured there under a strong guard.

The policy of Aurengzebe was not restricted to the retaining of Dara in a state of captivity, similar to the other princes of the blood. The aversion, he had to this prince, was more a personal antipathy, than the result of ambition. However, in order to give to his conduct a colour of justice, he caused a general council to be assembled, composed of all the nobles of his court, and of the principal commanders of his armies. He proposed to them, with great apparent indifference, the question; whether it would be better to retain Dara in a state of perpetual captivity, or to take away his life. The object of Aurengzebe was to detect, by this means, those who secretly favored the prince; having resolved not to spare one, who, from any remains of attachment to him, should give his voice for the preservation of his life. The council guessed the motive of the Emperor. Every one voted for putting him to death. One person only, who had been his particular enemy, was bold enough to advocate the cause of the unfortunate prince. Whether it was through a refinement in policy, or by an effort of probity, it is difficult to decide; but, it is certain, that this conduct appeared to Aurengzebe himself so truly generous, that he placed him among the number of his friends.

Dara was waiting in his prison the decision of his fate, when his son was taken from his arms, to be conveyed to the citadel of Guallier, the ordinary place of confinement for unfortunate princes. When the father found himself deprived of his son, he rightly judged, that it was time to think of preparing for death. The Christian sentiments, with which the missionaries had endeavoured to inspire him, were revived in the closing hour of his life. He requested to be allowed a conversation with Father Busée, a Flemish jesuit, who had formerly instructed him in our sacred mysteries. All communication with the Europeans was denied him. In this universal desolation, the prince sought for consolation in God. He was heard to say, more than once:—"Mahomet has destroyed me; Jesus Christ, the son of the Eternal, will save me." A few hours before he was put to death, Aurengzebe caused a captious question to be put to his brother:—"What would you have done to the Emperor," they said to him, "had he fallen into your hands, as you have fallen into his?"—"He is a rebel, and a parricide," said Dara; "let him judge of the treatment he has merited, by reflecting upon his crimes; and such deserts he would have received with the utmost rigour at my hands." This answer exasperated Aurengzebe. He only now sought a minion, who would have the barbarity to execute his orders. Nazar, one of the slaves of Cha-Jaham, whose occupation was that of a writer to the Emperors, offered himself for this cruel service. He proceeded to the spot, where Dara was expecting the moment, which was to terminate his miseries. He found the prince in his apartment, raising his eyes to Heaven, and repeating these words:—"Mahamet mara mïcuchet, e ben alla Marïam mi bacchet;" which is, "Mahomet gives me death, and the

Son of God will give me life." He had scarcely finished these words, when the executioner threw him to the earth, and cut off his head. Such was the termination of the life of a prince, in whose character was blended such a mixture of virtues and defects, as to render him more capable of reigning over the Mogul states, than adapted for maintaining himself in the possession of them. He died on the 22d of October, in the year 1657, lamented by the people; and regretted even by those who had abandoned, and betrayed him.

The hatred, which Aurengzebe had conceived against his brother, did not end with the life of that unfortunate prince. He caused the head of Dara to be brought to him; he examined it with an air of satisfaction; he touched it with the point of his sword; he opened his closed eyes to observe a speck, that he might be convinced that another head had not been substituted in the place of the one he had ordered to be struck off. He added, at last, insult to cruelty. "Here are then," he exclaimed, "the remains of that imbecile man, who would have deprived me of a crown, which he was incapable himself of wearing." He followed afterwards the counsel of Roxanara Begom, an ancient enemy of her brother Dara, and always attached to the cause of her brother Aurengzebe. He caused the head of the prince to be embalmed, and conveyed to Cha-Jaham, enclosed in a box. The poor Emperor, at that time a prisoner in the citadel of Agra, was at table, when he received the present, which they came to offer him in the name of Aurengzebe. Before the box was opened; "It is at least a consolation," he said, "for an unhappy father, to find that the usurper has not wholly forgotten me." But, when, on opening the packet, he beheld the head of Dara, that son so tenderly beloved, the good old man fell into a swoon. The Princess Begom-Saeb, always faithful to the cause of Dara, made the air resound with her cries. Nothing, indeed, could be more affecting, than the melancholy and despair, excited by so tragical a spectacle, in the prison of Agra.

All which now remained to Aurengzebe, in order to secure to himself the permanent possession of the empire of the Moguls, was to compel Cha-Chuia to desist from carrying arms against him; and to get into his power Sultan Chacu, the eldest son of Dara. It has been already stated, that this prince had retired to the kingdom of the mountains, the territory of the Raja of Sirinagar. The Emperor succeeded in both enterprises, partly by force, and partly by artifice. Disembarrassed from the long war, which he had been obliged to wage against Dara, he caused all his troops to march on the side of Bengal. Mirza-Mula kept the Prince Cha-Chuia in a state of blockade in that country. This prince, with the utmost difficulty, preserved alive the remains of his almost expiring faction. As soon as he received the news of the reinforcements, which had arrived from all quarters to the assistance of Mirza-Mula, he found that he had no other resource but to take to flight. The kingdom of Arracan, till then impenetrable to the arms of the Moguls, offered him an asylum. This country is on every side surrounded by mountains and forests. Its situation, in consequence, shelters it from insult. As it borders upon the territory of Bengal, it was easy for the prince to retire to it. He, therefore, wrote to the king of this region, the most uncultivated in all the Indies, to entreat that he would grant him a temporary asylum in his dominions. He promised, that 'ere long, he would leave Arracan, and embark for Moca; from which place, he should take his departure, to implore the assistance of the King of Persia. The perfidious monarch meditated profiting, on this occasion, by the spoils of the fugitive prince. He offered Cha-Chuia a retreat in his states, and promised to defend him against all the persecutions of Aurengzebe. The retreat of Cha-Chuia had all the appearance of a precipitate flight. The Portuguese, who at that time inhabited Chitagong, a maritime city of the kingdom of Arracan, and the nearest to the states of Bengal, took upon themselves the charge of conveying the prince, his wives, his treasures, and some officers of his household, in some small barks, which they were accustomed to use in carrying on a trade of piracy. It is said, that the Portuguese caused the brigantine, freighted with the money and the jewels of the prince, to founder, and then plundered it. Cha-Chuia arrived with great difficulty in the kingdom of Arracan, where he found in the monarch of the country, as dangerous an enemy, as the one from whom he fled. After some shew of affection and respect, submissions were exacted, derogatory to a prince of his rank. They wished to compel him, to attend, and pay his court regularly to this petty sovereign. His daughter was demanded, that she might be numbered among the wives of the prince of Arracan, the eldest son of the king. They were displeased at his complaining of the repasts, which were served up to him, in the Indian fashion. Lastly, they imputed to him as a crime, the Mahometan sect to which he belonged. These mortifications, occasioned the prince, at first, some discontent, which broke out afterwards into murmurs. It is even said, that Cha-Chuia had formed designs upon the life of the king. Whether this be true or not, the imprudence of Cha-Chuia cost him his life. The subjects of the king of Arracan invested on all sides the palace in which the Mogul was residing. The unfortunate Cha-Chuia, found no longer any security, but by flying to the forests. He saved himself in their sequestered haunts; but these tigers pursued him; and after having

T

massacred, without pity, his wives and his children, they deprived him of life on the 7th of February, in the year 1658. Cha-Chuia was the second of the three brothers of Aurengzebe, who fell a sacrifice to his ambition. It may be said, that this poor prince merited the punishment inflicted upon him by Providence. It was he, who, by his rashness, and his revolt, originated that cruel war; the result of which was, to arm the sons against the father, and brothers against brothers. It is even probable, that his bad example paved the way for the invasion of Aurengzebe. Cha-Chuia dearly paid for the first shock which was given by him to the authority of the Emperor his father. Always vanquished, he found his death in a foreign land; and massacred by the hands of barbarians, he spared Aurengzebe the obnoxious measure of staining his hands anew with the blood of a brother.

Sultan Chacu, the eldest son of Dara, was not safe in the kingdom of Sirinagar, from the artifices of Aurengzebe. This prince had too much merit, to hope to escape the enmity of the usurper. His first essay in arms had been distinguished by the defeat of Cha-Chuia. Aurengzebe was interested in preventing a shoot of the royal family from taking root in the neighbourhood of his states. The difficulty was, to wrest him out of the hands of the king of Sirinagar, who loved him tenderly, and guarded him from the dangers that menaced him with the greatest vigilance. Independently of the natural mildness and compassionate temper of the Raja, the levity and perfidy so common to the Indians was corrected by his attachment to the principles of Christianity. He was, therefore, far from having any inclination to deliver up the prince Chacu to Aurengzebe; regarding him as a precious deposit, that Providence had entrusted to his care. The difficulty was still greater to wrest him out of his hands by force. The Moguls had formerly made some attempts upon this kingdom; but their armies, unable to obtain subsistence in an uncultivated country, had either perished from hunger, or the soldiers had returned with the loss of their ears and noses, through the severity of the climate. Aurengzebe, unable to succeed in obtaining the co-operation of the father, endeavoured to carry off the Mogul prince through the assistance of the son of the king of Sirinagar. He engaged him by presents, and by still greater promises, to betray Chacu into his hands. A hunting party was proposed; the two young princes separated from each other among the mountains, in the pursuit of their prey; soldiers, placed in ambuscade, seized upon Sultan Chacu, and conducted him to Aurengzebe. The fortress of Guallier became finally the place of his imprisonment; where a prince of the greatest merit, and who had given the highest hopes to the empire, was destined to be buried alive for ever.

Of the three brothers of Aurengzebe, Moradbax alone now remained alive. Although in a state of the strictest captivity, he was, notwithstanding, regarded as a subject for suspicion and uneasiness to the new Emperor. It was necessary, that he should be delivered from this state of inquietude. His death, therefore, was resolved upon, and the pretext, made use of for the commission of this crime, shall be related:—

The mask of justice was borrowed, in order to give a color to this iniquitous proceeding. It is a law with the Mahometans, that a new sovereign cannot make use of his right of life and death over his subjects, until he has received from the Cazi, or chief of the law, a species of consecration, which is regarded among the Moguls as sealing the Imperial jurisdiction. The good old man, who was, at that time, at the head of the religion, and the chief interpreter of the Alcoran, regarded with indignation the usurpation of Aurengzebe. He, therefore, obstinately refused to administer, during the life of Cha-Jaham, to the ceremony, which was necessary in order to put the Emperor in possession of absolute authority. Aurengzebe caused the old judge to be deposed, and a Cazi less scrupulous, and perfectly disposed to favor the inclinations of the court, to be elected in his room. It was from his hands, that Aurengzebe received, by a consecration, the power of disposing at his pleasure of the lives of his subjects.

The first use the Emperor made of his new authority, was to take away the life of his brother Moradbax. Two false witnesses were suborned, to give evidence against him. They deposed, that when the prince was acting as viceroy of Guzerat, he had caused a secretary of Cha-Jaham, who had been sent into his government for the express purpose of investigating his conduct, to be put to death. Aurengzebe heard the accusation with an air of great indignation against the witnesses; but, which he afterwards directed against the accused. "It is, however," he exclaimed, "my brother. Must I be compelled to shed the blood of all my race?" Whilst he was in this apparent affliction, his astrologers, accustomed to consider the language of the passions of princes as proceeding from Heaven, spoke to him after this manner:—"Be assured, my lord, that your reign cannot but be unfortunate, if a criminal compassion hinders you from revenging the very first crime, which has been deferred to your tribunal." Aurengzebe, at last, sighing, appeared reluctantly to yield to the unhappy necessity. Some tears were seen to flow down his cheeks, when he gave orders to some soldiers of his guard, to transport themselves to Guallier, and cause his brother to be stung by one of those adders, whose poison is quick, and mortal. The death of the unfortunate Moradbax placed Aurengzebe, at last, in quiet possession of the throne. Cha-Jaham was suffered to live out the remainder of his days, in a state of captivity. He was an imbecile old man, whose incapacity for holding the reins of government was known to the whole empire. Become, thus, tranquil possessor of the richest monarchy in the world, by the means of intrigue; Aurengzebe rules it at the present day, and sustains by his ability, a sceptre, of which he obtained possession by his policy and valour.

The first care of the Emperor, when he found himself at peace, and without competitors to the throne, was to build his glory on solid foundations. He assembled the historians of the palace, whose office it is to write the Chronicles of the empire. These have been my guides throughout the whole of this work. "Deliver down," he said to them, "to posterity, the history of my conquests; and let my attainment of the crown serve as an example to my successors." The chief of the historians took the liberty of asking the sultan, what complexion he should give to the imprisonment of his own father, and the massacre of his three brothers. "Know," he said to him, "that my conduct was authorised by the condition of the state; and by the support which it was necessary to give to our religion, then in a declining state. An imbecile parent, and brothers the enemies of Mahomet, efface the guilt of my offences. The whole glory of my reign is derived from the protection of the Eternal. It is he, who has conducted by his hand, a poor Faquir, to the possession of the throne; to instruct posterity, that he humbles the proud, and exalts the lowly."

DESCRIPTION

OF THE

Court, of the Military Force, of the Revenue, and of the Government

OF THE

MOGUL EMPERORS.

It was not possible to write a general history of the Mogul Empire, without giving some idea of the court, of the forces, of the resources, and of the government of the Emperors. The elements of what it is now purposed to enlarge upon will, doubtless, have been found dispersed throughout the body of the work. It must, however, be confessed, that the little, which has been inserted, was rather calculated to excite the curiosity of the reader, and to awaken a desire of learning in detail, what it was, then, only possible to touch upon cursorily. The laws of narration do not allow of long digressions for the purpose of entering into detailed descriptions. It was determined, therefore, rather than interrupt the narrative, by distracting the attention of the reader, during its perusal, to reserve any enlargement on these topics, till the conclusion of the history.

There appeared, also, a propriety, in representing under one aspect, the plan of the court; the magnificence, the interests, and the government of the Emperors, whose lives have been just recorded. An ambassador, or the envoy of a company at the court of the Mogul will find in these pages, competent information respecting the manners of the country, to which they may be delegated. Even the simple traveller in Delhi, or at Agra, the merchant, or the missionary, will experience a satisfaction, in knowing the usages of a court, with which it is but too probable they may be compelled to have an intercourse. It is with a view to such usefulness, that M. Manouchi has written, separately, a description of the state of the haram, of the armies, the revenues, and the government of the Mogul, without blending these things with the Chronicle. The ensuing pages will furnish, in an abridged state, without however omitting any of the topics, the substance of whatever the Venetian has described at large. That the public may not be deceived on a subject, in which error might be more pernicious, than it would be in a point of history, he declares, that he relates nothing on the authority of another. All which he relates, he says, is derived from personal observation, and experience. When he wrote his memoirs in the year 1697, he had already resided forty-eight years in the Mogul states. He had travelled through nearly all the provinces of this great empire. He had occupied an honorable post, which had enabled him, with a greater facility than could fall to the lot of the ordinary class of European travellers, to obtain an acquaintance with the interior of the haram; a place most carefully secluded from the notice of the vulgar. It ought, then, not to excite surprise, that a more circumstantial detail should be traced in these pages, of the condition of the Mogul empire, than is to be found in the works of any other writer. It is proposed, in the first place, to give some idea of the court of the Emperors; to which will succeed, a description of their forces, and their armies; a detail of their revenues will then follow; and lastly, an account of their police; and the character of their government.

THE COURT OF THE MOGUL.

IT is not in Europe only, that splendor and magnificence reign at the court of sovereigns. Respect being had to the difference of manners, the court of the great princes of the east is not inferior to that of the monarchs of Europe. That of the Mogul has an air of splendor and magnificence, which dazzles the stranger, and truly astonishes a native of Italy.

The palaces of the Emperor at Delhi and in Agra have, indeed, nothing of the regularity and symmetry which are so much admired in the structure of the great edifices of Rome and Venice. It may be said, nevertheless, that those of the Mogul have their correct proportions, and peculiar beauties, according to the taste in architecture, which prevails in India. This style is not to be viewed contemptuously. In the construction of their edifices, no regard has been had to the Greek style of architecture, with which they are unacquainted throughout the regions of the east; a method has been pursued, that has nothing repulsive to the eye, and which, if respect be had to the usages and climate of the country, has, doubtless, a greater air of convenience than numerous stories, which can never be ascended without fatigue.

The palace of Agra, called in the language of the country, Mahal, serves also for a fortress to the capital. It is built on the banks of the Gemna, in the form of a cross. Viewing it on the side of the city, its form is circular. The walls are lofty, and of a breadth capable of supporting pieces of ordnance of a moderate size, which are planted at intervals throughout the whole length. A fortress of this description is sufficient in India to keep the people in awe. The Mahal may be seen from a great distance; and as the stones have a reddish tinge, and a resemblance to jasper, and are, besides, soft, and easily exfoliate, the whole palace is splendidly illuminated by the sun's rays. It is easily distinguished from the rest of the city. The trench filled with water surrounding it, and the terraced garden, which serves as a rampart round the palace, form, at a moderate distance, a mixed view of running water, verdure, and edifices, which might have a pleasing effect even in Europe.

A wide space of ground, the whole length of that side of the palace which fronts the capital, separates in some measure the Mahal from the city of Agra. It is on this spot, that the Rajas exercise their troops. These Indian princes, (each in his turn,) have their week of attendance as commanders of the guard, which is stationed at the outer gates of the palace. There are two, which open upon the place of exercise, and where the two principal streets of the capital terminate. After crossing the bridges, which are raised over the fosse, the Mahal is approached by these gates. A large canal, replenished with water from springs, and clear as crystal, is the first object which is presented to view, on entering the precinct of the palace. Its banks, coated with stone, serve as dykes raised to confine the water, and prevent its overflowing. It is upon these causeways, which are, on both sides, of a sufficient breadth, to allow a free passage for the elephants and troops, both cavalry and infantry, that a long suit of guard houses, habitations, and shops are seen disposed at intervals. Here are the apartments and the offices of the inferior officers of the court. There are also to be seen long galleries, in which those who manufacture for the Imperial family are employed. Every day, artisans of all descriptions come to labor in the palace for the Mogul. In one ward, are found painters and embroiderers; in another, goldsmiths and enamellers; there is one for silk weavers; in others, weavers of all descriptions, and such as are employed in the meanest trades. These wards, or galleries, have each their superintendant, who directs the labors, and watches over the conduct of the workmen. The silence which prevails, while each person is diligently occupied, is truly surprising. All the phlegm of a Hindoo would be requisite, to pass whole days in a single occupation; to labor in company, without uttering scarcely a syllable; and with no other exercise, than the movements required by the peculiar art which he is practising.

At the termination of the canal, a large parade extends itself in a circular form. It is here, that the Mahometan soldiery every day mount guard. The War-Omrhas, who are the principal officers of the armies, bring hither every day their troops, and take their turn to command. The entire circuit of the place is in consequence occupied by tents set up for the inferior Omrhas, and by huts for the private soldiers. This warlike display, which is seen continually, both within and without the palace, has an air of majesty, inspiring respect for the great monarch who inhabits it.

It is thus necessary to pass through a large encampment, to enter the Am-Kas; the first court of the Mahal being so named. It is spacious; the form is a square. As it is surrounded on every side by an arcade, it furnishes at all hours, at least on one of its sides, a place of shade. Here, from an elevated situation, at certain hours, a concert is heard of musical instruments, agreeably to the taste of the country. Perhaps the harmony would not find many admirers in Europe. But in the Indies, strangers even who are accustomed to it, become at last sensible of an indescribable majesty in this species of concert, which is pleasing to them. There is certainly an air of grandeur, in reminding the people of their sovereign by the aid of music, with which the palace is made to resound at different hours of the day.

The Am-Kas, which may be compared to the Place Royale of Paris, seems intended only to serve for an avenue to the magnificent hall of audience, where all the subjects of the Emperor have a right to attend, and claim redress of their grievances. This apartment is large and splendid. As it is entirely open on the side of the court, there is, in effect, no door of entrance, but you pass immediately between the double row of columns by which it is supported. The ceiling is painted, and the gilding, which is often renewed, has not been spared. At the further end of the hall of audience is seen the resplendent throne of the Emperor, which may be discovered at a considerable distance from the entrance of the Am-Kas. At a fixed hour, which is commonly about noon, all the Omrhas, who are then in the capital, make their appearance in the hall of audience. They are separated from the people, whom curiosity, or their particular interests, bring thither in crowds, by a ballustrade, or rather a lattice work of silver, of very delicate workmanship. A platform, which is ascended by several steps, approaches them more or less near to the person of the Emperor, according to their rank and dignity. The coming of the Mogul is expected in deep silence. At last, when it has been announced by the sound of instruments, a curtain is withdrawn. The Emperor then appears, seated upon his throne, after the fashion of the East, in a species of recess. The sultans, his sons, are at his feet, squatted on cushions of gold brocade; and a small number of eunuchs chace away the flies from around the throne, and promote a circulation of the air with their fans.

The beauty of the throne excels all the other objects in the apartment; upon which the Mogul shews himself every day, seated, to his people. The precious stones with which it is ornamented dazzle the sight of the beholder. It is said to have been the work of a French artisan, who lived in the Indies under the reign of the preceding Emperor. It is much to be desired, that the art displayed had been equal to the materials employed. The most ingenious part of the design consists in the figures of two peacocks, which serve for the crowning ornament to the throne. It is entirely covered with precious stones, inlaid; and on the presumption that no false have been substituted by the workman in the place of the genuine ones with which he was furnished, nothing can possibly exceed the splendor of this costly monument. It was Cha-Jaham who caused it to be made; but the first who seated himself upon it was Aurengzebe, on the day when he took public possession of the empire.

It is in this style of splendor and magnificence, that the Mogul dispenses justice to his people. The Omrhas, in few words, explain to him the causes, the offences, and the different subjects of dispute; and the Emperor gives his decision. Criminals are executed on the spot. Some are trampled to death under the feet of elephants; others are beheaded; or stung by adders, whose poison is mortal.

If his attention does not happen to be engrossed by the affairs passing, the Mogul takes a pleasure, during the time of audience, in seeing his horses and elephants pass in the court of the Am-Kas. His attention is indeed sometimes taken off by it, at a time when business of the most serious kind is going forward. However, generally speaking, all the Emperors have prided themselves on their love of equity, and their discernment in unravelling the merits of complicated causes. It may be asserted, that they have even attached less glory to the subjugation of new kingdoms, than to an exact administration of justice.

In subjecting themselves every day to the hours of audience, they have undoubtedly imposed upon themselves a severe duty. It is an institution with which no Emperor has ventured to dispense, except in cases of extreme illness. The Mogul sovereigns have often, indeed, been known to cause themselves to be carried and placed by their attendants upon the throne, at a time when their health appeared in the most languishing state.

From the hall of audience, the Emperor always passes to the apartments appropriated for his bath. Some Omrhas of the first rank are allowed to follow him. Here are discussed the interests of the empire, the extension or defence of the frontiers, the conduct of the young sultans, and the plans for their establishment; the dispatches of the viceroys are read, and the reports of the spies (a class of agents which is dispersed by the Emperor throughout the whole of his states, even into the meanest villages and towns) are examined. Such is the occupation of the secret council, which is held daily in the Imperial bathing apartments.

When the Emperor has taken his usual afternoon's repose, he returns again to these apartments, and then the attendance of all the Omrhas is required. This is a regulation which admits of no excuse. During the discussion of business, or their remaining in conference with the Mogul, the inferior officers of the soldiery, called Mansebdars, make the troops pass in review. A company of the guards, especially, which is always in attendance upon the Emperor, never fails on this occasion to be present. It makes its appearance with torches, and the arms by which it is distinguished; these are long clubs, or rather large staffs covered with silver. The usage must, doubtless, have been introduced into the palace by one of the Mogul monarchs not over scrupulous in the observance of the laws of Mahomet. These staffs are seen surmounted with figures of animals or constellations, serving them for ornaments. This description of officers appear always in the presence of the sovereign, holding in their hands their staff, in sign of being prepared to proceed in any direction for the execution of his orders. It is from this body, that the ambassadors for foreign courts, and the envoys to the Rajas of Indostan are chosen.

None of the nobles of the empire are permitted to follow in the suite of the Emperor beyond the saloon in which are his baths. The interior of the Mahal is a mysterious abode, which the eunuchs only are permitted to enter. It may with truth be asserted, that a faithful description of this place has never yet been given by any traveller who has visited India. A profession such as that of M. Manouchi, and the confidence reposed by the court in an aged physician, would be required to obtain access to the haram. It shall be described in his own words. It is, he says, inhabited by more than two thousand females, of which the different classes are as follow: In the first class are the queens, or the Emperor's wives of the first rank. In the second place, the coucubines, or the wives of the second rank. Thirdly, the princes and the princesses. Fourthly, the ladies of the palace, who are the duennas of the queens, and the governesses of the princesses. Fifthly, the musicians of the court. Sixthly, the female slaves and the eunuchs.

With respect to the queens, or the wives of the first rank, the Mogul has sometimes as many as six. The marriage takes place accompanied by ceremonies instituted for the occasion. They are commonly the daughters of Rajas, who, from considerations of birth, or the interests of the state, are raised immediately to the first rank, without having passed through the second. Sometimes they are favorite concubines, female musicians or dancers, whom the Emperor advances to the rank of queens from choice.

The children of these women only are looked upon in the empire as legitimate, bear the title of sultans, and have the right to succeed their father. It is remarkable, that of so many queens, no more than four sons have appeared to be born to any of the Mogul emperors; and that no mention has ever been made of a son born of so great a number of concubines. Doubtless, a law must have been instituted in the haram, that no more than four princes should be allowed to survive, and that all the male children of the wives of the second rank should be destroyed. The names, by which the queens are designated, (which are invariably changed on being advanced to the first rank) are bestowed by the Emperor himself. The name of the wife of Jehan-Guir was Nur-Jaham; and that of the wife of Cha-Jaham was Taigé-Mahal. The first means, The Light of the World, and the second, The Crown of the Haram. The apartments of the queens are magnificent; and whatever can contribute either to convenience or pleasure has been consulted in their arrangement. It may be said, that the ardour of a burning climate is never experienced in these abodes. Here are to be seen running streams, shadowy groves, fountains, and subterraneous grottos for securing the enjoyment of a delicious coolness.

The women of the second rank differ little from those of the first rank, with the exception of the inferior distinction which they hold in the haram. Their apartments are less adorned, their pensions less considerable, their wardrobe not so magnificent, and they have fewer slaves to attend them. These, indeed, defray themselves the expenses attending their subsistence. The queens and the princesses of Mogul blood only are served from the Imperial kitchen. They are called, for this reason, "Begom;" which means Free from Care or Solicitude. The Emperor gives names, likewise, to his wives of the second rank. One, for instance, has the name of Ranadel, which signifies, The Faithful; another, Matlub, which is, Given by destiny.

The princes and the princesses of the blood are treated with the same magnificence as the queens. The young sultans inhabit the haram till the time of their marriage only. They pass the most tender years of their youth only near the Mogul. As soon as they have attained the age of thirteen or fourteen years, they are provided with a separate haram; and their court is not at all inferior to that of the Emperors. Those who are not destined, by the preference of the sovereign, to succeed him in the empire, are sent in the quality of viceroys into the most distant provinces. These sultans are rich from the moment of their leaving the palace. The occasion of their sudden opulence arises from the custom of assigning to them a revenue, which commences from the very day of their birth, and is always more considerable than the allowances to the first officers of the empire. This revenue of the young prince is kept apart in a treasury by itself; and he is put in possession of the whole of this accumulated wealth, on the day of his marriage. The eldest son of the Emperor now reigning possesses a revenue of twenty millions of rupees, which is nearly equal to thirty millions of our money of France. This is a conduct very inconsiderate on the part of the Mogul Emperors, who, by their liberality in making provision for their children, put into their hands the instruments of rebellion. The Emperors too often experience the fatal effects of their liberality. Whilst the princes remain in the haram under the eye of their father, a eunuch is charged with their education. They are taught to read; and sometimes to write in Arabic and Persian. Their bodies are formed to military exercises, and they are instructed in the principles of equity. They are taught to decide rationally upon subjects of dispute which occur, or on supposititious suits at law. Finally, they are instructed in the Mahometan religion, and in the interests of the nation, which they may be called one day to govern.

With respect to the young sultanesses, their sisters, they are brought up in the greatest indolence. As they become usually the chief amusement of their father the Emperor, they make it their whole study to please him. It is by such means, that they obtain sometimes a greater degree of liberty than is usual for persons of their rank; and to oblige them, they relax greatly from the severity of their confinement. The indulgence of the Moguls has been known to extend even to a connivance at their irregularities; a conduct, which, commonly, entails upon it a dissolution of manners, throughout the haram. It is easy to conceive, that indolence, joined to a life passed in the softest and most voluptuous enjoyments, and exposed to conversation not the most pure, should be the source of vices among persons so secluded; and whose minds are uninfluenced by the principles of the true religion. However, it must be acknowledged, that there is more courtesy, and general amicability, than might be supposed to exist where so great a number of women are congregated, all of whom must be more or less subjected to envy and jealousy. Avowed and serious hostilities are rare; even trivial disputes occur among them but seldom. The governantes exercise an authority over all animosities; and the fear of punishment operates as a salutary check to passions which may exist, but which are constrained at least from exhibiting themselves outrageously, and violating the laws of decorum.

The same mode of adorning themselves is common to the queens, the wives of the second rank, and the princesses of the blood. The hair is formed in tresses, and perfumed with essences. With the permission of the Emperor, some ornament their heads with a turban, which is surmounted by a tuft of feathers, with a contour of pearls and precious stones. Others fasten on the top of the head, on the tresses of their hair raised in the fashion of a pyramid, flying scarfs of cloth of gold, which float on their shoulders and descend to the ground. Their hair is thickly sown with pearls, which also form a species of royal fillet upon their foreheads. In the centre is seen suspended a rich jewel, which has been formed to represent the sun, the crescent, a star, or some flower. It is a species of head-dress which is very graceful. Their necklaces are composed of the finest pearls of the east, sown at intervals with diamonds, rubies, and sapphires.

As the climate obliges the ladies of the haram to wear only very light dresses, there are some manufactured of silk, of so fine a texture, that the whole dress does not weigh more than an ounce. They repose in these dresses, which they change in the morning, casting aside entirely the former, as of no further use. Every day they assume a dress of a different colour. They are adorned, besides, with an immense quantity of jewels. The collar of their robe is bordered with two bands of diamonds, enchased in the centre of two rows of pearls, crossing upon the stomach. Their ear-rings and bracelets are of surprising beauty. Their fingers, and also their toes, which are bare (the feet being covered with sandals only), are ornamented, equally, with the most beautiful rings. All the wives of the Mogul, and all the princesses his daughters, carry on the thumb of the right hand, in the form of a ring, a small looking-glass, bordered with pearls. They cast their eyes incessantly upon this mirror; it is with them the occupation of every moment.

Their most becoming ornament is a golden girdle, of

the breadth of two fingers, enriched with jewels. Mantels of the same metal are suspended to it, sown with diamonds, whose points are terminated by knots of pearls. What is very surprising, is, that each of these ladies has a change of six or eight sets of these jewels. The reader may possibly here imagine, that it is intended to transport him into fairy land, where nothing is seen besides pearls and diamonds; but the description which is now given is still far below the truth. The court of the Moguls is richer in jewels than can possibly be imagined in Europe. Tamerlane, the founder of the empire, plundered the palaces of all the principal sovereigns of Asia. It is well known, that the great care of the princes of the east, was, and still is, to accumulate a great quantity of precious stones. Babar transported with him to the Indies, from Samarcand, all the treasure of Tamerlane; that is, the spoil of all the east. The Emperors, who have reigned since Babar, have been continually augmenting the treasure of their fathers. Aurengzebe, especially, who, by the conquest of the kingdom of Golconda, has made himself master of the diamond mines. Every year, the Mogul, besides the tribute he exacts from Golconda in jewels, purchases the finest, and the most perfect, for the adornment of his wives and his daughters. These jewels never leave the palace, not even on the decease of the queens, or the princesses. The Emperor is their sole heir. It may be added further, that the jewels of the haram have been placed in a condition, rendering them incapable of being brought to market. They are almost all perforated. Akebar having, on a time, occasion for a supply of money, to enable him to undertake the conquest of the kingdom of Guzurat, sent, it is said, to Goa, some rubies for sale. Their beauty appeared extraordinary, but having been pierced, no purchasers could be found for them. With respect to the jewels, which serve for the Emperor's particular use, they are the masterpieces of nature. A particular name has been assigned to each of them. One is called the sun, another the moon, some other the bull's-eye, or the constellation of the bear. It is always by appellations such as these, that they are designated by the Mogul.

The expense of the Emperor in perfumes, for the use of his wives and the princesses of the blood, would appear incredible in France. All the day and all the night long perfuming pans are kept burning in all the apartments. These, besides, are not perfumes of an ordinary kind, but in general the most exquisite that India produces. The pleasure to be derived from the sense of smelling may be said to have been carried in the haram of the Mogul to a degree of refinement which cannot be exceeded.

The ladies of the palace, who act as governesses to the young princesses, and as duennas to the queens, participate in a less degree of the luxuries, and of the magnificence of the haram; but they have a much greater share in the government of the empire. It is by their instrumentality, that intrigues of state are managed, that peace or war is declared, that viceroyalties and governments are bestowed; they are, indeed, the true dispensers of fortune's gifts. These ladies, venerable by their years, and respected for their discretion, have each an office, and a name, corresponding with the post and title of the chief ministers of the crown. Thus, one among them will perform in the interior of the haram, the function of first minister; another that of secretary of state; some other that of viceroy. The lady, for example, who is charged with the principal administration, is in correspondence with the chief minister. She has eunuchs at her command, who convey continually her letters to this principal Omrha, and bring back those of the minister to his correspondent.

It is by the means of the ladies of the palace, that the subjects, which have been slightly treated in the hall of audience, and the bathing apartment, are more particularly introduced to the notice of the Emperor. They are, properly speaking, the privy council of the Mogul. By the means of those, whose title corresponds with that of viceroy, the Emperor learns all the news from the frontiers. They are entitled to dispatch couriers for the places pertaining to their department. It may be easily conceived, that the chief officers of the crown pay the greatest attention to cultivate, each, his lady of the palace. The least variance with her entails upon him, sooner or later, some serious injury, or reverse of fortune. Happy the minister, whose good fortune it may be to escape being dependant on a correspondent of a capricious disposition. The Emperor bestows upon them all names descriptive of their character. That of Faima Banu is one of the most honorable, which signifies, the Philosophic Lady.

The musicians and dancers are separated into distinct bands. Each troop has its directress for singing, and dancing. She acts as the governess, and the directress of those young females, who are chosen indifferently from the Mahometan, or the Pagan families, for the purpose of being transplanted to the haram. The salary of the intendants of music is equal to that of the ladies of the palace, but the former are never admitted to the councils of the Emperor; their whole employment consists in regulating the concerts, teaching their pupils how to perform on a species of lute, the sound of which is harmonious, and furnishing new airs for the pleasures of the queen and the princesses. All the wives, indeed, of the Mogul, and all the princesses of the blood, have each a troop of musicians appointed for their particular service, which is obedient to their command only. It is from these, that they select their confidants. All these musical corps reunite on certain days of festival, either to sing hymns to the Eternal, or to celebrate the praises of the Emperor. There is no œconomy of flattery in these compositions in honor of the Mogul. When he walks, they say, the four elephants, who are the supporters of the earth, tremble. The sun serves him for a cushion on which to repose his head; when he mounts his horse, the moon is his stirrup. The names of these female musicians are always of the invention of the Emperor. One is called, Saroc Bay, the melodious voice; another, Gian-Bay, the inventive mind. The principal merit, indeed, of these females, is, in inventing diversions for their mistresses, and especially, comic spectacles, in which they excel. The Emperor is present on these occasions; and a pleasant drama, well represented, intermixed with music and dancing, has often been known to procure some one of the actresses, a place among the women of the first, or of the second rank.

The female slaves of the haram perform the meanest offices to the queens, the concubines, the princesses, and the ladies of the palace. It is the Emperor who names them. One is called Golal, the rose; another, Narguis, the tulip; some other, Chambeli, the jessamine. They are separated into troops, composed each of ten or twelve females, under the control of a mistress. The Emperor disposes according to his pleasure of these attendants, assigning a greater or a less number to any of his wives, or daughters. He is himself attended upon by women only; and what may appear not a little extraordinary, he is guarded always in the interior of the haram by a company composed of one hundred Tartar women, armed with the bow, a poignard, and a cimetar. Their leader has the same rank, and the same pay, as a War-Omrha. This guard is necessary to the Moguls, as a precaution against the rage and the treason of so many rivals, of which his court is constituted.

With respect to the eunuchs, they are very numerous in the interior of the palace. Some of them exercise the function of porters, which is a difficult service, and exposes them to great peril. It is equally dangerous to be wanting in fidelity in guarding the entrances of the haram, or to be too strict in the performance of their duty. By a too great severity, they draw upon themselves the aversion of the queens, and the princesses; and by too much complaisance, they are in danger of forfeiting their lives. Other eunuchs are superintendants of the haram. He, especially, who is called Nader, that is, the chief of the Mahal, is one of the first officers of the crown. His duty consists in preserving order in the haram; he establishes its discipline, and maintains it by severity; he regulates the expenses of the wives of the Emperor, and of the princesses; he is the guardian of the Imperial treasure, and grand master of the wardrobe. He prescribes the fashion of the dresses, and is responsible for all the jewels and precious stones of the empire. In fine, the expence of the haram; the provisions, the dresses, the linen, and the perfumes, are all entrusted to his attentions. The inferior eunuchs have all, under the Nader, some particular duty. Some have the charge of the essences, and the perfumed oils; others of the stuffs, and again, others of the furniture. Those, who are in the highest consideration with the princesses, have the composition and distribution of the liquors, which are drank in the haram. They procure, sometimes, through their means, wine and other beverages, of an intoxicating quality, which are a source of enjoyment, in proportion to the difficulty of obtaining, and the mystery which is required in the use of them. The remainder of the eunuchs of the lowest class are employed simply in executing the commissions of the ladies of the court. The number who are seen passing in the capital, on the business of the haram, is incredible. Whatever, therefore, is passing in the city, is certain of coming to the knowledge of the court; and it may be said, that none are better informed of the news, and especially of the intrigues which are passing in public, than these secluded females. The expence of the interior of the palace, defrayed every year by the Nader, scarcely exceeds fifteen millions.

Of the Armies of the Mogul.

The prodigious number of troops, which the Emperor always has in pay, renders him the most powerful sovereign in the Indies. It is commonly reported in Europe, that his armies are more formidable from their numbers, than their valour. But the truth is, that the Mogul soldiery are less deficient in courage, than in the science of war, and that skill which is so necessary to make the best use of one's weapons. In comparing the armies of Indostan with those of Europe, it may be said, that in an engagement they would prove much inferior to ours. Still, not any of the nations beyond the Indus, can be compared with the subjects of the Mogul Emperors for bravery. War, as a science, is even better understood among them, than it is among their neighbours. It is by the greater discipline of their armies, that Akebar and Aurengzebe have so much extended the limits of their empire, and that the latter, at this very time, fills the whole east with the terror of his name.

The soldiery, of this great empire, may be said to be composed of three descriptions of troops. The first, is that army which the Mogul always maintains in his capital, and which every day mounts guard before the palace. The second, are those soldiers who are dispersed throughout the different provinces of the empire. The third, are the auxiliary Indian troops, whom the Rajas, the vassals of the Emperor, are obliged to furnish to the Mogul.

The army, which is encamped every day at the gates of the palace, whether the court reside at Delhi or Agra, is composed at least of fifty thousand horse; there are also a prodigious number of foot soldiers, that throng the two capitals. Whenever the Emperor takes the field, the two cities have the appearance of two deserted camps, from which a great army has broken up. The multitude follow the court; and with the exception of the quarter inhabited by the Banians, who are the rich traders, the rest of the city appears depopulated. A prodigious number of sutlers, bearers of burdens, slaves, and small merchants of every description, follow in the rear of the armies, with a view of rendering them the same services, which they are accustomed to do in the cities. This soldiery of the royal guard are not all on the same establishment. The four thousand, who are distinguished by the appellation of the Emperor's slaves, a term to express their devotedness to his person, compose the most important corps among the troops of the Mogul. Their chief, who is called Daroga, is an officer of high rank, to whom the command of armies is often entrusted. All the soldiers, who are selected for admission into so distinguished a corps, are marked in the forehead. It is from this body, that the Mansebdars, or subaltern officers are chosen, preparatory to their being advanced by gradation to the dignity of War-Omrhas: this is a rank in the army, that nearly corresponds with that of a general officer in the European armies.

The guards of the Golden Mace, of the Silver Mace, and of the Iron Mace compose also three different companies, the soldiers belonging to which are diversely marked in the forehead. The estimation in which they are held, as well as their pay, is governed by the value of the metal with which their maces are ornamented. All these corps are filled with picked soldiers, selected from such as have distinguished themselves by their valour. It is necessary to have served, and to have distinguished himself in some one of these corps, in order to arrive at the high dignities of the state. Birth does not confer rank in the armies of the Mogul; pre-eminence is the reward of merit alone. The son of an Omrha of the first rank, often finds himself confounded with the lowest grades of the soldiery. Among the Mahometans of India, certain descendants of Mahomet, who are esteemed in every place where the Alcoran is confessed, are the only persons in whom an inherent nobility is acknowledged.

In order to ascertain the number of the troops maintained by the Emperor, at a distance from the court, it will be necessary to enumerate the kingdoms which compose the extensive empire of the Mogul. If the historians of the country are to be credited; in the vast extent of lands, which at the present day are subject to the power of the Emperor, there are no less than fifty-four. In this place, a less detailed distribution of the soil will be given. The numerous kingdoms, included within the circuit of the Mogul territory, will be reduced to twenty; for the others are little more, in fact, than large provinces dependant on some one of the kingdoms which will be enumerated.

The kingdom of Delhi, situated in the centre of the empire, has for its capital a city of the same name, and is often the residence of the Mogul Emperors. Whenever the court resides there, it may be asserted, that the Emperor keeps in pay in that kingdom, even in time of peace, nearly two hundred thousand men. When the city of Agra, in its turn, is inhabited by the Emperor, the kingdom of that name may be said to contain the same number of soldiers. But when the court is absent, the garrison consists commonly of fifteen thousand horse, and double the number of infantry. It is here necessary to remark, in the enumeration of the troops of the Mogul, that the foot soldiers, reckoning all descriptions, are generally twice the number of the cavalry. Mention will, therefore, be made of the number of the cavalry only, as the memory of the reader will then be able to supply the number of infantry. Two reasons oblige the Moguls to keep, always, on foot in Agra a small army. The first is, that the treasure of the empire is kept and guarded in that capital; the second is the war which they are almost constantly obliged to wage with the peasants of the country; an intractible and warlike race of people, which has never been brought completely under their yoke, since the conquest of Indostan.

The court sometimes takes up its residence in Lahor. When it is absent, the Emperor maintains, at all times, in that kingdom, twelve thousand cavalry and infantry in proportion. The kingdom of Asmir is garrisoned by six thousand horse, and that of Guzurat by ten thousand. Seven thousand horse are maintained in that of Mallua; and as many in the kingdom of Patna. Six thousand defend the kingdom of Multan. With regard to the kingdom of Cabul; the army which protects it is always very considerable. The most formidable enemy, which the Mogul has, is, doubtless, the Persian. In order, therefore, to prevent him from extending his conquests beyond Candahar; as well as, with the object of bridling the incursions of the Tartars, and containing the Patans in their duty, the Moguls maintain in this kingdom, (otherwise sterile, and of a very moderate revenue,) an army of sixty thousand horse. The kingdoms of Tata, Bacar, Urecha, and Cachemire have to garrison them, each, four thousand horse. Eight thousand horse are reckoned for the kingdom of the Decan; seven thousand for that of Barar; six thousand for Brampour; four thousand for the protection of Ragemul, and six thousand for the defence of the kingdom of Nandé.

The kingdoms of Bengal, Ugen, Visapour, and Golconda have stronger garrisons. Bengal, which is bordered on one side by that part of India which is situated beyond the Ganges, and on the other by the kingdom of Arracan, and the city of Chitagong, as well as by some Portuguese colonies, has occasion for a greater number of soldiers for its protection. An army of forty thousand horse is therefore maintained constantly for its defence. Although the situation of Ugen, in respect to the Mogul territories, is rather centrical; yet is it locked within the lands of the most powerful Rajas. A moderate army, capable of making head against the enterprises of the Indian princes, is always maintained for the security of this kingdom. The strength of the protecting force is never less than fifteen thousand horse. As Visapour, at the time of writing these Memoirs, was the theatre of the war against the Sevagi, Aurengzebe had transported into that province his court and his armies. Lastly, the kingdom of Golconda, a new conquest atchieved by the reigning Emperor, is preserved to the empire by a garrison of twenty thousand horse.

Certain it is, that this multitude of soldiers and officers, which are maintained by the sovereign; although it protects, in some measure, the tranquillity of the state, is, nevertheless, often the bane of its peace. Whilst the viceroys are kept to their allegiance, and the troops remain faithful, there is no danger of the people revolting; but, when the princes of the Mogul blood conspire against their legitimate sovereign, and enter upon hostilities, they find frequently in the military an instrument prepared to second their designs. It was by their assistance, that Aurengzebe raised himself to the throne; having gained the affection of the principal officers of the empire, and the governors of the provinces, all the forces, which his father maintained for his defence, declared in favor of the son. It seems, nevertheless, that the Moguls have, by a particular providence, given the preference to this species of government. Being the proprietors of all the lands of the empire, it was, doubtless, but just, that they should maintain a considerable portion of their subjects out of their own revenues.

The auxiliary troops, which the Rajas, who are vassals of the empire, are obliged to furnish to the Mogul, augment still further the strength of his forces. It is true, that the use made of them in their wars is not unfrequently more through ostentation, than from necessity. It is a tribute, which it is always honorable to exact; and the retention of these troops in their service secures the fidelity of the tributary prince. There are calculated to be, in all Indostan, as many as twenty-four of these Indian princes, who still preserve a species of sovereignty in their native country. It may, however, be said, that the greater number of them are distinguished at the court of the Mogul from the other Omrhas, by the contempt only in which they are held by the prince, and the bad treatment which they receive from the great officers of the palace. The Rajas, it is true, possess lands in their own right, and their posterity inherit their territory, which is almost the only advantage that their character as sovereigns gives them over the Mahometan Omrhas; a class which makes its way to power by courting fortune, and whose children often relapse into that obscurity, from which merit or favor had raised their fathers. Some of these idolatrous Rajas still maintain, in the presence of the Mogul, a shadow of greatness. Three, especially, whose states are equally populous, wealthy, and impregnable, pay their court to the Emperor with dignity. The first, who pretends to derive his origin from Porus, and who styles himself the son of him who escaped from the deluge, (as if this were a title of nobility distinguishing him from other men) is sovereign of the kingdom of Sedussia. His capital is Usepour. All the princes of this large territory, from father to son, take the name of Rana, which signifies, The Handsome Man. He maintains, at all times, fifty thousand horse, and two hundred thousand infantry. He is the only Indian prince, who has been able to retain the privilege of walking under the shade of the parasol; an honor reserved only for the sovereign of Indostan.

In wealth and in power the Raja of Rator is equal to the Raja of Sedussia. He governs in sovereignty nine provinces. His name, when Aurengzebe mounted the throne, was Jacont-Sing; which means, The King Lion. As he is able to bring into the field an army, in strength equal to that of Rana, he is as highly esteemed at the court of the Mogul as the descendant of Porus. One day that Cha-Jaham threatened Jacont-Sing with a visit to his states, the Indian, it is said, fiercely answered, that he would present to him the next morning a sight, which might, probably, prevail upon him to spare himself the trouble of the journey. It was the turn of the Raja to mount guard at the palace gates. He drew up twenty thousand of his cavalry upon the banks of the river, and begged the Emperor to view from a balcony the appearance of the troops of his states. Cha-Jaham was astonished at the sight of the shining arms, and the warlike bearing of these brave Rajepoots. "My lord," said the Raja to the Mogul, "you have seen fearlessly from the windows of your palace the bold countenance of my Indians; you would not, perhaps, behold it without peril, should you attempt any violation of their liberties." The Raja was applauded, and had a present made to him.

The third Raja, who is held in high respect at the court of the Mogul, is able to bring into the field forty thousand cavalry. His state is called Chagué, and his capital, Amber. At the time of the wars of Aurengzebe, the prince who reigned there was the famous Ja-Sing, of whom so much has been spoken. Besides these principal Rajas, more than thirty others may be reckoned, whose forces are by no means contemptible. There are four, in particular, who keep each in pay twenty-five thousand cavalry. All these princes, on the urgènt occasions of the state, unite their troops to those of the Mogul, command them in person, give their Rajepoots the same pay as is received by the troops of the empire, and enjoy themselves appointments equal to those of the first Mahometan generals.

So great a number of auxiliary troops, and such formidable armies dispersed throughout Indostan, maintain, in general, the frontiers in security, and tend especially to preserve peace in the centre of the empire. The smallest hamlet has not less than two horsemen and four foot soldiers stationed in it. These act likewise as spies of the court, and are obliged to furnish an account of what passes. On the faith of their informations, orders are dispatched into the provinces.

The stables of the Emperor are suitable to the number of his cavalry, and are filled with a prodigious multitude of horses and elephants. His horses, it is said, are in number nearly twelve thousand. For the personal accommodation of the prince, there may not be more than twenty or thirty; the rest are for pomp, or destined to serve for presents. It is the custom of the Emperor to make a present of a dress and a horse to every one from whom he has received the slightest service. All these horses are brought from Persia, Arabia, and especially from Tartary. The horses, which are bred in India, besides being very stubborn and very shy, are weak and sluggish. Every year more than one hundred thousand are introduced from Balk, Bochara, and Cabul. This forms a considerable source of revenue to the customs of the empire. They are made to pay twenty-five per cent. on their value, on passing the Indus. The best are set apart for the service of the prince, and the remainder are sold to those persons whose office it is to keep up a supply for the cavalry. Horses are fed very differently in India from the mode followed in Europe. In a soil that is dry, and parched by the intense heat of the sun, very little forage is to be obtained, except on the banks of rivers: the want of it is supplied by a sort of seasoned paste. In the morning bread is prepared, compounded of sugar and butter, which is given to them by way of breakfast. In the evening rice milk is made, mixed with pepper and aniseed; this is for their supper. All the horses of the Emperor retain the name which he has bestowed upon them. One is called Rad-baftar, signifying, "fleet as the wind;" another Cha-Passand, meaning, "the prince's favorite."

The elephants of the Emperor form also a considerable accession of strength to his army, and an ornament to his palace. As many as five hundred are fed and lodged under large porches, built expressly for them. The Mogul bestows upon them very majestic appellations, and such as are appropriate to such prodigious animals. Memum-Babarecq is the name of one elephant, signifying, "he that marches with dignity;" Dul-Singer, is that of another, which is, "the terror of armies." The harness for these elephants is of astonishing magnificence. The one, especially, on which the Emperor is mounted, has upon its back a throne, shining with gold and precious stones. The others are covered with plates of gold and silver, housings with gold embroidery, tuffs and fringes of gold. The Mogul appears to have taken a pleasure in displaying the greatest possible magnificence in adorning these superb animals, which constitute, ordinarily, the means of his conveyance when he goes abroad. The elephant of the throne, that is called Orang-Gas, meaning, "the captain of the elephants," has always a large train in his suite, and a number of officers to attend on him. Whenever he marches, he is preceded by the sound of timbals and trumpets, and banners displayed. His pay is treble that of any other elephant. The nourishment for each elephant is estimated at twenty-five rupees each day; that is, of about thirty-three livres of French money. Ten valets are appointed to take charge of each elephant, and to attend to all his necessities. Two of them, who are called Cornaques, perform the duty of exercising, leading, and directing him. Two others bind on his chains; two help him to the water, and to the wine which is allowed for his drinking; two carry before him lances, with which they disperse the populace; two let off fireworks before his eyes, to accustom him to support the sight without terror; one is paid for furnishing him continually with fresh litter; and another for driving away the insects that molest him, and refreshing him at intervals by pouring water upon his body. These elephants are trained equally for hunting, and for war. They will attack lions, and tigers; and it is by such exercises that they are familiarised to carnage. The manœuvres, especially, by which they are taught to force the gates of cities, has something in it extremely military.

There are no arsenals in India. Every leader of a troop is obliged to provide his soldiers with arms. In their armies are seen a medley of musquets, bows, swords, cimetars, and lances. Different arms are often used, indeed, in the same troop. One, armed with the bow, will combat by the side of his comrade carrying a musquet or a lance. Aurengzebe has begun to reform this species of disorder. The Emperor's private arsenal is superb. His javelins, bows, quivers, and, especially, his sabres are ranged in the greatest order; the whole shining resplendently with precious stones. He gives names to his arms, as he does to every thing else. One of his cimetars is called Alanguír, which is, "the subduer of the earth;" another, Fate-Alam, "the conqueror of the world." Every Friday, in the morning, the Mogul says his prayers in the arsenal. He supplicates, that with his sabres, God will give him victory, and enable him to make his enemies fear the name of the Eternal.

The artillery of the Emperor is very numerous; and the pieces of ordnance, with which his armies are supplied, are for the most part more ancient than any which are in use in Europe. Cannon and powder were certainly known in India a long time prior to its conquest by Tamerlane. It is pretended that the Chinese, to whom they attribute the discovery, had cast pieces of ordnance at Delhi, during the time they were in possession of that city. Such is the tradition of the country. Names have been bestowed, according to the custom of the empire, on each piece of artillery. One is called, Orang-Var, that is, "the strength of the throne;" another, Bargisican, signifying, "he that breaks down bulwarks." The cannoneers of the empire, under the Emperors, the predecessors of Aurengzebe, were almost all Europeans. The zeal of the reigning sovereign for the Alcoran has prompted him to reject the services of all who are not Mahometans. Few Franguis are now seen at the court, with the exception of physicians, and jewellers. The rest have abandoned a country, in which their religion was no longer tolerated, as formerly. The Emperor has learnt with success, to dispense with the aid of the cannoneers, and with that in general of European artificers.

The description, which I have given of the forces, and of the armies of the Mogul, must, doubtless, instil a high opinion of the power of this great monarch. It is in his journies, and in his hunting parties, especially, that he makes the most magnificent display of his riches and splendour. On these occasions, he is attended by his armies. A palace is conveyed, in his train, not inferior in size to those which he inhabits in his capitals. This is every day erected in the centre of a camp, composed of the magnificent pavilions provided by the nobles of the court for their own accommodation. The bordering nations are appalled at this display; and he is almost certain of victory, when he takes arms against an Indian people.

Of the Revenues of the Mogul.

It may easily be conceived, that so magnificent a court, and such large armies, cannot be supported without immense revenues. Generally speaking, the people of Europe are sufficiently sensible of the great wealth of the Mogul; and, perhaps, the distance of the country, and the many fabulous relations, which have been given, may have too much exalted it in their imagination. In order to give a just idea of it, three things will be especially noticed; and first, the fertility of Indostan, and the abundant crops which its soil produces: secondly, the wealth which is introduced into it from Europe, Africa, and Asia, by the instrumentality of commerce: thirdly, the tributes exacted by the Emperor from his subjects.

It is well known, that the extent of the imperial domains is equivalent to that of the whole lands of the empire. The Mogul is the sole proprietor of the entire soil, and the only heir of his people. To form an idea, therefore, of his revenue, it will be necessary to estimate the produce extracted from the soil. The wealth of the sovereign may then be judged as nearly as possible, from the abundance of Indostan. With this view, a glance will be taken at the principal kingdoms of this great empire, explaining their situation, their produce, and the commerce carried on by them.

The kingdom of Delhi holds the first rank in India. Its capital is situated in the 31st degree 45 minutes of latitude, and in the 123rd degree of longitude. The soil is fertile in grain, and seems better cultivated than that of the more distant provinces.

The kingdom of Agra, whose capital of the same name is placed in the 29th degree 20 minutes of latitude, and in the 123rd degree of longitude, is less abundant than that of Delhi in wheat and rice. This is compensated by its producing indigo, and by the great commerce which it carries on from the produce of its manufactures. The muslins, silk stuffs, silver and gold cloths, which are especially in request for turbans; as well as the lace which is made there, render Agra one of the most opulent provinces of all India.

The kingdom of Pangiab has for its capital the city of Lahor. It is situated in the 33rd degree of latitude, and in the 119th degree 40 minutes of longitude. Fine cloths are here manufactured, pieces of silk of every colour, embroidery work, carpets of different patterns, and thick woollen stuffs. It is from thence that the rock salt is extracted, which is sent to every part of the empire.

The city of Asmir gives its name to a kingdom. It is

in the 30th degree of latitude, and in the 121st degree of longitude. This country abounds in grain and in pasturage.

The kingdom of Guzurat does not yield in riches to any other in the empire. Its capital, called Amadabat, is in the 23rd degree of latitude, and in the 117th degree 30 minutes of longitude. The great abundance of grain which is raised here, and the precious merchandise which it manufactures, give a great reputation to this kingdom. Gold and silver cloths, and silk stuffs, are exported. Jewellery work of all sorts is here carried on.

Mallua is the capital of a kingdom which bears the same name. It is in the 26th degree of latitude, and in the 103rd degree 50 minutes of longitude. The country is fruitful in grain, and abundant in plain and coloured cloths.

The kingdom of Bear has the city of Patna for its capital. This city is situated in the 25th degree of latitude, and in the 132d degree of longitude. Saltpetre is found here, with which vessels are freighted for Europe; and a species of pottery with an agreeable smell is made, almost as fine as paper. It is in use in the haram of the Mogul, and in the palaces of the princes.

Multan, whose principal city is in the 33rd degree 40 minutes of latitude, and in the 115th degree 20 minutes of longitude, furnishes scarcely any articles of commerce, except a few horses, and some camels without hair.

Cabulestan, abounding in pasturages, produces good horses, and haired camels. Its capital, Cabul, is in latitude 36 degrees 20 minutes, and longitude 113 degrees 50 minutes.

The kingdoms of Tata and of Bacar are equally rich in excellent corn, and in cattle. The capital of the last of these kingdoms is in latitude 28 degrees 30 minutes, and longitude 112 degrees 25 minutes.

Urecha is the name of a kingdom, and of a pretty considerable city, situated in latitude 20 degrees 25 minutes, and in longitude 125 degrees 20 minutes. The soil is fertile in rice.

In the city of Benares, situated in the kingdom of Illavas, latitude 29 degrees 25 minutes, and longitude 129 degrees 15 minutes, vegetables and most sorts of grain are produced in abundance. The silk stuffs, gold and silver cloths, magnificent turbans, beautiful girdles, and light dresses for the ladies of the haram, which are here made, render the country one of the richest in all India.

Orangabad is the capital of the kingdom of the Decan. It was built by the reigning Emperor, and is in latitude 19 degrees 25 minutes, and in longitude 120 degrees 25 minutes. Silk stuffs and fine cloths are made here.

One of the most productive kingdoms of Indostan is that of Barar. Corn and rice are raised, and it is planted with vegetables. It is here, that the poppy, from which opium is extracted, abounds. Sugar canes are produced, almost without the trouble of cultivation. The capital of this fertile kingdom is in latitude 23 degrees, and in longitude 129 degrees 40 minutes.

The kingdom of Brampour is fertile in grain; its capital, of the same name, is in latitude 23 degrees, and in longitude 123 degrees 30 minutes.

Baglana and Nande, two kingdoms, celebrated for the plain and coloured cloths which are manufactured in them, bear the same name as their capitals. The first is in latitude 19 degrees, and in longitude 118 degrees; the second in 27 degrees latitude, and 124 degrees 20 minutes of longitude.

Bengal, of all the kingdoms of the Mogul empire, is the best known in France. The prodigious riches, which are transported from that country every year into Europe, are a proof of its fruitfulness. It may be said to be nothing inferior in fertility to Egypt, and even to surpass it in the production of silks, cottons, sugar and indigo. Every thing is most abundant; fruits, vegetables, grain, fine cloths, and gold silk stuffs. Its capital, Daca, is in latitude 23 degrees 20 minutes, and in longitude 123 degrees 40 minutes.

The kingdom of Ugen produces salt and grain only. Its capital, of the same name, a very ancient city, is in latitude 28 degrees 25 minutes, and in longitude 122 degrees 30 minutes.

The fine cloths of the kingdom of Ragemal are highly esteemed, and rice is produced in abundance. Its capital is in latitude 24 degrees 20 minutes, and longitude 132 degrees.

The kingdoms of Visapour and Golconda are newly acquired territories, added by Aurengzebe to the Mogul empire. The diamond mine is a dependancy of the latter kingdom, and is a source of great wealth to the conqueror. The plain and coloured cloths which are manufactured there; iron, in which it abounds; the bezoar stones which are found there; augment the value of so fine a conquest. The capital of Visapour is in latitude 17 degrees 25 minutes, and in longitude 118 degrees 50 minutes. Baganagar, the principal city of Golconda, is commonly placed in latitude 19 degrees 40 minutes, and in longitude 124 degrees 40 minutes.

This short review of so many kingdoms, all the lands of which are the property of the sovereign, has, doubtless, furnished some idea of his opulence. The revenues, which are drawn from the territory of Indostan, cannot, however, be estimated on the same principle as that of land to the same extent in France. In India, large tracts of country are met with, which are not susceptible of cultivation. Others are found, possessing great fertility, but unproductive, through the neglect of the inhabitants. The people of Indostan cannot be expected to give the same application to the cultivation of the patrimony of the

Emperor, as would be employed by an individual in Europe, to render productive a soil of which he is himself the rightful possessor. This is a vice naturally resulting from that species of despotism established by the Moguls on the theatre of their conquests. Akebar, who introduced reforms into the finances of his empire, for the purpose of remedying this evil, no longer paid his viceroys and governors in money. He relinquished to them some of the lands of their departments, to be cultivated on their own account, and exacted for the remainder a fixed sum. The conditions were regulated on the principle of the greater or less fertility of their province. These governors, who are, properly speaking, only the farmers of the empire, let out in their turn these lands. The great difficulty is, to find labourers in the country, who are willing to engage in the cultivation of the lands, for the sole advantage of obtaining a mere subsistence. Violence, in consequence, is obliged to be resorted to; and the peasants are compelled to labour upon them. Hence their revolts, and frequent emigrations to the countries of the Indian Rajas, who are accustomed to treat them with rather more humanity. Thus the population of the territory of the Mogul insensibly diminishes, and the lands lie fallow and uncultivated.

The gold and silver, which is introduced into Indostan by the instrumentality of commerce, supply abundantly the defect of cultivation, and augment, infinitely, the riches of the sovereign. If, upon this subject, M. Bernier may be believed, who is not prone to a vice common to travellers, and is thought not to exaggerate the advantages of this empire; Indostan is an abyss that engulphs all the treasures which are transported to the rest of the world, from the American continent. All the silver of Mexico, and all the gold of Peru, he says, after having circulated for a time in Europe and in Asia, find their way to the dominions of the Mogul, and never afterwards leave the country. It is well known, he says, that a part of these treasures are transported to Turkey, in payment for the merchandise which is received from that country. Thence, by the way of Smyrna, they pass into Persia in payment for its silks. They then enter Indostan, by the intercourse of commerce carried on with Moka, Babelmandel, Bassora, and Bender Abassi. Much treasure is, besides, conveyed direct from Europe to the Indies, especially through the commerce carried on by the Dutch, and the Portuguese. Almost all the money drawn by the former from Japan remains on the territory of the Mogul. They find their advantage in taking the produce of the country, and leaving gold and silver in its stead. Indostan, it is true, notwithstanding its fertility, receives certain commodities from the countries of Europe, and Asia. Copper is introduced from Japan; lead from England; cinnamon, nutmeg, and elephants, from Ceylon: horses from Arabia, Persia, and Tartary. The traders, however, commonly take the produce of the country in exchange, with which they relade the same vessels that have carried out to India the commodities of their respective countries. Thus, the greater part of the gold and silver of the universe finds innumerable channels by which it may enter Indostan, and scarcely a single one for escaping from it.

The following reflection of M. Bernier merits attention: —Notwithstanding the astonishing quantity of gold and silver which finds its way to the Mogul states, and never afterwards leaves them; it is wonderful, he says, that a larger treasure should not be found in the hoards of individuals, than is common in other countries. It must, indeed, be admitted, that the cloths, and gold and silver brocades, which are manufactured in such abundance, the jewellery work, and especially the gildings, must consume a pretty considerable quantity of these metals; but it will still be necessary to recur to other causes. The Indians are known to entertain a superstitious notion, which prompts them to bury their treasures; this may account, partially, for the disappearance of the money they may have amassed. They imagine that their souls after death will animate the body of some other Indian, and that they may thus find in a time of adversity, a resource in this concealed wealth. It is acknowledged, that by these practices, a part of the precious metals, which have been extracted from the bowels of the earth in America, returns into its bosom in Indostan. But what chiefly contributes to the scarcity of specie, in the empire of the Mogul, is to be found in the conduct of the court. The Emperors amass great treasures, and although no one of them, with the exception of Cha-Jaham, has been accused of being violently addicted to avarice, they all like to secure gold and silver in subterraneous vaults, considering a too great abundance of them in the hands of the public as pernicious. The fact then is, that the precious metals, which are introduced into India by the operations of commerce, are all finally swallowed up by the coffers of the prince. All that remains, after defraying the expenses of the government, is carefully reserved, and used only when required by the very pressing exigencies of the state.

All which has hitherto been advanced, on the subject of the finances of the Mogul, will have prepared the reader for giving credence to what is about to be related. The immense revenues which the Mogul collects from his states will, doubtless, no longer excite surprise. The list here recorded is extracted from the archives of the empire. The actual produce of the domains in the entire extent of his sovereignty, and of which the Emperor was sole proprietor, was exactly such in the year 1697, as is about to be described. For a proper understanding, it is necessary to premise two things. First, that all the kingdoms of the empire are divided into Circars, or Provinces; that the Circars are again divided into Parganas, or Governments within the circuit of a province. These latter are, properly speaking, the lands let out by the Emperor. Secondly, it is necessary to be understood, that according to the manner of reckoning in Indostan, a Carol is equal to one hundred Lacks, or ten millions; that a Lack is equivalent to one hundred thousand Rupees; lastly, that a Rupee is equal to thirty sols, money of France.

The kingdom of Delhi has, within its circuit, eight Circars, and 220 Parganas, which furnish one carol, 25 lacks, and 50,000 rupees.

In the kingdom of Agra are 14 Circars, and 278 Parganas, which pay to the Emperor, two carols, 22 lacks, and 3,550 rupees.

Within the extent of the kingdom of Lahor are five Circars, and 314 Parganas, paying two carols, 33 lacks, and 5,000 rupees.

The Circars and Parganas of the kingdom of Asmir pay two carols, 19 lacks, and two rupees.

The kingdom of Guzurat, which has nine Circars and 19 Parganas, pays the Emperor two carols, 33 lacks, and 95,000 rupees.

Mallua contains 11 Circars, and 250 small Parganas, and pays only 99 lacks, and 6,250 rupees.

Bear, eight Circars, 245 small Parganas, pays one carol, 21 lacks, and 50,000 rupees.

Multan, fourteen Circars, 96 Parganas, 50 lacks, 25,000 rupees.

Cabul, thirty-five Parganas, 32 lacks, 7,250 rupees.

Tata pays 60 lacks, 2,000 rupees.

Bacar pays 24 lacks.

Urecha has eleven Circars, and a great number of Parganas, and pays 57 lacks, 7,500 rupees.

Cachemire, 46 Parganas, pays only 35 lacks, and 5,000 rupees.

Illavas, with its dependancies, pays 77 lacks, and 38,000 rupees.

The kingdom of the Decan has eight Circars, and 79 Parganas, and pays one carol, 62 lacks, 4,750 rupees.

Barar, ten Circars, 191 small Parganas, one carol, 58 lacks, 7,500 rupees.

Candis, a great province, pays one carol, 11 lacks, 5,000 rupees.

Baglana, 43 Parganas, 68 lacks, 85,000 rupees.

Nandé, pays 72 lacks.

Bengal pays four carols.

Ugen, two carols.

Ragemal, one carol, 50,000 rupees.

Visapour, and a moiety of the province of the Carnatic pays five carols.

Lastly, Golconda and the other moiety of the Carnatic pays five carols.

The sum total, makes, 387 millions, 194 thousand rupees. Estimating the rupee at 30 French sols, the domain of the Mogul Emperor furnishes yearly a revenue of 580 millions 791,000 livres.

The casualities of the empire are another source of revenue, in addition to the beforementioned, derived solely from the produce of the soil. In the first place, a pole tax is levied upon every Indian idolater. As the accidents of death, travelling, and emigration cause much confusion in the collection, fraudulent returns are very liable to be made; the governors of the provinces often availing themselves of such circumstances to disguise, and diminish the actual receipt. Secondly, all the merchandise, exported by the idolatrous traders, pays to the customs five per cent. on its value. The Mahometans have been exempted from this species of impost by Aurengzebe. Thirdly, the bleaching of that infinite quantity of linen cloths, which are manufactured in the Indies, is another source of taxation. Fourthly, the diamond mine pays a heavy duty to the Emperor. He exacts for his own use, the finest and the most perfect, that is to say, all those which are in size more than three eighths. Fifthly, the sea ports, and particularly those of Sindi, Barocha, Surat, and Cambaye are heavily taxed. Surat, alone, pays in general thirty lacks for port entries, and eleven lacks on account of the profit arising from coinage. Sixthly, the whole coast of Coromandel, and the ports situated on the banks of the Ganges, produce a considerable revenue. Seventhly, the monarch's universal heirship to the property of all his Mahometan subjects, who are in his pay, augments greatly his revenue. The furniture, the money, and all the effects of the deceased belong of right to the Emperor. The wives of governors of provinces, and of the commanders of armies, are in consequence often reduced to subsist on a small pension; and their children, if destitute of talent, fall into poverty. Eighthly, the tributes of the Rajas are of sufficient consequence to be classed among the principal sources of revenue to the Mogul.

All these adventitious sources of revenue, nearly equal, or even exceed the wealth derived by the Emperor from the soil of his domains. A wealth, so prodigious, is, doubtless, a matter of astonishment; but, it must be recollected, that a great part of these riches flow only into the treasury of the Mogul, again every year to leave it, and circulate anew upon the lands. One half of the population are supported by the liberalities of the prince, or, at least, are in his pay. Independently of the great number of officers and soldiers who live on their pay, all the peasants who labour on the lands on account of the sovereign, are nourished at his charge; and nearly all the artisans in the cities, who are obliged to labour for the royal family, are paid out of the Imperial treasury. This will give a sufficient idea of the state of dependance in which his subjects are held, and of the depth of their subjection to their Sovereign Imperial Lord.

OF THE GOVERNMENT, AND OF THE POLICE OF THE MOGUL EMPIRE.

THERE remains little to be added on the subject of the species of government, and of the police established by the Moguls in India. Nothing certainly can be more simple than the springs which move this great empire. The Emperor is the soul of the whole. As his rule is as absolute, as his right over the soil, the whole authority is concentrated in his person alone; and, properly speaking, there is but one master in Indostan. All the rest are more entitled to be regarded as slaves, than subjects.

The affairs of the state are entirely confided to three or four Omrhas of the first rank at court, who administer them under the direction of the prince. The Etmadoulet has the rank of first minister to the Emperor, and occupies in India, in the service of the Mogul, the same place, which the chief vizier holds in Turkey, in the service of the Grand Seignour.

This is often, however, a title without employment, and a dignity without office. A man without experience is sometimes selected for Etmadoulet; and who has no further concern with the post, than to receive its emoluments. Sometimes it is a prince of the Mogul blood, who has been suffered quietly to attain to an advanced age; sometimes it is the father of a favorite queen, taken perhaps from the lowest rank of the soldiery, or from the meanest of the populace. In these cases, the whole weight of the government devolves upon the two secretaries of state. One collects the treasures of the empire; the other disburses them. This pays the officers of the crown, the troops, and the labourers; the other receives the tributes, collects the revenue from the lands, and that arising from the imposts. A third minister of finance, but of inferior rank to the secretaries of state, has the duty of collecting the inheritances of all those who die in the service of the prince. This is a profitable, yet an odious service. These eminent offices of the empire are only attained by a course of military service. The ministers who rule the state, and the generals who command the troops, are all equally chosen from among the officers of the army. Whenever their interest with the monarch is solicited, they are never approached without a present. This is rather reputed a mark of respect on the part of the petitioner, than charged to a base passion of avarice on the side of the Omrhas. The value of the present is little regarded, the chief matter is, not to appear empty-handed in the presence of the great officers of the court.

The command of the armies, when the Emperor is not himself at the head of his troops, is often confided to a prince of the blood. In the absence of a Sultan of the Imperial family, two generals are chosen by the sovereign; one from the Mahometan Omrhas, the other from the Indian Rajas. The troops of the empire are commanded by the Omrha; and the Rajepoot auxiliaries obey only a Raja of their own nation. It was the Emperor Akebar who instituted the discipline of their armies, and who established in them the order about to be described. He directed that all the officers of his troops should be paid under three different heads. The first, under the head of twelvemonths; the second under that of six months; and the third under that of four months. Thus, when the Emperor directs to be paid to a Mansebdar, (which is the name given to the inferior officers) twenty rupees a month under the first head, his pay for the year amounts to seven hundred and fifty rupees; ten rupees being added over and above. He, to whom the twenty rupees a month are assigned, under the second head, receives yearly three hundred and seventy-five rupees; and he, whose pay is under the third head, has yearly only two hundred and fifty rupees. This is a capricious arrangement; for the services of those, who are paid only on the footing of four months, are equally severe throughout the year with that of the officers of the same rank, who receive pay upon the footing of twelve months. The Emperors have proposed by this means, to give themselves an air of dignity, and of regard to justice, which is suitable to the genius of the Orientals. They would have it to be supposed, that if they gave less to some of their officers than to others, it is because they receive from them less constant services. The Mogul, besides, when he orders the pension of a Mansebdar, never uses the term of rupees. He always makes use of the word Dams, which is the term for a small coin but little used in commerce. Forty of them make a rupee. Thus, when the Emperor orders an officer a pension of a thousand rupees; "I assign him," he says, "fifty thousand dams for his pay," an emphatic style of expression, which does not augment the value of the gift.

When the pension of an officer of the army, or of the court, amounts monthly to a thousand rupees under the first head; that is, according to the manner of reckoning in the Mogul states, to an Azari Omarhao, he is no longer rated in the class of Mansebdars; he has the quality of

Omrha. This dignity is thus attached to the amount of pay received. He is then obliged to maintain an elephant, and two hundred and fifty horsemen for the service of the prince. These fifty thousand rupees of yearly pension, would, doubtless, be insufficient, even in the Indies, to support the charge of so considerable a corps; for the Omrha is obliged to provide at least two horses for each of his soldiers. The Emperor furnishes the means from other sources. He assigns to the officer some lands from his domains. The expence of each horseman is calculated on the principle of ten rupees a day; but the property in land, which is relinquished for the Omrhas to cultivate on their own account, produces much beyond what would be required to defray the expences of their horsemen.

The Omrhas, moreover, do not always receive the same pay. There are some, whose pay amounts to two azaris; others, to three azaris; some to four; others again to five. Lastly, those of the first rank receive as much as six. That is to say, all advantages included, the pension of these last may amount to three millions of rupees yearly. Their suit is, therefore, very magnificent, and the cavalry in their pay is equal to a small army. Certain Omrhas have sometimes proved formidable to the sovereign by the means of such an auxiliary. The example of Mahobet-Cham ought, doubtless, to have corrected so dangerous a liberality, which elevates the subject too near the throne. But, the institution was introduced by Akebar, and no Emperor has ventured its innovation. There are, generally speaking, six Omrhas, who enjoy the largest pension. The etmadoulet, the two secretaries of state, and the viceroys of Cabul, Bengal, and Ugen. The pay of the horsemen, and of the rest of the soldiery, is at the discretion of the Omrhas, who levy and who maintain them. The law requires that they should be paid every day; but it is ill observed.

Some money is, indeed, distributed to them every month; but they are often obliged to accept in payment the antique furniture of the palaces, and the dresses which the wives of the Omrhas have cast aside. It is by such impositions, that the first officers of the empire accumulate great wealth, which passes at their death into the coffers of the sovereign.

Nothing can possibly be more uniform than the administration of justice in the States of the Mogul. The viceroys, the governors of provinces, the chiefs of the cities, and of the smallest towns, perform precisely in the place of their department, (subject always to the Emperor) the part acted by the Mogul in Agra or in Delhi. They alone administer justice, and decide causes which concern the property and the life of the subject. It is true, that in all the cities of the empire, a Cotwall and a Cazi have been established for judging certain causes. Nevertheless, nothing is decided at their tribunals, but such causes as it has pleased the parties to carry before them. Every one has the right to carry his cause at once, either before the Emperor himself, in whatever place he may reside, or before the viceroys, in the capital of their viceroyalty, or before the governors, in the place of their superintendance.

The Cotwall fills, at the same time, the office of police magistrate, and of grand provost. At the present day, under Aurengzebe, a zealous observer of the laws of the Alcoran, the principal duty of the judge of police is to prevent drunkenness, to exterminate the wine shops, and all places of debauchery, and to punish those who distil arrack, a species of brandy extracted from sugar. It is his duty to make a report to the Emperor of all the domestic disorders which occur in families; of disputes, of seditions, and of nocturnal assemblages. With this view he maintains, in every quarter of the city, a prodigious number of spies. Those, of whose services he chiefly avails himself, are a class of persons called Alarcors, whose employment consists in cleansing the houses, and putting the furniture in order. Every morning, they enter the residences of the citizens, inform themselves of the secrets of the families, interrogate the slaves, and make their report to the Cotwall. This chief officer of justice, in his capacity of grand provost, is responsible, on the strength of the gratuities of his post, for all the robberies which occur in his district, both in the city and in the country. His zeal and his vigilance may, therefore, be easily imagined. He has always soldiers dispersed throughout the country, and persons in disguise in the cities, whose care it is to keep watch, and preserve good order. The jurisdiction of the Cari seldom extends beyond matters of religion, and the dissolution of marriages. It is not permitted to either of these inferior judges to pronounce sentences of death, without having first made a report to the Emperor. The sovereign must himself have given his assent to the decree of condemnation, three times, on three different days, before they are suffered to put it into execution. The same law prevails in the provinces, and the power of life and death is reserved to the viceroys, and governors alone.

Justice is administered in the Mogul States with promptitude. Without having recourse to a number of formalities, each person gives an exposition of his own case, or causes it to be explained by the Omrhas. Witnesses are heard, and a decision is given on the spot, which is almost always as just as it is prompt. Corruption in the judges, and the perjury of witnesses, it must be acknowledged, have place in Indostan as well as in other countries; but, false evidence, and the taking of bribes by the judges, subject the parties to the penalty of death, if detected. All which can be done to remedy these evils, is effected by the severity of this law. Unjust decisions are, it seems, a universal grievance, which the tediousness of processes does not always correct. Besides, this small number of judicial officers, which, in the largest, as well as in the smallest cities, is limited to three, have not even so much employment as the least of our judges; a class which is so numerous in Europe.

Such are the institutions of the great empire, whose history has been recorded. They have not been represented as free from defect; but as exhibiting rather a state, in which barbarism was so qualified by the equity which pervaded the administration of justice, as to render the government of the Mogul empire little inferior to that of any other nation. The Emperor, who now rules the realms of Indostan, sustains by his ability, and is extending daily by his valour, an empire, which has never suffered any diminution of its prosperity since his accession.

FINIS.